WORKING PAPERS
Volume I, Chapters 1-12
to accompany

ACCOUNTING

PRINCIPLES

10th Edition

Jerry J. Weygandt PhD, CPA
Arthur Andersen Alumni Professor of Accounting
University of Wisconsin
Madison, Wisconsin

Donald E. Kieso PhD, CPA
KPMG Peat Marwick Emeritus Professor of Accountancy
Northern Illinois University
DeKalb, Illinois

Paul D. Kimmel PhD, CPA
Associate Professor of Accounting
University of Wisconsin--Milwaukee
Milwaukee, Wisconsin

Prepared by
Dick D. Wasson, M.B.A., C.P.A.
Southwestern College
University of Phoenix

WILEY
John Wiley & Sons, Inc.

COVER PHOTO: ©Bill Stevenson/Photolibrary

CONTENTS

Working Paper templates are provided for end-of-chapter brief exercises, exercises, problems, and broadening your perspective problems. Working Paper templates are not provided for solutions that are textual in nature.

BE1-1		Assets	Liabilities	Owner's Equity	
1	(a)	$ 90 0 0 0	$ 50 0 0 0		1
2					2
3	(b)		4 0 0 0 0	7 0 0 0 0	3
4					4
5	(c)	9 4 0 0 0		5 3 0 0 0	5
6 **BE1-2**					6
7	(a)		$ 1 2 0 0 0 0	$ 2 3 2 0 0 0	7
8	(b)	1 9 0 0 0 0		9 1 0 0 0	8
9	(c)	8 0 0 0 0 0			9
10					10
11 **BE1-3**					11
12	(a)				12
13					13
14	(b)				14
15					15
16	(c)				16
17					17
18 **BE1-4**	See next page				18
19					19
20 **BE1-10**					20
21		**George Company**			21
22		Balance Sheet			22
23		December 31, 2012			23
24		Assets			24
25					25
26					26
27					27
28					28
29					29
30		Liabilities and Owner's Equity			30
31					31
32					32
33					33
34					34
35					35
36					36
37					37
38					38
39					39
40					40

Expanded Accounting Equations

BE1-4

	Assets	=	Liabilities	+	Owner's Capital	–	Owner's Drawings	+	Revenues	–	Expenses
					Owner's Equity						

(a)

(b)

(c)

1 2 3 4 5 6 7 8 9 10 11 12 13 14 15 16 17 18 19 20 21 22 23

Do It! 1 - 3

Orlando Bloom and Co.

See Appendix

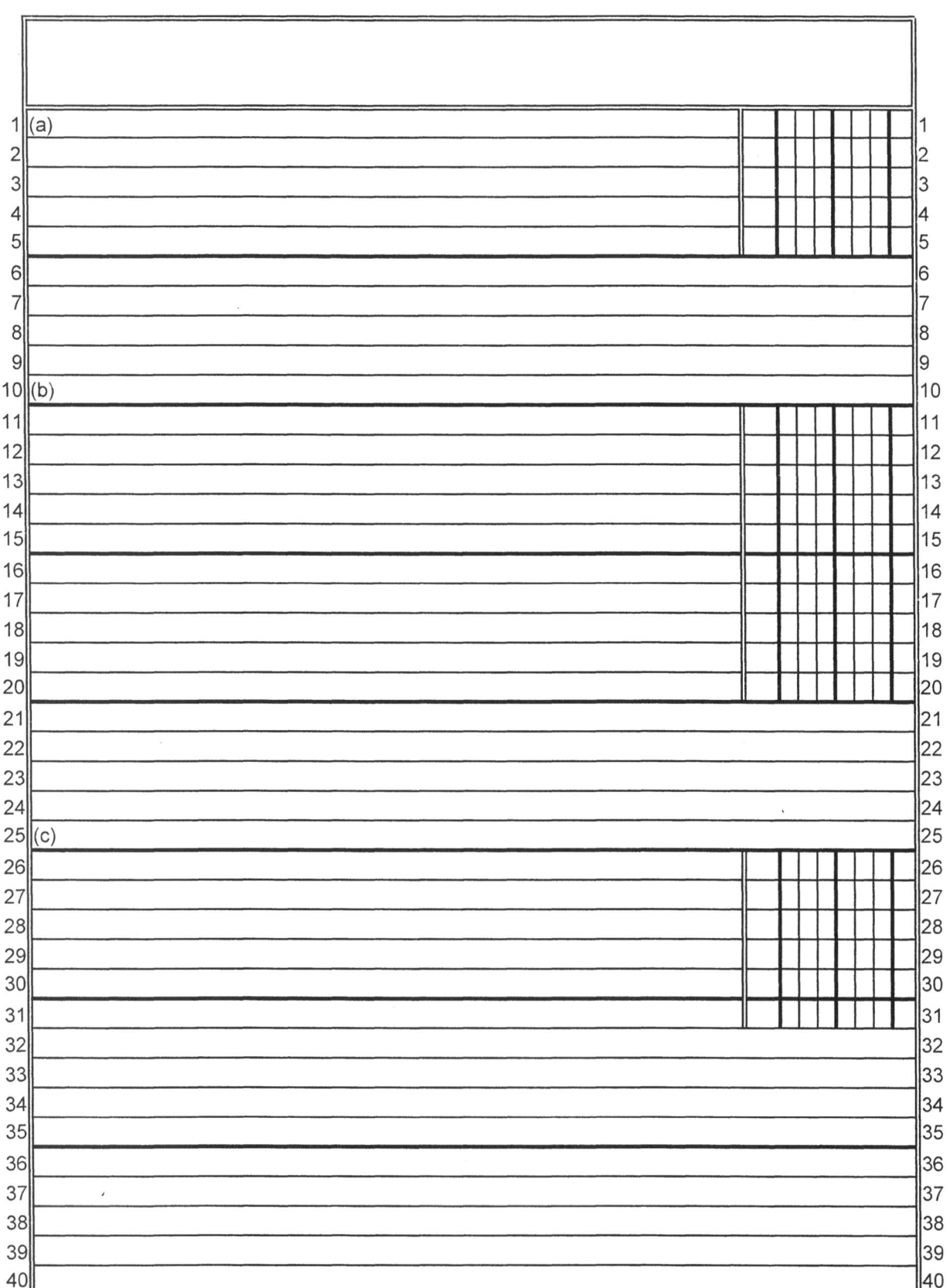

(a)

1.

2.

3.

4.

5.

6.

7.

8.

9.

10.

(b)

(c)

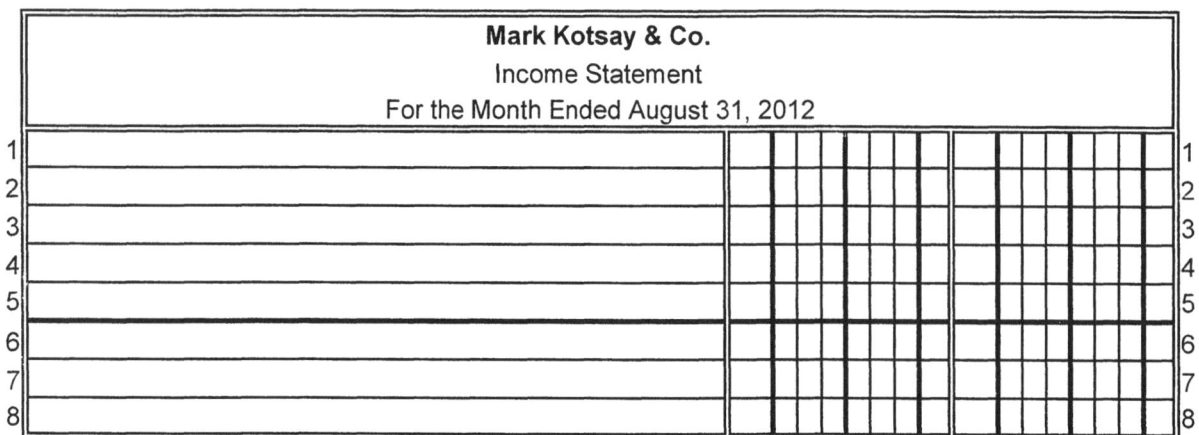

Mark Kotsay & Co.

Income Statement

For the Month Ended August 31, 2012

Mark Kotsay & Co.

Owner's Equity Statement

For the Month Ended August 31, 2012

Mark Kotsay & Co.

Balance Sheet

August 31, 2012

Assets

Liabilities and Owner's Equity

1	(a)		1
2			2
3			3
4			4
5			5
6			6
7			7
8			8
9			9
10			10
11	(b)		11
12			12
13			13
14			14
15			15
16			16
17			17
18			18
19			19
20			20
21	(c)		21
22			22
23			23
24			24
25			25
26			26
27			27
28			28
29			29
30			30
31			31
32			32
33			33
34			34
35			35
36			36
37			37
38			38
39			39
40			40

	(a)										
1											1
2											2
3											3
4											4
5											5
6	(b)										6
7											7
8											8
9											9
10											10
11											11
12											12
13											13
14											14
15											15
16											16
17											17
18											18
19											19
20											20
21	(c)										21
22											22
23											23
24											24
25											25
26	(d)										26
27											27
28											28
29											29
30											30
31											31
32											32
33											33
34											34
35											35
36											36
37											37
38											38
39											39
40											40

Jake Peavy Co.
Income Statement
For the Year Ended December 31, 2012

1		
2		
3		
4		
5		
6		
7		
8		
9		
10		

Jake Peavy Co.
Owner's Equity Statement
For the Year Ended December 31, 2012

1	
2	
3	
4	
5	
6	
7	
8	
9	
10	

E1-13

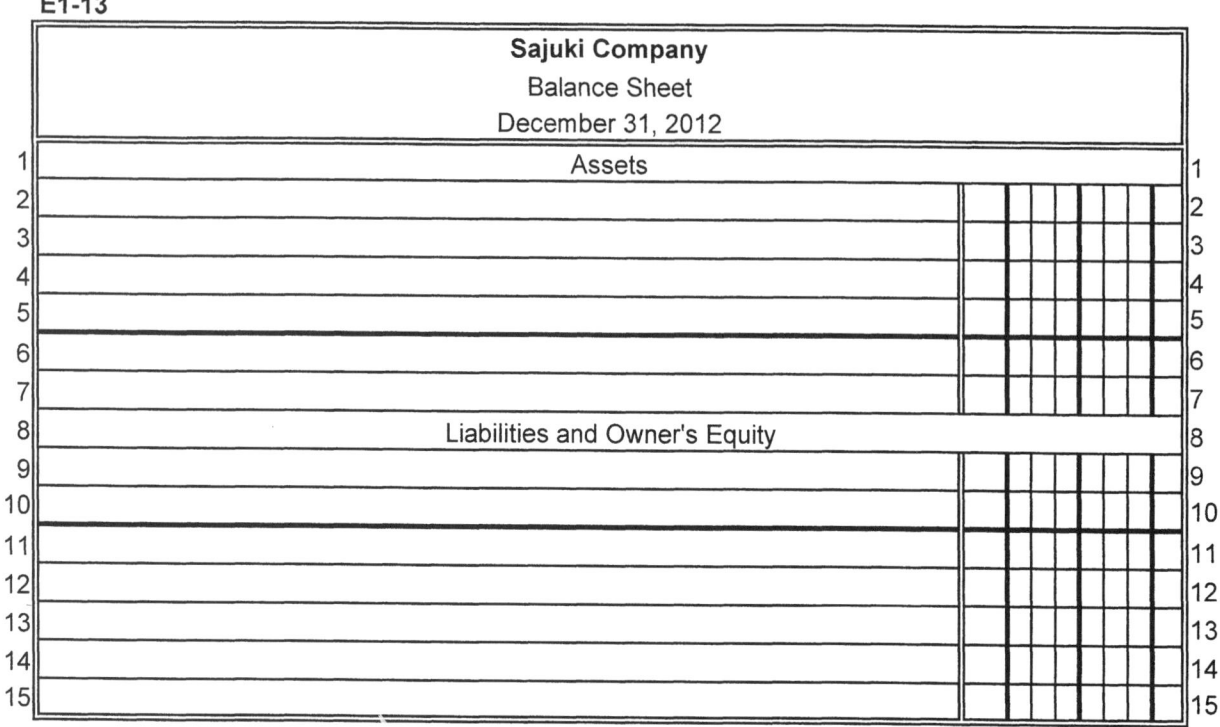

Sajuki Company
Balance Sheet
December 31, 2012

Assets

Liabilities and Owner's Equity

E1-15

J. J. Putz Cruise Company
Income Statement
For the Year Ended December 31, 2012

(a)

	1
1	
2	
3	
4	
5	
6	
7	
8	
9	
10	

(b)

Deer Park
Balance Sheet
December 31, 2012

Assets

Liabilities and Owner's Equity

Sergio Santos, Attorney
Owner's Equity Statement
For the Year Ended December 31, 2012

1								
2								
3								
4								
5								
6								
7								
8								
9								
10	Supporting Computations							
11								
12								
13								
14								
15								
16								
17								
18								
19								
20								
21								
22								
23								
24								
25								
26								
27								
28								
29								
30								
31								
32								
33								
34								
35								
36								
37								
38								
39								
40								

Problem 1-1A

Threet's Repair Shop

See Appendix

(b)

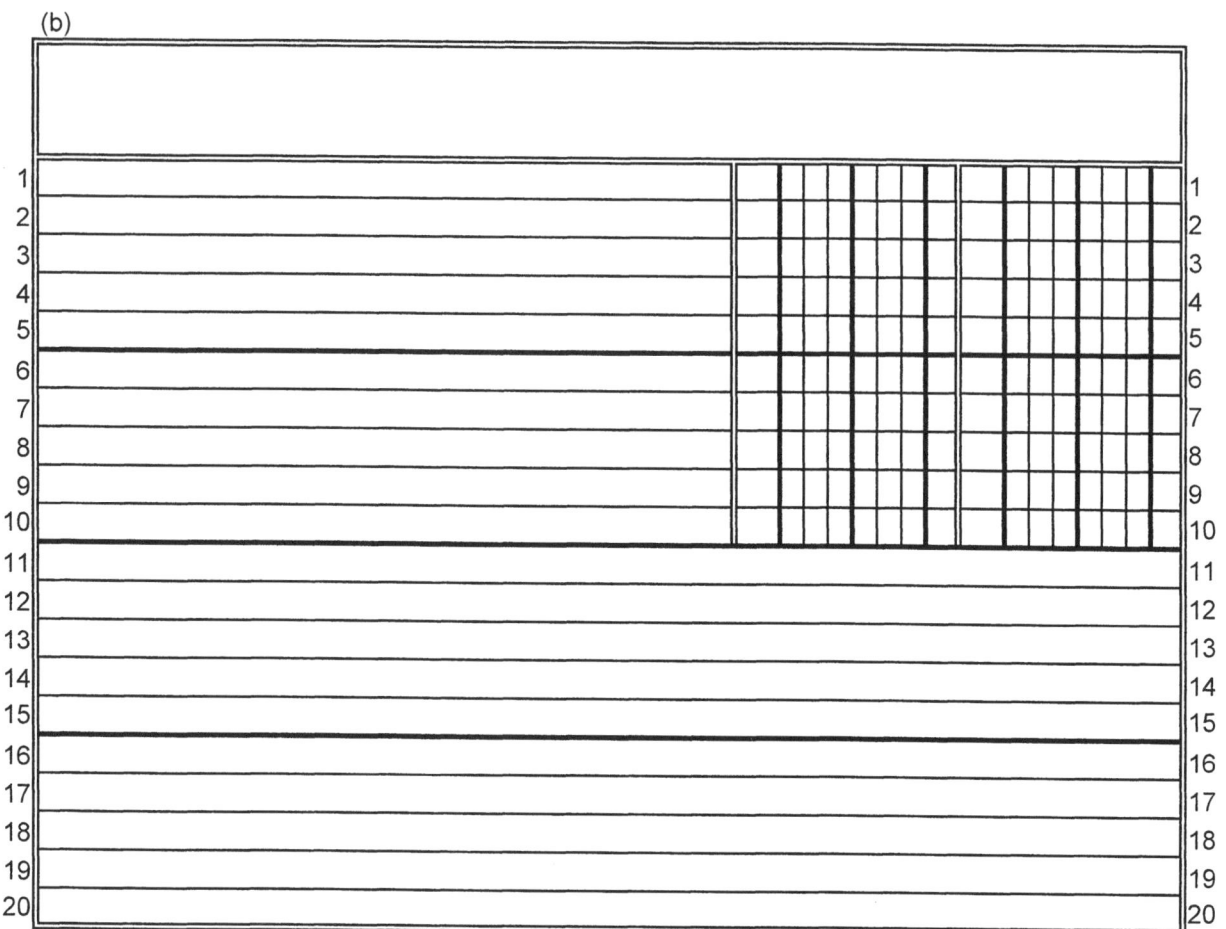

Problem 1-2A

Ramona Castro, Veterinarian

See Appendix

(b)

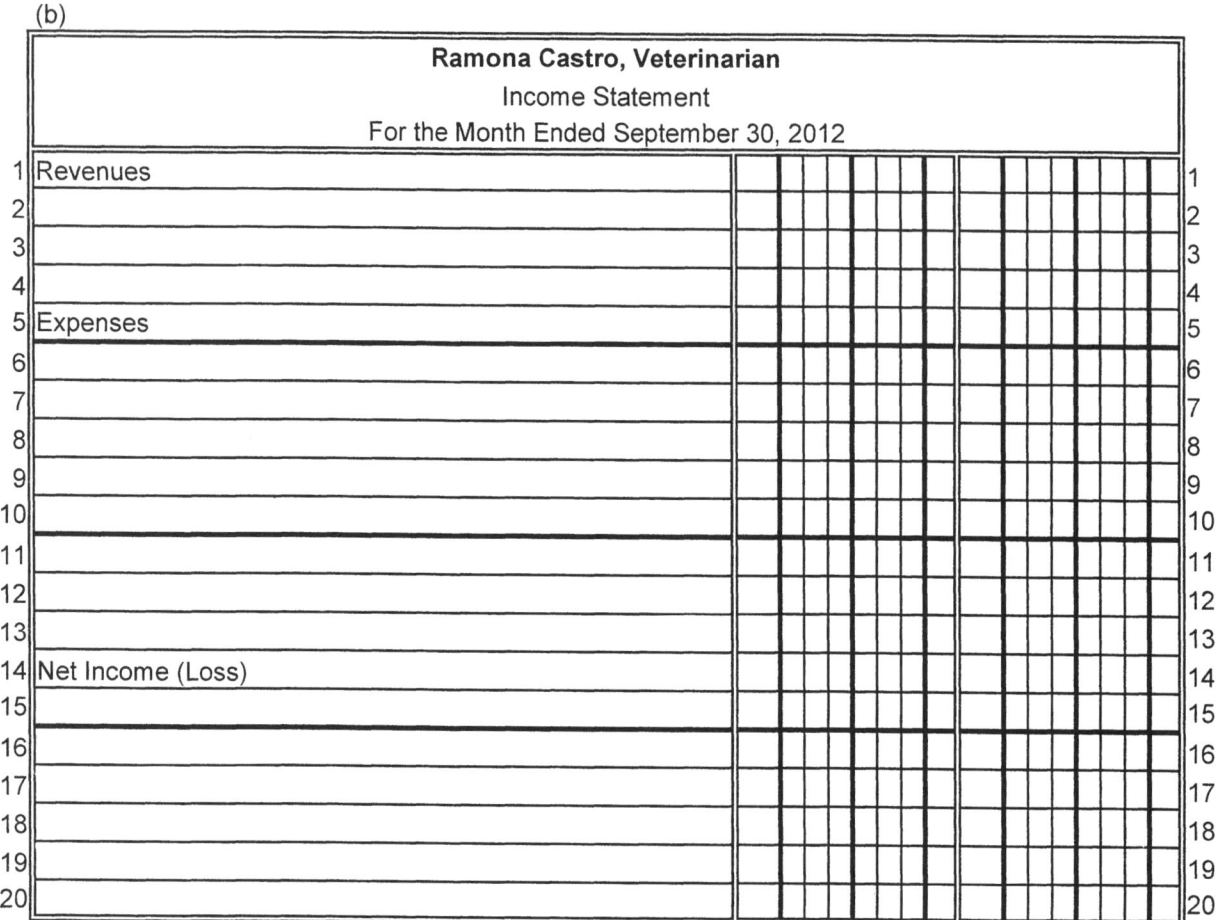

Ramona Castro, Veterinarian
Income Statement
For the Month Ended September 30, 2012

Revenues			
Expenses			
Net Income (Loss)			

Ramona Castro, Veterinarian
Owner's Equity Statement
For the Month Ended September 30, 2012

Problem 1-4A

Beckham Deliveries

See Appendix

(b)

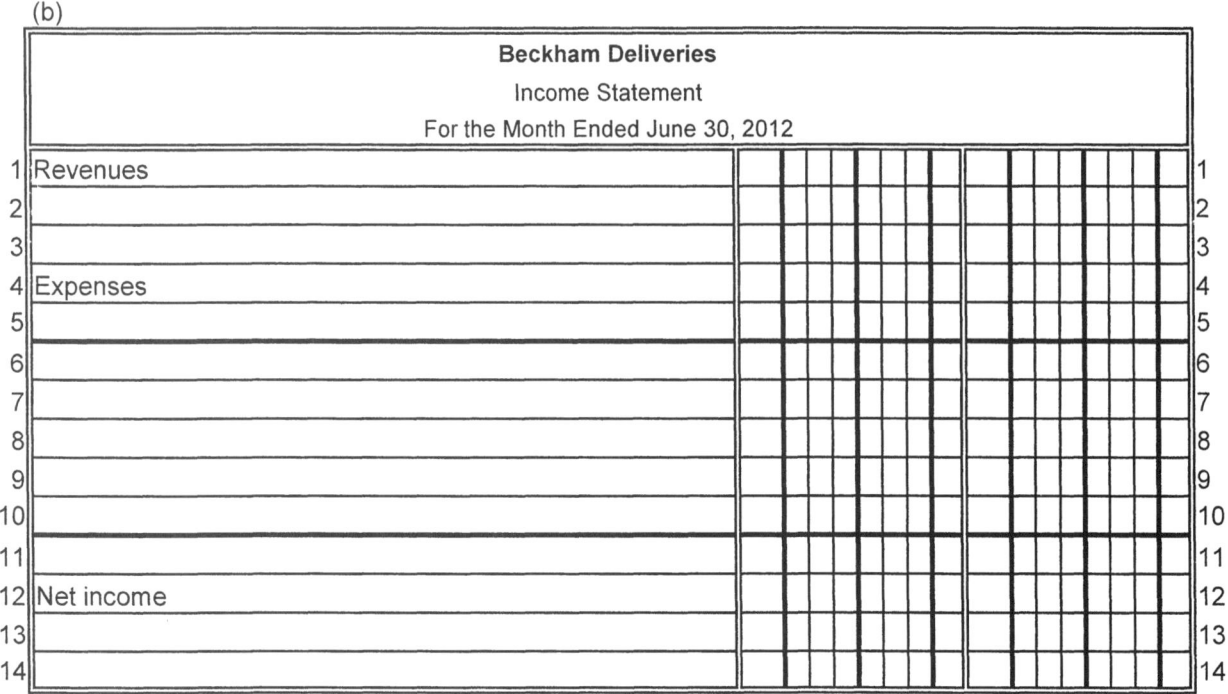

Beckham Deliveries

Income Statement

For the Month Ended June 30, 2012

	Revenues		
1	Revenues		
2			
3			
4	Expenses		
5			
6			
7			
8			
9			
10			
11			
12	Net income		
13			
14			

Beckham Deliveries

Balance Sheet

June 30, 2012

	Assets		
1	Assets		
2			
3			
4			
5			
6			
7			
8	Liabilities and Owner's Equity		
9			
10			
11			
12			
13			
14			
15			
16			
17			
18			

(a)

	Alexei Company	Ramirez Company	Dayan Company	Viciedo Company	
1	January 1, 2012					1
2	Assets	$ 95 000	$ 110 00		$ 170 000	2
3	Liabilities	50 000		75 000		3
4	Owner's Equity		60 00	45 000	90 000	4
5	December 31, 2012					5
6	Assets		141 000	200 000		6
7	Liabilities	55 000	75 000		80 000	7
8	Owner's Equity	63 000		130 000	162 000	8
9	Owner's equity changes					9
10	in year					10
11	Add'l investment		15 000	10 000	15 000	11
12	Drawings	25 000		14 000	20 000	12
13	Total revenues	350 000	420 000		520 000	13
14	Total expenses	320 000	385 000	342 000		14
15						15

(b)

Ramirez Company
Owner's Equity Statement
For the Year Ended December 31, 2012

1		1
2		2
3		3
4		4
5		5
6		6
7		7
8		8
9		9
10		10

(c)

11		11
12		12
13		13
14		14
15		15
16		16
17		17
18		18
19		19
20		20

Problem 1-1B

Vince's Travel Agency

See Appendix

(b)

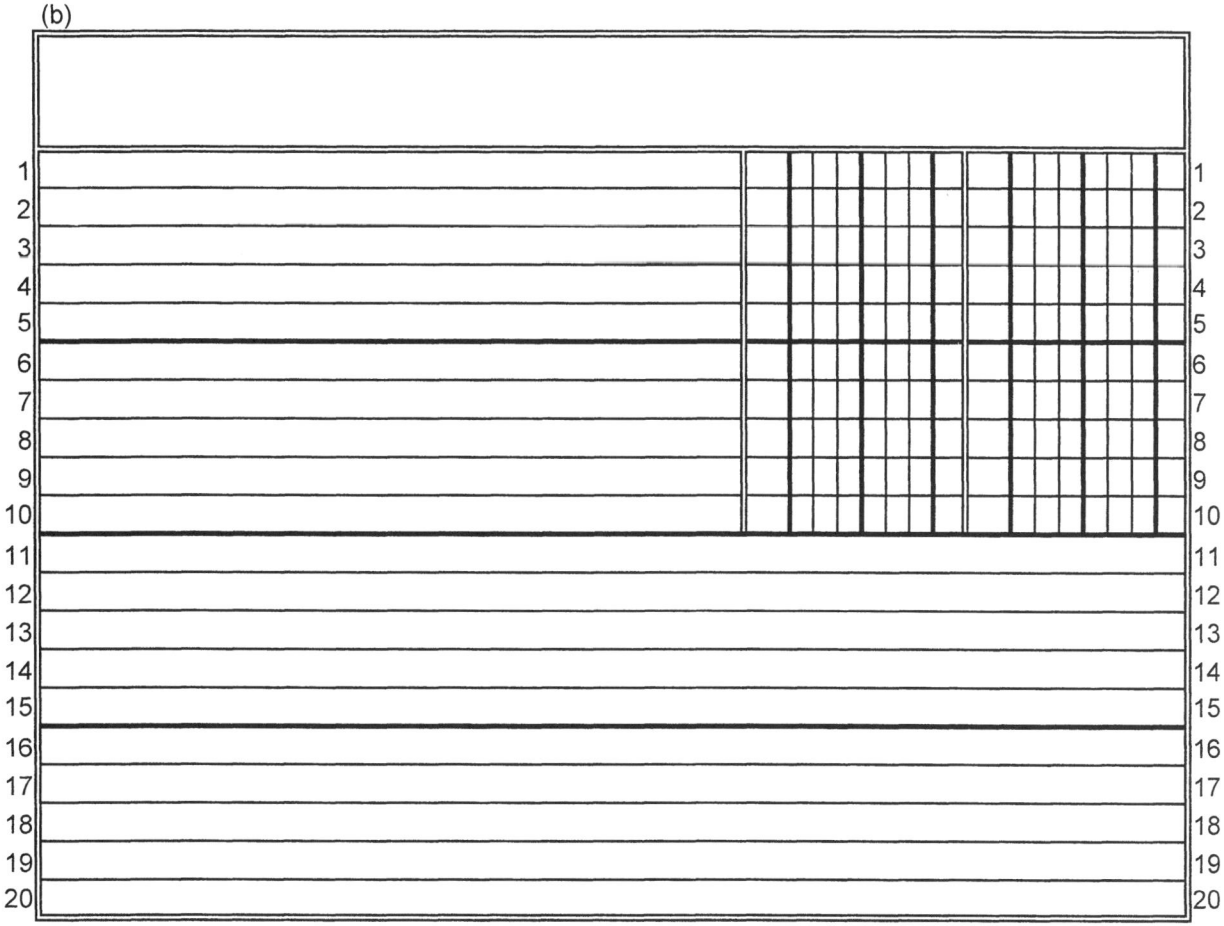

Problem 1-2B

Juanita Pierre, Attorney at Law

See Appendix

(b)

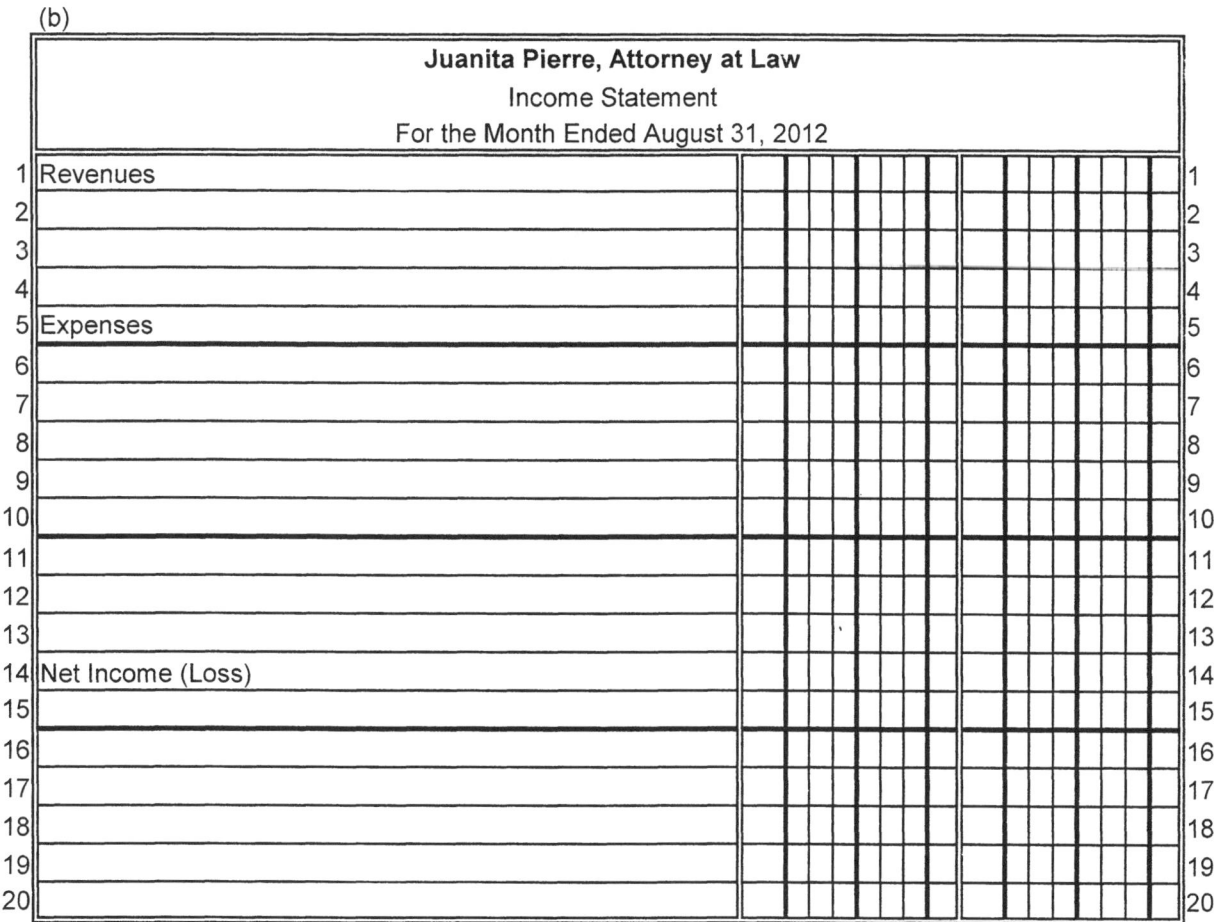

Juanita Pierre, Attorney at Law
Income Statement
For the Month Ended August 31, 2012

1	Revenues		
2			
3			
4			
5	Expenses		
6			
7			
8			
9			
10			
11			
12			
13			
14	Net Income (Loss)		
15			
16			
17			
18			
19			
20			

Juanita Pierre, Attorney at Law
Owner's Equity Statement
For the Month Ended August 31, 2012

1			
2			
3			
4			
5			
6			
7			
8			
9			
10			

(b) (Continued)

Juanita Pierre, Attorney at Law
Balance Sheet
August 31, 2012

	Assets										
1											1
2											2
3											3
4											4
5											5
6											6
7											7
8											8
9											9
10											10
11	Liabilities and Owner's Equity										11
12											12
13											13
14											14
15											15
16											16
17											17
18											18
19											19
20											20
21											21
22											22
23											23
24											24
25											25
26											26
27											27
28											28
29											29
30											30

(a)

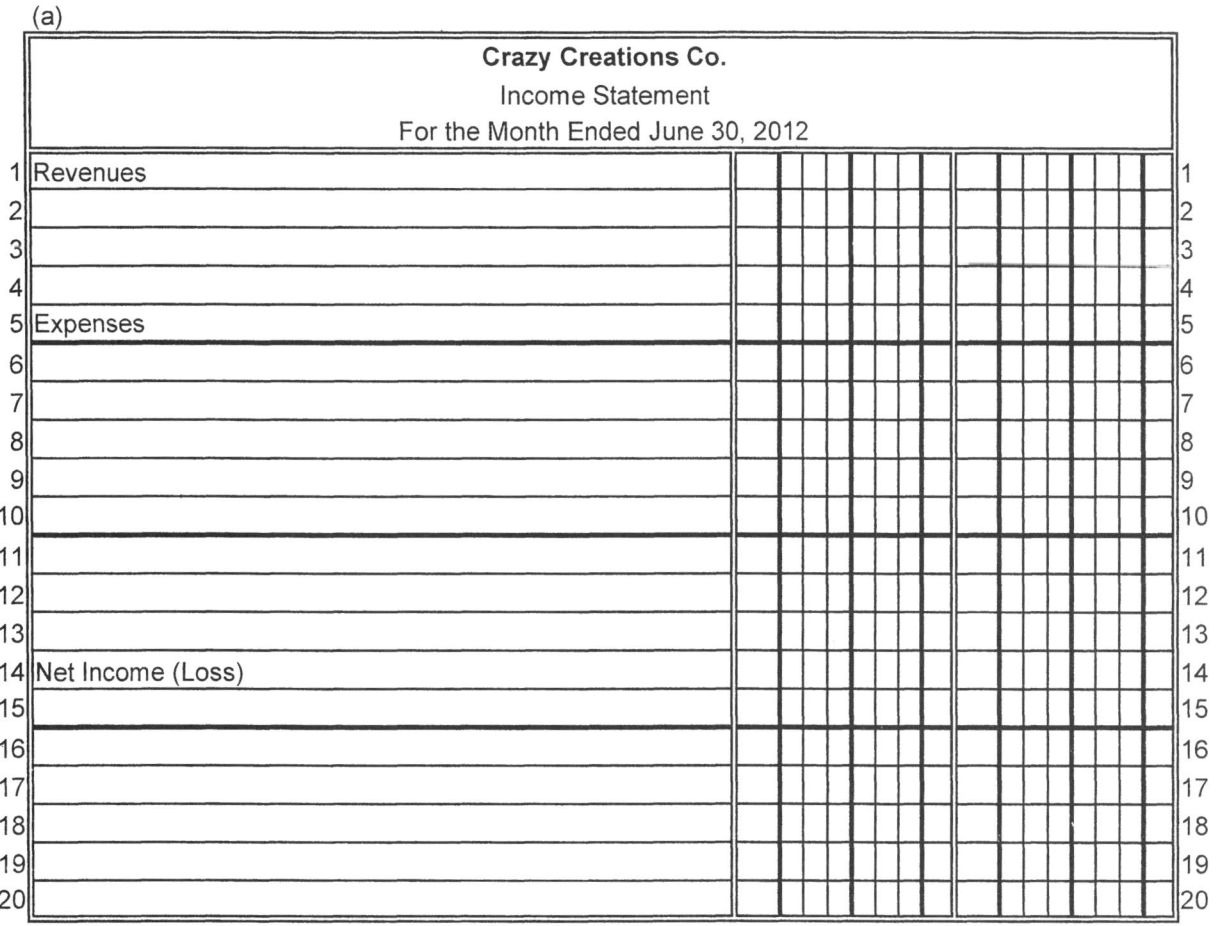

Crazy Creations Co.
Income Statement
For the Month Ended June 30, 2012

1 Revenues			
2			
3			
4			
5 Expenses			
6			
7			
8			
9			
10			
11			
12			
13			
14 Net Income (Loss)			
15			
16			
17			
18			
19			
20			

Crazy Creations Co.
Owner's Equity Statement
For the Month Ended June 30, 2012

1			
2			
3			
4			
5			
6			
7			
8			
9			
10			

(a) Continued

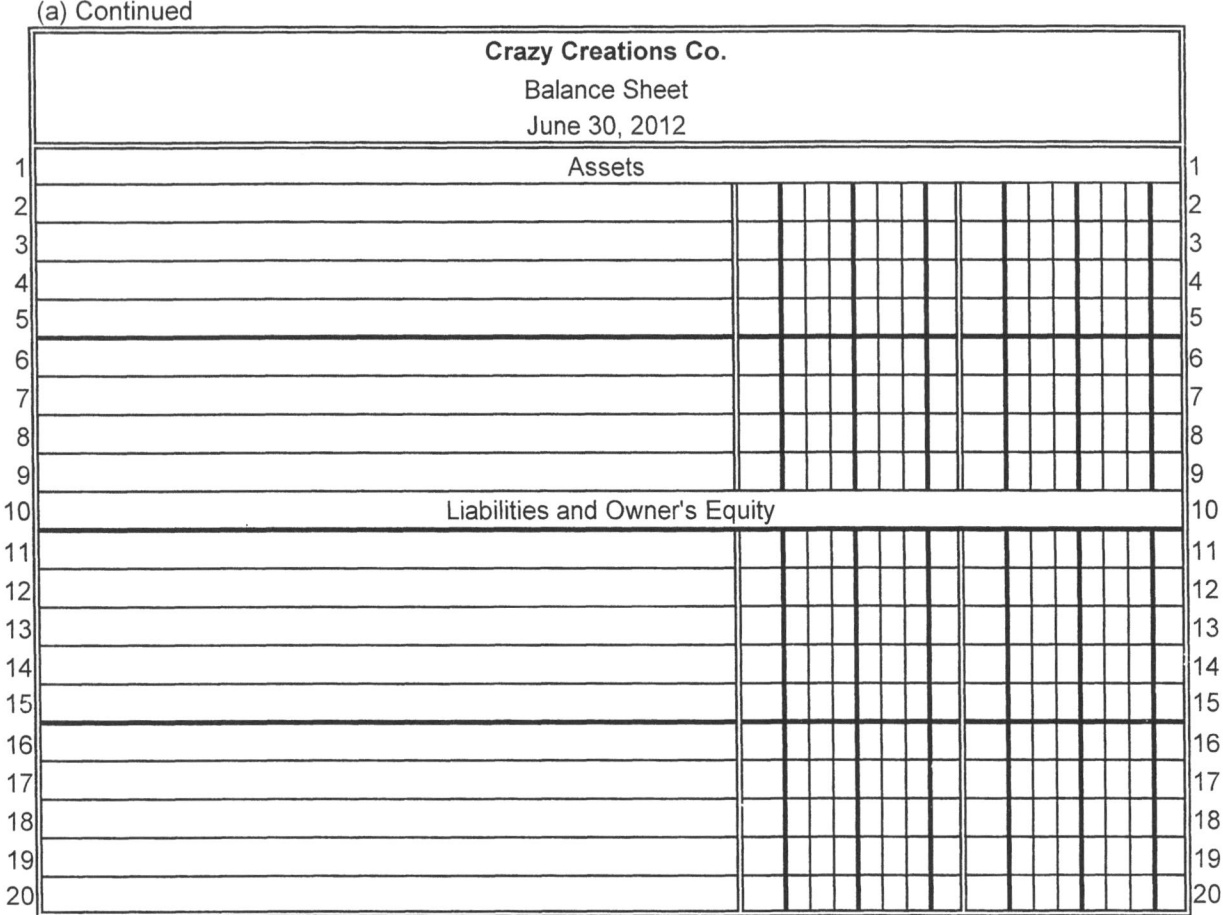

Crazy Creations Co.

Balance Sheet

June 30, 2012

	Assets				
1					1
2					2
3					3
4					4
5					5
6					6
7					7
8					8
9					9
10	Liabilities and Owner's Equity				10
11					11
12					12
13					13
14					14
15					15
16					16
17					17
18					18
19					19
20					20

(b)

Crazy Creations Co.

Income Statement

For the Month Ended June 30, 2012

1	Revenues				1
2					2
3					3
4	Expenses				4
5					5
6					6
7					7
8					8
9					9
10					10
11					11
12	Net Income (Loss)				12
13					13
14					14
15					15

(b) Continued

	Crazy Creations Co.									
	Owner's Equity Statement									
	For the Month Ended June 30, 2012									

Problem 1-4B

Quentin Consulting

See Appendix

(b)

Quentin Consulting		
Income Statement		
For the Month Ended May 31, 2012		

1	Revenues		
2			
3			
4	Expenses		
5			
6			
7			
8			
9			
10			
11			
12	Net income		
13			
14			

(c)

Quentin Consulting		
Balance Sheet		
May 31, 2012		

1	Assets		
2			
3			
4			
5			
6			
7			
8	Liabilities and Owner's Equity		
9			
10			
11			
12			
13			
14			
15			
16			
17			
18			

(a)

	Brent Company	Lillibridge Company	Omar Company	Vizquel Company
January 1, 2012				
Assets	$ 80000	$ 90000		$ 150000
Liabilities	48000		80000	
Owner's Equity		40000	49000	90000
December 31, 2012				
Assets		112000	180000	
Liabilities	60000	72000		100000
Owner's Equity	50000		82000	151000
Owner's equity changes				
in year				
Add'l investment		8000	10000	15000
Drawings	15000		12000	10000
Total revenues	350000	410000		500000
Total expenses	333000	385000	350000	

(b)

Brent Company

Owner's Equity Statement

For the Year Ended December 31, 2012

(c)

1	(a)
2	
3	
4	
5	
6	(b)
7	
8	
9	
10	
11	(c)
12	
13	
14	
15	
16	(d) Net sales - 2007:
17	
18	2008:
19	
20	2009:
21	
22	
23	
24	
25	
26	(e)
27	
28	
29	
30	
31	
32	
33	
34	
35	
36	
37	
38	
39	
40	

	PepsiCo	Coca-Cola
(a) (in millions)		
1. Total assets		
2. Accounts receivable(net)		
3. Net sales		
4. Net income		
(b)		

(a)

1	1
2	2
3	3
4	4
5	5

(b)

Chip-Shot Driving Range
Balance Sheet
March 31, 2012

	Assets		
1			1
2			2
3			3
4			4
5			5
6			6
7			7
8			8
9			9
10			10
11	Liabilities and Owner's Equity		11
12			12
13			13
14			14
15			15
16			16
17			17
18			18
19			19
20			20
21			21
22			22
23			23
24			24
25			25
26			26
27			27
28			28
29			29
30			30

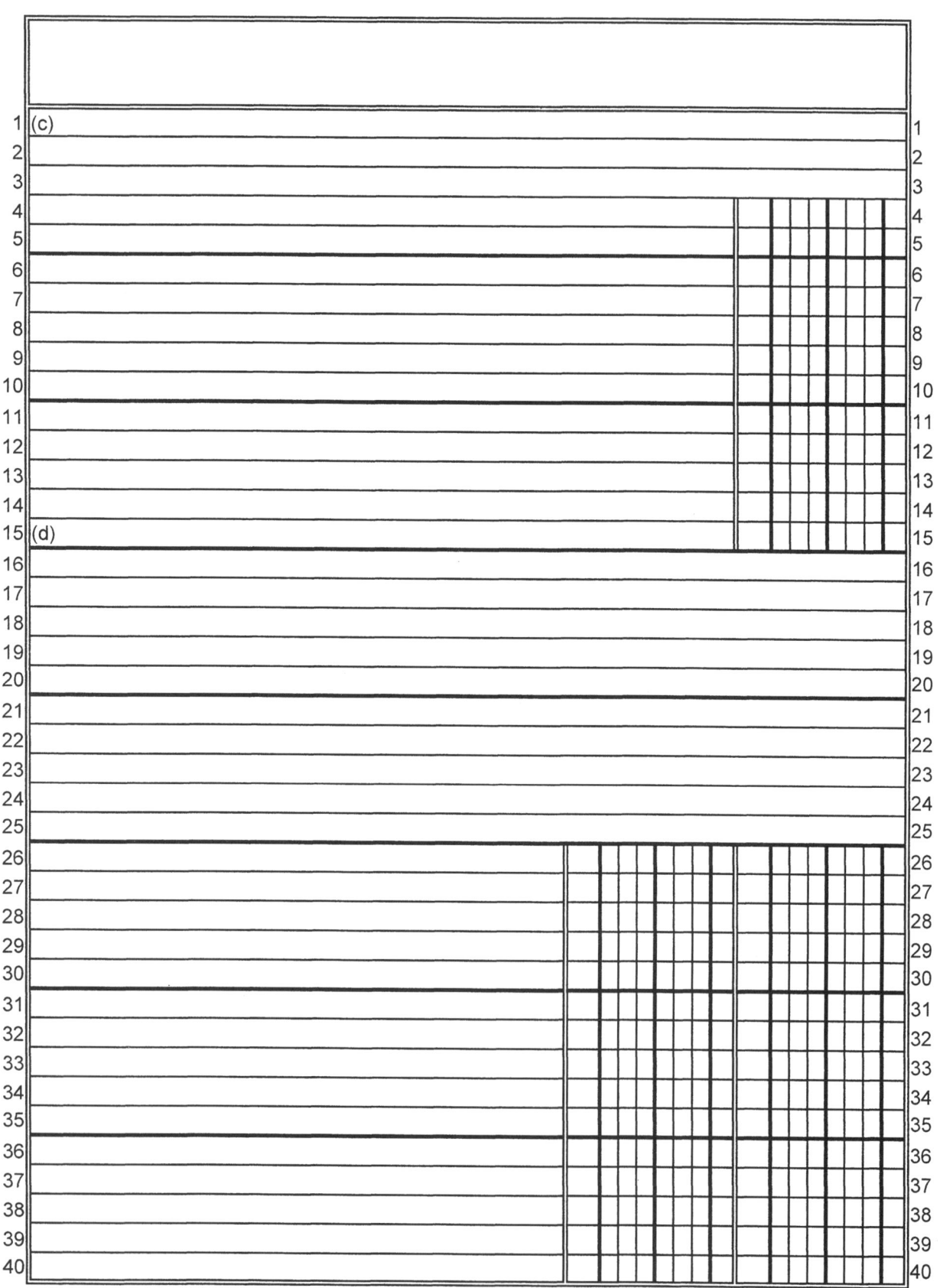

Name

Section

Date

1	1
2	2
3	3
4	4
5	5
6	6
7	7
8	8
9	9
10	10
11	11
12	12
13	13
14	14
15	15
16	16
17	17
18	18
19	19
20	20
21	21
22	22
23	23
24	24
25	25
26	26
27	27
28	28
29	29
30	30
31	31
32	32
33	33
34	34
35	35
36	36
37	37
38	38
39	39
40	40

	New York Company		
	Balance Sheet		
	December 31, 2012		
1	Assets		
2			
3			
4			
5			
6			
7			
8			
9	Liabilities and Owner's Equity		
10			
11			
12			
13			
14			
15			
16			
17			
18			
19			
20			
21			
22			
23			
24			
25			
26			
27			
28			
29			
30			
31			
32			
33			
34			
35			
36			
37			
38			
39			
40			

BE2-9

	Afalava Company Trial Balance June 30, 2012	Debit	Credit	
1				1
2				2
3				3
4				4
5				5
6				6
7				7
8				8
9				9
10				10
11				11
12				12

BE2-10

	Walter Company Trial Balance December 31, 2012	Debit	Credit	
1				1
2				2
3				3
4				4
5				5
6				6
7				7
8				8
9				9
10				10
11				11

DO IT! 2-2

	Trans.	Account Titles	Debit	Credit	
1	1.				1
2					2
3					3
4	2.				4
5					5
6					6
7					7
8	3.				8
9					9

DO IT 2-3

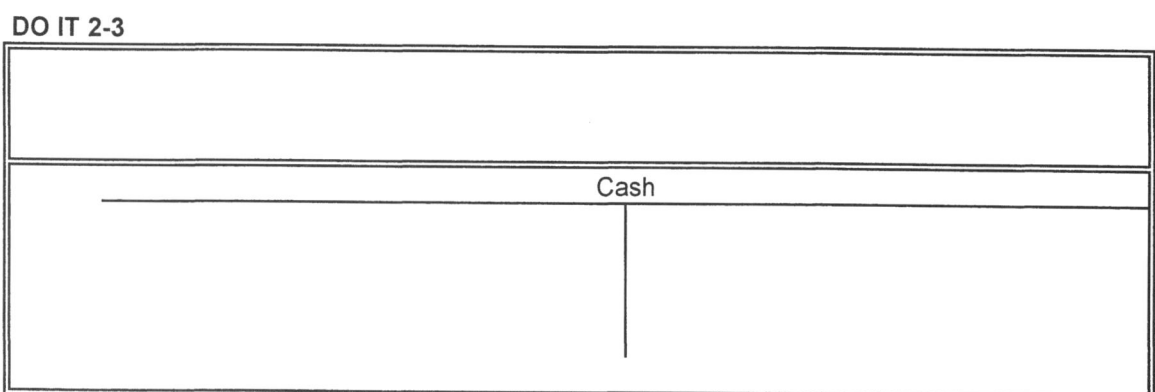

Cash

DO IT 2-4

	Angulo Company Trial Balance December 31, 2012			
1				1
2				2
3				3
4				4
5				5
6				6
7				7
8				8
9				9
10				10
11				11
12				12
13				13
14				14
15				15

Section

Date   M. Anderson, Interior Decorator

	Date	Account Titles	Ref.	Debit	Credit	
1	Jan. 2					1
2						2
3						3
4	3					4
5						5
6						6
7	9					7
8						8
9						9
10	11					10
11						11
12						12
13	16					13
14						14
15						15
16	20					16
17						17
18						18
19	23					19
20						20
21						21
22	28					22
23						23
24						24

General Journal   J1

	Date	Account Titles	Ref.	Debit	Credit	
1	Oct. 1					1
2						2
3						3
4	2					4
5						5
6	3					6
7						7
8						8
9	6					9
10						10
11						11
12	27					12
13						13
14						14
15	30					15
16						16
17						17

	(a)			
1	1.			
2				
3	2.			
4				
5	3.			
6				
7	(b)	Account Titles	Debit	Credit
8	1.			
9				
10				
11	2.			
12				
13				
14	3.			
15				
16				
17				
18				

(a)		Assets =	Liabilities +	Owners' Equity	
1.					1
					2
2.					3
					4
3.					5
					6
4.					7
					8
					9
(b)	Account Titles		Debit	Credit	10
1.					11
					12
					13
2.					14
					15
					16
3.					17
					18
					19
4.					20
					21
					22
					23

(a)

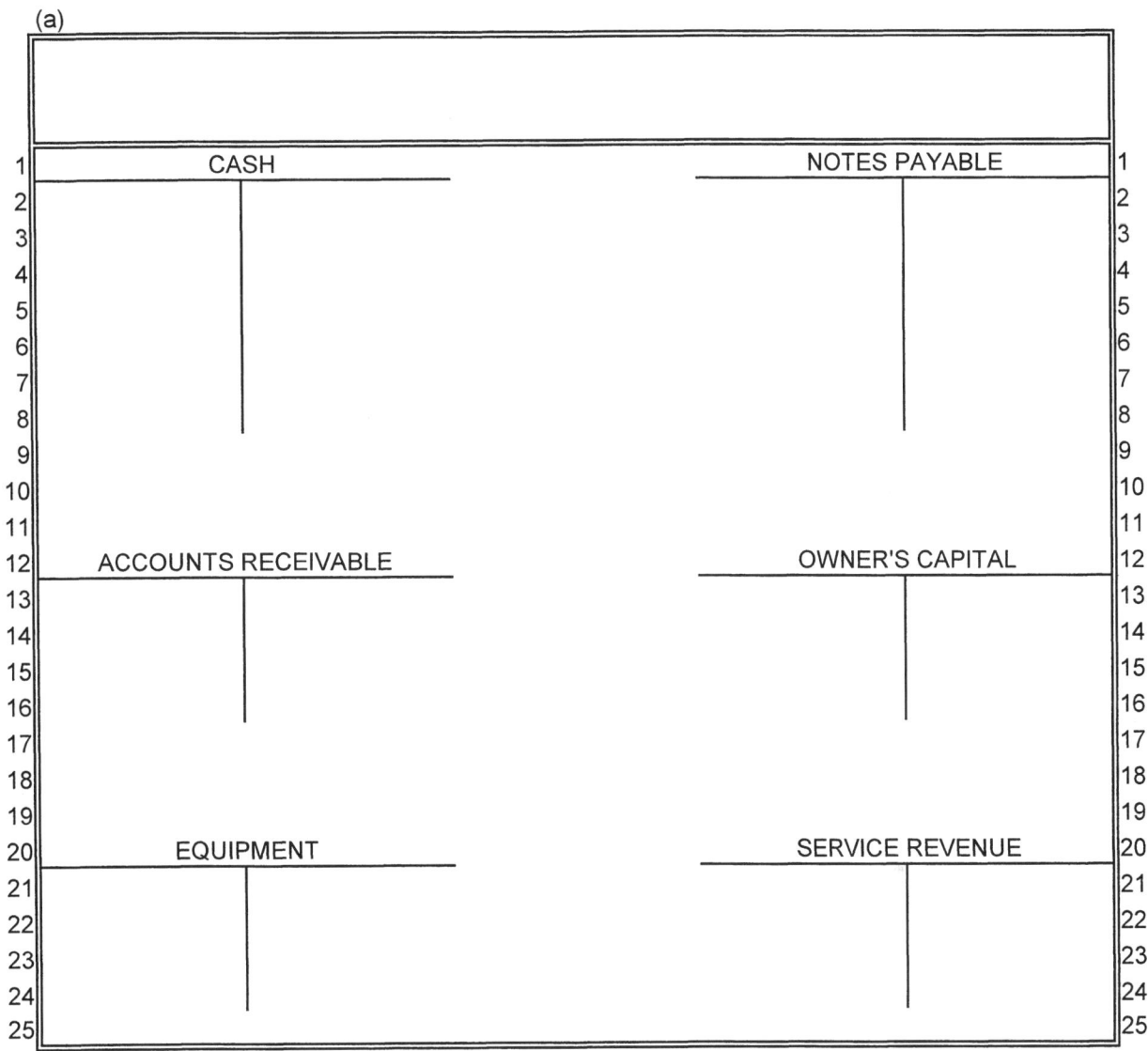

	CASH			NOTES PAYABLE	
1					1
2					2
3					3
4					4
5					5
6					6
7					7
8					8
9					9
10					10
11					11
12	ACCOUNTS RECEIVABLE			OWNER'S CAPITAL	12
13					13
14					14
15					15
16					16
17					17
18					18
19					19
20	EQUIPMENT			SERVICE REVENUE	20
21					21
22					22
23					23
24					24
25					25

(b)

Consuela Brown, Investment Broker

Trial Balance

August 31, 2012

		Debit	Credit	
1				1
2				2
3				3
4				4
5				5
6				6
7				7
8				8
9				9
10				10

(a)   General Journal

	Date	Account Titles	Ref.	Debit	Credit	
1	Apr. 1					1
2						2
3						3
4						4
5	12					5
6						6
7						7
8						8
9	15					9
10						10
11						11
12						12
13	25					13
14						14
15						15
16						16
17	29					17
18						18
19						19
20						20
21	30					21
22						22
23						23
24						24
25						25
26						26

(b)

	Bennet Landscaping Company Trial Balance April 30, 2012	Debit	Credit	
1				1
2				2
3				3
4				4
5				5
6				6
7				7
8				8
9				9

(a)   General Journal   J1

	Date	Account Titles	Ref.	Debit	Credit	
1	May 1					1
2						2
3						3
4						4
5	2					5
6						6
7	3					7
8						8
9						9
10						10
11	7					11
12						12
13						13
14						14
15	11					15
16						16
17						17
18						18
19	12					19
20						20
21						21
22						22
23	17					23
24						24
25						25
26						26
27	31					27
28						28
29						29
30						30
31	31					31
32						32
33						33
34						34
35						35
36						36
37						37
38						38
39						39
40						40

(b)

Cash   No. 101

Date	Explanation	Ref.	Debit	Credit	Balance

Accounts Receivable   No. 112

Date	Explanation	Ref.	Debit	Credit	Balance

Supplies   No. 126

Date	Explanation	Ref.	Debit	Credit	Balance

Accounts Payable   No. 201

Date	Explanation	Ref.	Debit	Credit	Balance

Unearned Service Revenue   No. 205

Date	Explanation	Ref.	Debit	Credit	Balance

Owner's Capital   No. 301

Date	Explanation	Ref.	Debit	Credit	Balance

(b) (Continued)

Service Revenue   No. 400

Date	Explanation	Ref.	Debit	Credit	Balance

Salaries and Wages Expense   No. 726

Date	Explanation	Ref.	Debit	Credit	Balance

Rent Expense   No. 729

Date	Explanation	Ref.	Debit	Credit	Balance

(c)

Desiree Clark, CPA
Trial Balance
May 31, 2012

		Debit	Credit	
1	Cash			1
2	Accounts Receivable			2
3	Supplies			3
4	Accounts Payable			4
5	Unearned Service Revenue			5
6	Owner's Capital			6
7	Service Revenue			7
8	Salaries and Wages Expense			8
9	Rent Expense			9
10				10
11				11

(a) & (c)

Cash		Owner's Capital	
Bal. 8,000			Bal. 40,000

Accounts Receivable		Owner's Drawings	
Bal. 15,000			

		Service Revenue	

Supplies		Advertising Expense	
Bal. 13,000			

Prepaid Rent		Miscellaneous Expense	
Bal. 3,000			

		Supplies Expense	

Equipment		Salaries and Wages Expense	
Bal. 20,000			

Accounts Payable	
	Bal. 19,000

(b)

	Date	Account Titles	Ref.	Debit	Credit	
1	1.					1
2						2
3						3
4	2.					4
5						5
6						6
7	3.					7
8						8
9						9
10	4.					10
11						11
12						12
13	5.					13
14						14
15						15
16	6.					16
17						17
18						18
19	7.					19
20						20
21						21
22						22
23	8.					23
24						24
25						25
26	9.					26
27						27
28						28
29						29
30						30
31						31
32						32
33						33
34						34
35						35
36						36
37						37
38						38
39						39
40						40

General Journal J1

(d)

Mega Repair Service Trial Balance January 31, 2012	Debit	Credit
1 Cash		
2 Accounts Receivable		
3 Supplies		
4 Prepaid Rent		
5 Equipment		
6 Accounts Payable		
7 Owner's Capital		
8 Owner's Drawings		
9 Service Revenue		
10 Advertising Expense		
11 Miscellaneous Expense		
12 Supplies Expense		
13 Salaries and Wages Expense		
14 Totals		
15		
16		
17		

(a) and (c) (Continued)

Mortgage Payable No. 275

Date	Explanation	Ref.	Debit	Credit	Balance
Apr. 1	Balance	√			8 0 0 0

Owner's Capital No. 301

Date	Explanation	Ref.	Debit	Credit	Balance
Apr. 1	Balance	√			1 8 0 0 0

Service Revenue No. 405

Date	Explanation	Ref.	Debit	Credit	Balance

Rent Revenue No. 429

Date	Explanation	Ref.	Debit	Credit	Balance

Advertising Expense No. 610

Date	Explanation	Ref.	Debit	Credit	Balance

Rent Expense No. 632

Date	Explanation	Ref.	Debit	Credit	Balance

Salaries and Wages Expense No. 726

Date	Explanation	Ref.	Debit	Credit	Balance

(b)

General Journal

J1

	Date	Account Titles	Ref.	Debit	Credit	
1	Apr. 2					1
2						2
3						3
4						4
5	3					5
6						6
7	9					7
8						8
9						9
10						10
11	10					11
12						12
13						13
14						14
15						15
16						16
17	11					17
18						18
19	12					19
20						20
21						21
22						22
23	20					23
24						24
25						25
26						26
27	25					27
28						28
29						29
30						30
31	29					31
32						32
33						33
34						34
35	30					35
36						36
37						37
38						38
39	30					39
40						40
41						41

(d)

Chicago Theater Trial Balance April 30, 2012	Debit	Credit	
1 Cash			1
2 Accounts Receivable			2
3 Prepaid Rent			3
4 Land			4
5 Buildings			5
6 Equipment			6
7 Accounts Payable			7
8 Mortgage Payable			8
9 Owner's Capital			9
10 Service Revenue			10
11 Rent Revenue			11
12 Advertising Expense			12
13 Rent Expense			13
14 Salaries and Wages Expense			14
15			15
16			16
17			17

General Journal   J1

	Date	Account Titles	Ref.	Debit	Credit	
1	Mar. 1					1
2						2
3						3
4						4
5	3					5
6						6
7						7
8						8
9						9
10						10
11	5					11
12						12
13						13
14						14
15	6					15
16						16
17						17
18						18
19	10					19
20						20
21						21
22						22
23	18					23
24						24
25						25
26						26
27	19					27
28						28
29						29
30						30
31	25					31
32						32
33						33
34						34
35	30					35
36						36
37						37
38						38
39						39
40						40

	Date	Account Titles	Ref.	Debit	Credit	
1	Mar. 30					1
2						2
3						3
4						4
5	31					5
6						6
7						7
8						8
9						9
10						10
11						11
12						12
13						13
14						14
15						15
16						16
17						17
18						18
19						19
20						20
21						21
22						22
23						23
24						24
25						25
26						26
27						27
28						28
29						29
30						30
31						31
32						32
33						33
34						34
35						35
36						36
37						37
38						38
39						39
40						40

General Journal   J1

(a)

General Journal

J1

	Date	Account Titles	Ref.	Debit	Credit	
1	Apr. 1					1
2						2
3						3
4						4
5	1					5
6						6
7	2					7
8						8
9						9
10						10
11	3					11
12						12
13						13
14						14
15						15
16	10					16
17						17
18						18
19						19
20	11					20
21						21
22						22
23						23
24	20					24
25						25
26						26
27						27
28	30					28
29						29
30						30
31						31
32	30					32
33						33
34						34
35						35
36						36
37						37
38						38
39						39
40						40

(b)

Cash   No. 101

Date	Explanation	Ref.	Debit	Credit	Balance

Accounts Receivable   No. 112

Date	Explanation	Ref.	Debit	Credit	Balance

Supplies   No. 126

Date	Explanation	Ref.	Debit	Credit	Balance

Accounts Payable   No. 201

Date	Explanation	Ref.	Debit	Credit	Balance

Unearned Service Revenue   No. 205

Date	Explanation	Ref.	Debit	Credit	Balance

Owner's Capital   No. 301

Date	Explanation	Ref.	Debit	Credit	Balance

(b) (Continued)

Service Revenue   No. 400

Date	Explanation	Ref.	Debit	Credit	Balance

Salaries and Wages Expense   No. 726

Date	Explanation	Ref.	Debit	Credit	Balance

Rent Expense   No. 729

Date	Explanation	Ref.	Debit	Credit	Balance

(c)

		Debit	Credit	
	Victoria Hall, Dentist Trial Balance April 30, 2012			
1	Cash			1
2	Accounts Receivable			2
3	Supplies			3
4	Accounts Payable			4
5	Unearned Service Revenue			5
6	Owner's Capital			6
7	Service Revenue			7
8	Salaries and Wages Expense			8
9	Rent Expense			9
10				10
11				11

(a)   General Journal

	Trans.	Account Titles	Ref.	Debit	Credit	
1	1.					1
2						2
3						3
4	2.					4
5						5
6	3.					6
7						7
8						8
9	4.					9
10						10
11						11
12						12
13	5.					13
14						14
15						15
16	6.					16
17						17
18						18
19	7.					19
20						20
21						21
22	8.					22
23						23
24						24
25						25
26	9.					26
27						27
28						28
29	10.					29
30						30
31						31
32	11.					32
33						33
34						34
35	12.					35
36						36
37						37
38						38
39						39
40						40

(b)

Cash		Accounts Payable

Accounts Receivable		Owner's Capital

Supplies		Service Revenue

Prepaid Insurance		Salaries and Wages Expense

Prepaid Rent		Utilities Expense

Equipment

(c)

San Jose Services		
Trial Balance		
May 31, 2012		
	Debit	Credit
1 Cash		
2 Accounts Receivable		
3 Supplies		
4 Prepaid Insurance		
5 Prepaid Rent		
6 Equipment		
7 Accounts Payable		
8 Owner's Capital		
9 Service Revenue		
10 Salaries and Wages Expense		
11 Utilities Expense		

		Debit	Credit
1			
2			
3			
4			
5			
6			
7			
8			
9			
10			
11			
12			
13			
14			
15			
16	Journal Entry Aids:		
17			
18			
19			
20			
21			
22			
23			
24			
25			
26			
27			
28			
29			
30			
31			
32			
33			
34			
35			
36			
37			
38			
39			
40			

Robbie Gould Co.
Trial Balance
June 30, 2012

(a) and (c)

Cash No. 101

Date	Explanation	Ref.	Debit	Credit	Balance
Mar. 1	Balance	√			3 0 0 0

Accounts Receivable No. 112

Date	Explanation	Ref.	Debit	Credit	Balance

Land No. 140

Date	Explanation	Ref.	Debit	Credit	Balance
Mar. 1	Balance	√			2 4 0 0 0

Buildings No. 145

Date	Explanation	Ref.	Debit	Credit	Balance
Mar. 1	Balance	√			1 0 0 0 0

Equipment No. 157

Date	Explanation	Ref.	Debit	Credit	Balance
Mar. 1	Balance	√			1 0 0 0 0

Accounts Payable No. 201

Date	Explanation	Ref.	Debit	Credit	Balance
Mar. 1	Balance	√			7 0 0 0

Owner's Capital No. 301

Date	Explanation	Ref.	Debit	Credit	Balance
Mar. 1	Balance	√			4 0 0 0 0

(a) and (c) (Continued)

Service Revenue   No. 405

Date	Explanation	Ref.	Debit	Credit	Balance

Rent Revenue   No. 429

Date	Explanation	Ref.	Debit	Credit	Balance

Advertising Expense   No. 610

Date	Explanation	Ref.	Debit	Credit	Balance

Rent Expense   No. 632

Date	Explanation	Ref.	Debit	Credit	Balance

Salaries and Wages Expense   No. 726

Date	Explanation	Ref.	Debit	Credit	Balance

(b)

General Journal

J1

	Date	Account Titles	Ref.	Debit	Credit	
1	Mar. 2					1
2						2
3						3
4						4
5						5
6	3					6
7						7
8	9					8
9						9
10						10
11						11
12	10					12
13						13
14						14
15						15
16	11					16
17						17
18	12					18
19						19
20						20
21						21
22	20					22
23						23
24						24
25						25
26	20					26
27						27
28						28
29						29
30	31					30
31						31
32						32
33						33
34						34
35						35
36						36
37						37
38						38
39						39
40						40

(b) General Journal — J1

	Date	Account Titles	Ref.	Debit	Credit	
1	Mar. 31					1
2						2
3						3
4						4
5						5
6						6
7	31					7
8						8
9						9
10						10
11						11
12						12
13						13
14						14
15						15
16						16

(d)

Cora Theater
Trial Balance
March 31, 2012

		Debit	Credit	
1	Cash			1
2	Accounts Receivable			2
3	Land			3
4	Buildings			4
5	Equipment			5
6	Accounts Payable			6
7	Owner's Capital			7
8	Service Revenue			8
9	Sales Revenue			9
10	Advertising Expense			10
11	Rent Expense			11
12	Salaries and Wages Expense			12
13				13
14				14
15				15
16				16
17				17

(a)

	Date	Account Titles	Debit	Credit	
1	May 1				1
2					2
3					3
4	5				4
5					5
6					6
7	7				7
8					8
9					9
10	14				10
11					11
12					12
13	15				13
14					14
15					15
16	20				16
17					17
18					18
19	30				19
20					20
21					21
22	31				22
23					23
24					24
25					25

(b)

1		1
2		2
3		3
4		4
5		5

(c)

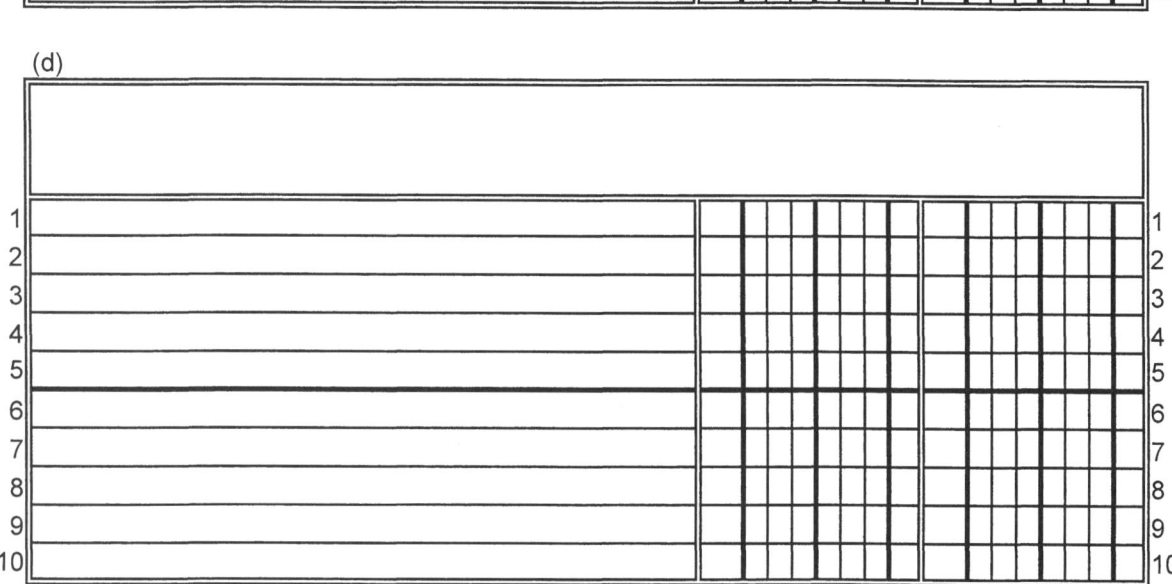

(d)

BE3-3

	Date	Account Titles	Debit	Credit	
1	Dec. 31				1
2					2
3					3
4					4

5		5
6	Supplies	Supplies Expense	6
7		7
8		8
9		9
10		10

BE3-4

	Date	Account Titles	Debit	Credit	
12	Date	Account Titles	Debit	Credit	12
13	Dec. 31				13
14					14
15					15

16			16
17	Depr. Expense	Accum. Depreciation - Equipment	17
18			18
19			19
20			20
21			21
22	Balance Sheet:		22
23			23
24			24
25			25
26			26

BE3-5

	Date	Account Titles	Debit	Credit	
28	Date	Account Titles	Debit	Credit	28
29	July 1				29
30					30
31					31
32	Dec. 31				32
33					33
34					34

35			35
36	Prepaid Insurance	Insurance Expense	36
37			37
38			38
39			39
40			40

BE3-6

	Date	Account Titles	Debit	Credit	
1	July 1				1
2					2
3					3
4					4
5	Dec. 31				5
6					6
7					7
8					8
9					9
10					10

	Unearned Service Revenue		Service Revenue	
11				11
12				12
13				13
14				14
15				15

BE3-7

	Date	Account Titles	Debit	Credit	
17	Date	Account Titles	Debit	Credit	17
18	Dec. 31				18
19					19
20					20
21	31				21
22					22
23					23
24	31				24
25					25
26					26
27					27
28					28
29					29
30					30
31					31
32					32
33					33
34					34
35					35
36					36
37					37
38					38
39					39
40					40

BE3-9

	Iwuh Company		
	Income Statement		
	For the Year Ended December 31, 2012		

1			
2			
3			
4			
5			
6			
7			
8			
9			
10			
11			
12			
13			
14			

BE3-10

	Iwuh Company		
	Owner's Equity Statement		
	For the Year Ended December 31, 2012		

19			
20			
21			
22			
23			
24			
25			

*BE3-11

Date	Account Titles	Debit	Credit
(a)			
Apr. 30			
(b)			
Apr. 30			

DO IT! 3-2

	Trans.	Account Titles	Debit	Credit	
1	1.				1
2					2
3					3
4					4
5	2.				5
6					6
7					7
8					8
9	3.				9
10					10
11					11
12					12
13	4.				13
14					14
15					15

DO IT! 3-3

	Trans.	Account Titles	Debit	Credit	
1	1.				1
2					2
3					3
4					4
5	2.				5
6					6
7					7
8					8
9	3.				9
10					10
11					11
12					12
13					13
14					14
15					15
16					16
17					17
18					18
19					19
20					20

(a)		
1 Revenues:		
2		
3		
4		
5 Expenses:		
6		
7		
8		
9		
10		
11		
12		
13 Net income (loss)		
14		
15 (b)		
16 Assets:		
17		
18		
19		
20		
21		
22		
23		
24		
25 Liabilities:		
26		
27		
28		
29		
30		
31		
32		
33 (c)		
34		
35		
36		
37		
38		
39		
40		

1	a. Cash-basis net income:						1
2							2
3							3
4							4
5							5
6							6
7							7
8							8
9							9
10	b. Accrual-basis net income:						10
11							11
12							12
13							13
14							14
15							15
16							16
17							17
18							18
19							19
20							20

Item	Account Titles	Debit	Credit
1.			
2.			
3.			
4.			
5.			
6.			
7.			

	Date	Account Titles	Debit	Credit	
1	Mar. 31				1
2					2
3					3
4					4
5	31				5
6					6
7					7
8	31				8
9					9
10					10
11	31				11
12					12
13					13
14	31				14
15					15
16					16

E3-8

	Date	Account Titles	Debit	Credit	
1	Jan. 31				1
2					2
3					3
4	31				4
5					5
6					6
7	31				7
8					8
9					9
10	31				10
11					11
12					12
13	31				13
14					14
15					15
16	31				16
17					17

E3-9

	Date	Account Titles	Debit	Credit	
1	Oct. 31				1
2					2
3					3
4	31				4
5					5
6					6
7	31				7
8					8
9					9
10	31				10
11					11
12					12
13	31				13
14					14
15					15
16	31				16
17					17
18					18
19	31				19
20					20

E3-10

	Brandon Co.				
	Income Statement				
	For the Month Ended July 31, 2012				
1	Revenues:				1
2					2
3	Expenses:				3
4					4
5					5
6					6
7					7
8					8
9					9
10					10

E3-11

	Answer	Computation	
1	(a)		1
2			2
3			3
4			4
5			5
6	(b)		6
7			7
8			8
9			9
10			10
11			11
12			12
13			13
14	(c)		14
15			15
16			16
17			17
18			18
19			19
20	(d)		20
21			21
22			22
23			23
24			24
25			25

	Date	Account Titles	Debit	Credit	
1	(a)				1
2	July 10				2
3					3
4					4
5	14				5
6					6
7					7
8	15				8
9					9
10					10
11	20				11
12					12
13					13
14					14
15					15
16	(b)				16
17	July 31				17
18					18
19					19
20	31				20
21					21
22					22
23	31				23
24					24
25					25
26	31				26
27					27
28					28
29					29
30					30
31					31
32					32
33					33
34					34
35					35
36					36
37					37
38					38
39					39
40					40

E3-13

	Date	Account Titles	Debit	Credit	
1	Aug. 31				1
2					2
3					3
4	31				4
5					5
6					6
7	31				7
8					8
9					9
10	31				10
11					11
12					12
13					13
14	31				14
15					15
16					16
17	31				17
18					18
19					19
20					20

E3-14

	Matthews Company Income Statement For the Year Ended August 31, 2012			
1	Revenues:			1
2				2
3				3
4				4
5	Expenses:			5
6				6
7				7
8				8
9				9
10				10
11				11
12				12
13				13
14				14
15				15

Matthews Company

Owner's Equity Statement

For the Year Ended August 31, 2012

1		1
2		2
3		3
4		4

Matthews Company

Balance Sheet

August 31, 2012

	Assets		
1			1
2			2
3			3
4			4
5			5
6			6
7			7
8			8
9			9
10	Liabilities and Owner's Equity		10
11			11
12			12
13			13
14			14
15			15
16			16
17			17
18			18
19			19
20			20

Section

Date

E3-15

		Account Titles	Debit	Credit	
1	(a)				1
2	1.				2
3					3
4					4
5	2.				5
6					6
7					7
8	3. (a)				8
9					9
10					10
11	(b)				11
12					12
13					13
14					14
15	4.				15
16					16
17					17
18	5.				18
19					19
20					20
21					21
22	(b)				22
23					23
24					24
25					25

*E3-16

		Account Titles	Debit	Credit	
1	1.				1
2					2
3					3
4	2.				4
5					5
6					6
7	3.				7
8					8
9					9
10					10

(a)

	Date	Account Titles	Debit	Credit	
1	Jan. 2				1
2					2
3					3
4	10				4
5					5
6					6
7	15				7
8					8
9					9

(b)

	Date	Account Titles	Debit	Credit	
11	Jan. 31				11
12					12
13					13
14					14
15	31				15
16					16
17					17
18	31				18
19					19

CASH

PREPAID INSURANCE   INSURANCE EXPENSE

SUPPLIES   SUPPLIES EXPENSE

UNEARNED SERVICE REVENUE   SERVICE REVENUE

(c)

1	Insurance Expense						1
2	Supplies Expense						2
3	Service Revenue						3
4	Prepaid Insurance						4
5	Supplies						5
6	Unearned Service Revenue						6
7							7
8							8
9							9
10							10

(a)   General Journal   J3

	Date	Account Titles	Ref.	Debit	Credit	
1	2012					1
2	June 30					2
3						3
4						4
5	30					5
6						6
7						7
8	30					8
9						9
10						10
11	30					11
12						12
13						13
14	30					14
15						15
16						16
17	30					17
18						18
19						19
20	30					20
21						21
22						22
23						23
24						24
25						25
26						26
27						27
28						28
29						29
30						30
31						31
32						32
33						33
34						34
35						35
36						36
37						37
38						38
39						39
40						40

(b)

Cash   No. 101

Date	Explanation	Ref.	Debit	Credit	Balance
2012					
June 30	Balance	√			7150

Accounts Receivable   No. 112

Date	Explanation	Ref.	Debit	Credit	Balance
2012					
June 30	Balance	√			6000

Supplies   No. 126

Date	Explanation	Ref.	Debit	Credit	Balance
2012					
June 30	Balance	√			2000

Prepaid Insurance   No. 130

Date	Explanation	Ref.	Debit	Credit	Balance
2012					
June 30	Balance	√			3000

Equipment   No. 157

Date	Explanation	Ref.	Debit	Credit	Balance
2012					
June 30	Balance	√			15000

Accumulated Depreciation - Equipment   No, 158

Date	Explanation	Ref.	Debit	Credit	Balance

Accounts Payable   No. 201

Date	Explanation	Ref.	Debit	Credit	Balance
2012					
June 30	Balance	√			4500

(b) (Continued)

Unearned Service Revenue — No. 209

Date	Explanation	Ref.	Debit	Credit	Balance
2012					
June 30	Balance	√			4 0 0 0

Salaries and Wages Payable — No. 212

Date	Explanation	Ref.	Debit	Credit	Balance

Utilities Payable — No. 244

Date	Explanation	Ref.	Debit	Credit	Balance

Owner's Capital — No. 301

Date	Explanation	Ref.	Debit	Credit	Balance
2012					
June 30	Balance	√			2 1 7 5 0

Service Revenue — No. 400

Date	Explanation	Ref.	Debit	Credit	Balance
2012					
June 30	Balance	√			7 9 0 0

Supplies Expense — No. 631

Date	Explanation	Ref.	Debit	Credit	Balance

Depreciation Expense — No. 711

Date	Explanation	Ref.	Debit	Credit	Balance

(b) (Continued)

Insurance Expense   No. 722

Date	Explanation	Ref.	Debit	Credit	Balance

Salaries and Wages Expense   No. 726

Date	Explanation	Ref.	Debit	Credit	Balance
2012					
June 30	Balance	√			4 0 0 0

Rent Expense   No. 729

Date	Explanation	Ref.	Debit	Credit	Balance
2012					
June 30	Balance	√			1 0 0 0

Utilities Expense   No. 732

Date	Explanation	Ref.	Debit	Credit	Balance

(c)

McGee Company Adjusted Trial Balance June 30, 2012	Debit	Credit
1 Cash		
2 Accounts Receivable		
3 Supplies		
4 Prepaid Insurance		
5 Equipment		
6 Accumulated Depreciation - Equipment		
7 Accounts Payable		
8 Unearned Service Revenue		
9 Salaries and Wages Payable		
10 Owner's Capital		
11 Service Revenue		
12 Supplies Expense		
13 Depreciation Expense		
14 Insurance Expense		
15 Salaries and Wages Expense		
16 Rent Expense		
17 Utilities Expense		
18 Totals		

(a)   General Journal   J1

	Date	Account Titles	Ref.	Debit	Credit	
1	Aug. 31					1
2						2
3						3
4	31					4
5						5
6						6
7	31					7
8						8
9						9
10	31					10
11						11
12						12
13	31					13
14						14
15						15
16	31					16
17						17
18						18
19	31					19
20						20
21						21
22	31					22
23						23
24						24
25						25
26						26

(b)

Cash   No. 101

Date	Explanation	Ref.	Debit	Credit	Balance
Aug. 31	Balance	√			1 9 6 0 0

Accounts Receivable   No. 112

Date	Explanation	Ref.	Debit	Credit	Balance

Name   Problem 3-2A Continued

Section

Date   Melton River Resort

(b) (Continued)

Supplies   No. 126

Date	Explanation	Ref.	Debit	Credit	Balance
Aug. 31	Balance	√			3 3 0 0

Prepaid Insurance   No. 130

Date	Explanation	Ref.	Debit	Credit	Balance
Aug.31	Balance	√			6 0 0 0

Land   No. 140

Date	Explanation	Ref.	Debit	Credit	Balance
Aug.31	Balance	√			2 5 0 0 0

Buildings   No. 143

Date	Explanation	Ref.	Debit	Credit	Balance
Aug. 31	Balance	√			1 2 5 0 0 0

Accumulated Depreciation - Buildings   No. 144

Date	Explanation	Ref.	Debit	Credit	Balance

Equipment   No. 149

Date	Explanation	Ref.	Debit	Credit	Balance
Aug. 31	Balance	√			2 6 0 0 0

Accumulated Depreciation - Equipment   No. 150

Date	Explanation	Ref.	Debit	Credit	Balance

Accounts Payable   No. 201

Date	Explanation	Ref.	Debit	Credit	Balance
Aug. 31	Balance	√			6 5 0 0

Unearned Rent Revenue   No. 209

Date	Explanation	Ref.	Debit	Credit	Balance
Aug. 31	Balance	√			7 4 0 0

Salaries and Wages Payable   No. 212

Date	Explanation	Ref.	Debit	Credit	Balance

(b) (Continued)

Interest Payable   No. 230

Date	Explanation	Ref.	Debit	Credit	Balance

Mortgage Payable   No. 275

Date	Explanation	Ref.	Debit	Credit	Balance
Aug. 31	Balance	√			8 0 0 0 0

Owner's Capital   No. 301

Date	Explanation	Ref.	Debit	Credit	Balance
Aug. 31	Balance	√			1 0 0 0 0 0

Owner's Drawing   No. 306

Date	Explanation	Ref.	Debit	Credit	Balance
Aug. 31	Balance	√			5 0 0 0

Rent Revenue   No. 429

Date	Explanation	Ref.	Debit	Credit	Balance
Aug. 31	Balance	√			8 0 0 0 0

Depreciation Expense   No. 620

Date	Explanation	Ref.	Debit	Credit	Balance

Maintenance and Repairs Expense   No. 622

Date	Explanation	Ref.	Debit	Credit	Balance
Aug. 31	Balance	√			3 6 0 0

Supplies Expense   No. 631

Date	Explanation	Ref.	Debit	Credit	Balance

Interest Expense   No. 718

Date	Explanation	Ref.	Debit	Credit	Balance

(b) (Continued)

Insurance Expense   No. 722

Date	Explanation	Ref.	Debit	Credit	Balance

Salaries and Wages Expense   No. 726

Date	Explanation	Ref.	Debit	Credit	Balance
Aug. 31	Balance	√			5 1 0 0 0

Utilities Expense   No. 732

Date	Explanation	Ref.	Debit	Credit	Balance
Aug. 31	Balance	√			9 4 0 0

(c)

Melton River Resort
Adjusted Trial Balance
August 31, 2010

		Debit	Credit	
1	Cash			1
2	Accounts Receivable			2
3	Supplies			3
4	Prepaid Insurance			4
5	Land			5
6	Buildings			6
7	Accumulated Depreciation - Buildings			7
8	Equipment			8
9	Accumulated Depreciation - Equipment			9
10	Accounts Payable			10
11	Unearned Rent			11
12	Salaries and Wages Payable			12
13	Interest Payable			13
14	Mortgage Payable			14
15	Owner's Capital			15
16	Owner's Drawing			16
17	Rent Revenue			17
18	Depreciation Expense			18
19	Maintenance and Repairs Expense			19
20	Supplies Expense			20
21	Interest Expense			21
22	Insurance Expense			22
23	Salaries and Wages Expense			23
24	Utilities Expense			24
25	Totals			25
26				26

(d)

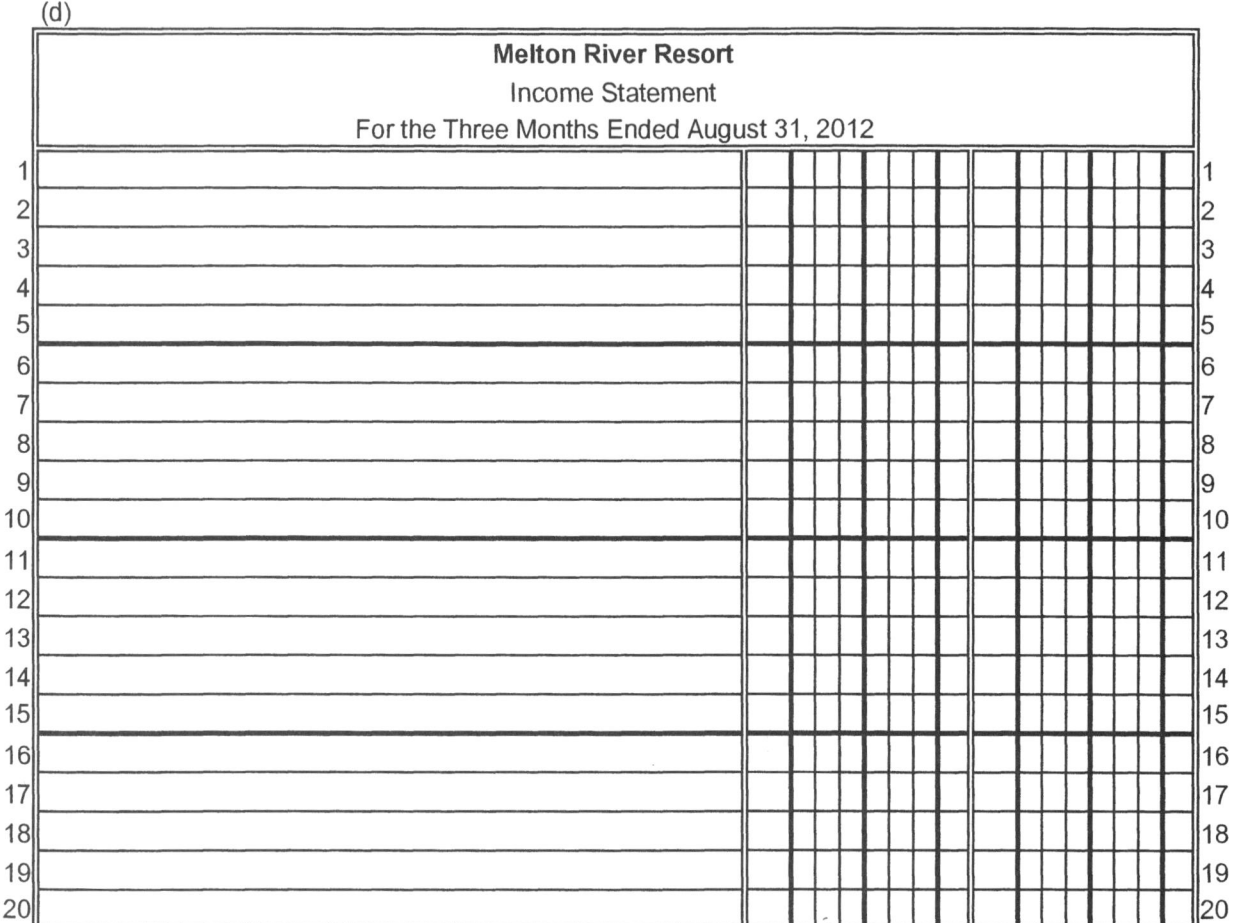

Melton River Resort

Income Statement

For the Three Months Ended August 31, 2012

Melton River Resort

Owner's Equity Statement

For the Three Months Ended August 31, 2012

(d) (Continued)

Melton River Resort
Balance Sheet
August 31, 2012

	Assets	
1		
2		
3		
4		
5		
6		
7		
8		
9		
10		
11		
12		
13		
14		
15		
16	Liabilities and Owner's Equity	
17		
18		
19		
20		
21		
22		
23		
24		
25		
26		
27		
28		
29		
30		
31		
32		
33		
34		
35		
36		
37		
38		
39		
40		

(a)

	Date	Accounts Titles	Debit	Credit	
1	Dec. 31				1
2					2
3					3
4	31				4
5					5
6					6
7	31				7
8					8
9					9
10	31				10
11					11
12					12
13	31				13
14					14
15					15
16	31				16
17					17
18					18
19	31				19
20					20
21					21

(b)

	Minor Advertising Agency Income Statement For the Year Ended December 31, 2012			
1				1
2				2
3				3
4				4
5				5
6				6
7				7
8				8
9				9
10				10
11				11
12				12
13				13
14				14

(b) (Continued)

Minor Advertising Agency		
Owner's Equity Statement		
For the Year Ended December 31, 2012		
1		
2		
3		
4		
5		
6		

Minor Advertising Agency		
Balance Sheet		
December 31, 2012		
Assets		
2		
3		
4		
5		
6		
7		
8		
9		
Liabilities and Owner's Equity		
11		
12		
13		
14		
15		
16		
17		
18		
19		
20		
21		

(c)

General Journal

	Date	Accounts Titles	Debit	Credit	
1	1.				1
2	Dec. 31				2
3					3
4					4
5					5
6	2.				6
7	Dec. 31				7
8					8
9					9
10					10
11	3.				11
12	Dec. 31				12
13					13
14					14
15					15
16	4.				16
17	Dec. 31				17
18					18
19					19
20					20
21					21
22					22
23					23
24					24
25					25
26					26
27					27
28					28
29					29
30					30
31					31
32					32
33					33
34					34
35					35
36					36
37					37
38					38
39					39
40					40

(a), (c) and (e)

Cash   No. 101

Date	Explanation	Ref.	Debit	Credit	Balance
Sept. 1	Balance	√			4 8 8 0

Accounts Receivable   No. 112

Date	Explanation	Ref.	Debit	Credit	Balance
Sept. 1	Balance	√			3 5 2 0

Supplies   No. 126

Date	Explanation	Ref.	Debit	Credit	Balance
Sept. 1	Balance	√			2 0 0 0

Equipment   No. 153

Date	Explanation	Ref.	Debit	Credit	Balance
Sept. 1	Balance	√			1 5 0 0 0

Accumulated Depreciation - Equipment   No. 154

Date	Explanation	Ref.	Debit	Credit	Balance
Sept. 1	Balance	√			1 5 0 0

Accounts Payable   No. 201

Date	Explanation	Ref.	Debit	Credit	Balance
Sept. 1	Balance	√			3 4 0 0

(a), (c) and (e) (Continued)

Unearned Service Revenue   No. 209

Date	Explanation	Ref.	Debit	Credit	Balance
Sept. 1	Balance	√			1 4 0 0

Salaries and Wages Payable   No. 212

Date	Explanation	Ref.	Debit	Credit	Balance
Sept. 1	Balance	√			5 0 0

Owner's Capital   No. 301

Date	Explanation	Ref.	Debit	Credit	Balance
Sept. 1	Balance	√			1 8 6 0 0

Service Revenue   No. 407

Date	Explanation	Ref.	Debit	Credit	Balance

Depreciation Expense   No. 615

Date	Explanation	Ref.	Debit	Credit	Balance

Supplies Expense   No. 631

Date	Explanation	Ref.	Debit	Credit	Balance

Salaries and Wages Expense   No. 726

Date	Explanation	Ref.	Debit	Credit	Balance

Rent Expense   No. 729

Date	Explanation	Ref.	Debit	Credit	Balance

(b)   General Journal   J1

	Date	Account Titles	Ref.	Debit	Credit	
1	Sept. 8					1
2						2
3						3
4						4
5	10					5
6						6
7						7
8	12					8
9						9
10						10
11	15					11
12						12
13						13
14	17					14
15						15
16						16
17	20					17
18						18
19						19
20	22					20
21						21
22						22
23	25					23
24						24
25						25
26	27					26
27						27
28						28
29	29					29
30						30
31						31
32						32
33						33
34						34
35						35

(d) & (f)

Moore Equipment Repair

Trial Balances

September 30, 2012

	Before Adjustment		After Adjustment		
	Dr.	Cr.	Dr.	Cr.	
1 Cash					1
2 Accounts Receivable					2
3 Supplies					3
4 Equipment					4
5 Accumulated Depreciation - Equipment					5
6 Accounts Payable					6
7 Unearned Service Revenue					7
8 Salaries and Wages Payable					8
9 Owner's Capital					9
10 Service Revenue					10
11 Depreciation Expense					11
12 Supplies Expense					12
13 Salaries and Wages Expense					13
14 Rent Expense					14
15 Totals					15
16					16
17					17
18					18
19					19
20					20

(e)   General Journal   J1

	Date	Account Titles	Ref	Debit	Credit	
1	1.					1
2	Sept. 30					2
3						3
4						4
5						5
6						6
7	2.					7
8	Sept. 30					8
9						9
10						10
11						11
12						12
13	3.					13
14	Sept. 30					14
15						15
16						16
17						17
18						18
19	4.					19
20	Sept. 30					20
21						21
22						22
23						23
24						24
25						25

(g)

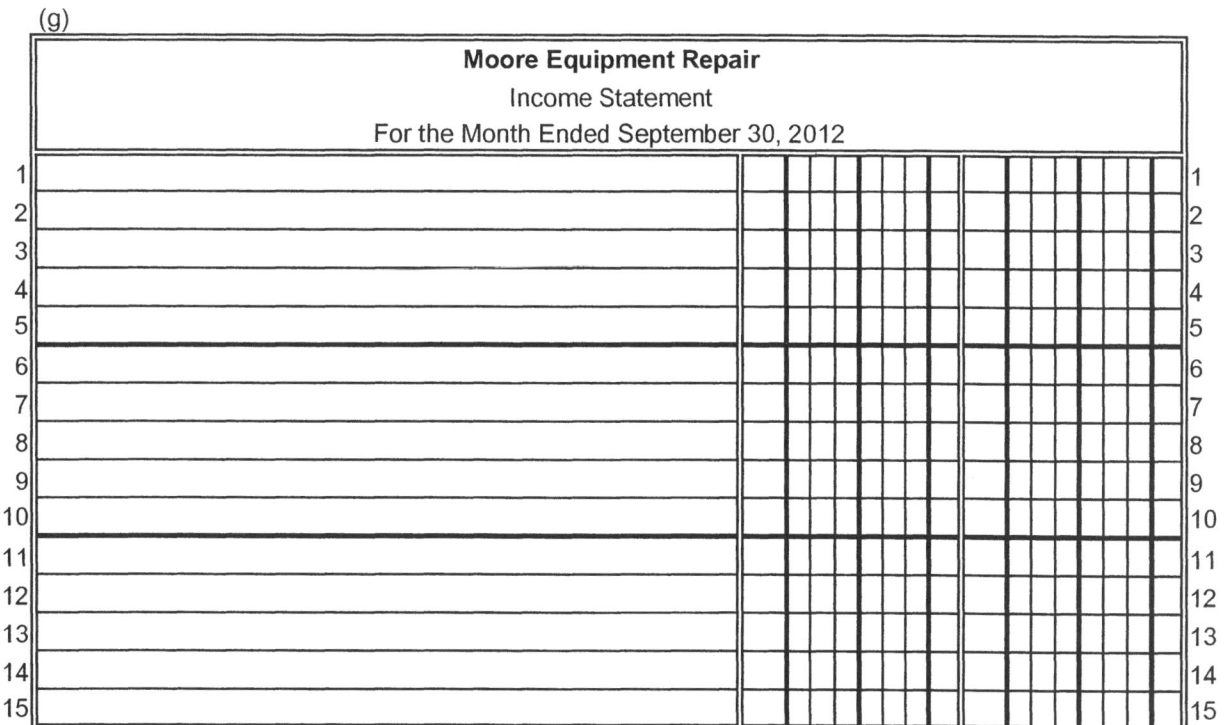

Moore Equipment Repair

Income Statement

For the Month Ended September 30, 2012

Moore Equipment Repair

Owner's Equity Statement

For the Month Ended September 30, 2012

(g) (Continued)

Moore Equipment Repair

Balance Sheet

September 30, 2012

Assets		

Liabilities and Owner's Equity		

(a)

	Date	Account Titles	Debit	Credit	
1	1.				1
2	June 30				2
3					3
4					4
5					5
6	2.				6
7	June 30				7
8					8
9					9
10					10
11	3.				11
12	June 30				12
13					13
14					14
15					15
16	4.				16
17	June 30				17
18					18
19					19
20					20
21	5.				21
22	June 30				22
23					23
24					24
25					25
26	6.				26
27	June 30				27
28					28
29					29
30					30
31					31
32					32
33					33
34					34
35					35
36					36
37					37
38					38
39					39
40					40

(b)

Olsen Graphics Company Adjusted Trial Balance June 30, 2012	Debit	Credit
1		
2		
3		
4		
5		
6		
7		
8		
9		
10		
11		
12		
13		
14		
15		
16		
17		
18		
19		
20		
21		
22		
23		
24		
25		

(c)

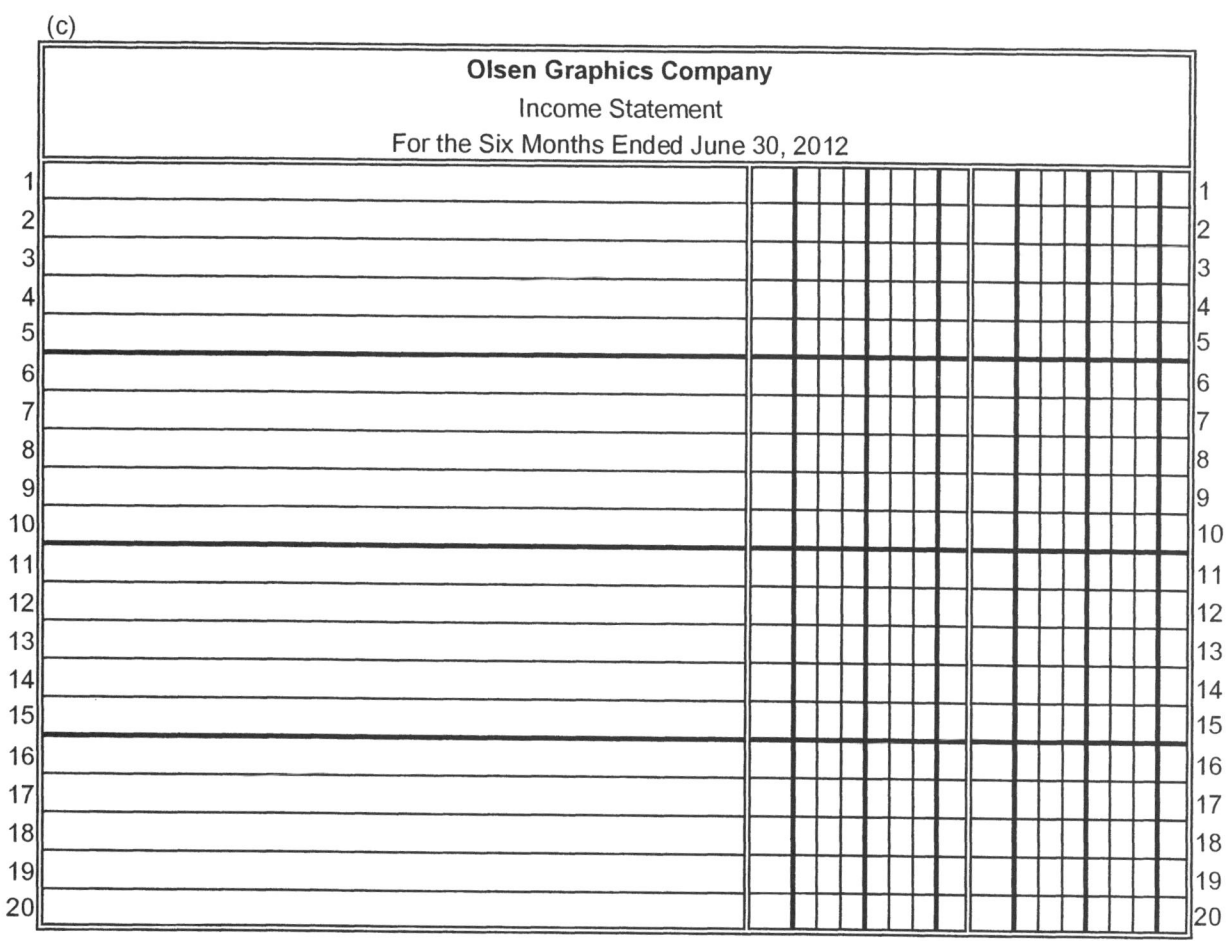

Olsen Graphics Company

Income Statement

For the Six Months Ended June 30, 2012

Olsen Graphics Company

Owner's Equity Statement

For the Six Months Ended June 30, 2012

(c) (Continued)

	Olsen Graphics Company							
	Balance Sheet							
	June 30, 2012							
1	Assets							
2								
3								
4								
5								
6								
7								
8								
9								
10								
11								
12								
13	Liabilities and Owner's Equity							
14								
15								
16								
17								
18								
19								
20								
21								
22								
23								
24								
25								
26								
27								

(a)

	Date	Account Titles	Ref.	Debit	Credit	
1	2012					1
2	May 31					2
3						3
4						4
5	31					5
6						6
7						7
8						8
9	31					9
10						10
11						11
12						12
13	31					13
14						14
15						15
16						16
17	31					17
18						18
19						19
20						20
21	31					21
22						22
23						23
24						24
25	31					25
26						26
27						27
28						28
29						29
30						30
31						31
32						32
33						33
34						34
35						35
36						36
37						37
38						38
39						39
40						40

General Journal

J4

(b)

Cash   No. 101

Date	Explanation	Ref.	Debit	Credit	Balance
2012					
May 31	Balance	√			4 5 0 0

Accounts Receivable   No. 112

Date	Explanation	Ref.	Debit	Credit	Balance
2012					
May 31	Balance	√			6 0 0 0

Supplies   No. 126

Date	Explanation	Ref.	Debit	Credit	Balance
2012					
May 31	Balance	√			1 9 0 0

Prepaid Insurance   No. 130

Date	Explanation	Ref.	Debit	Credit	Balance
2012					
May 31	Balance	√			3 6 0 0

Equipment   No. 149

Date	Explanation	Ref.	Debit	Credit	Balance
2012					
May 31	Balance	√			1 1 4 0 0

Accumulated Depreciation - Equipment   No, 150

Date	Explanation	Ref.	Debit	Credit	Balance

Accounts Payable   No. 201

Date	Explanation	Ref.	Debit	Credit	Balance
2012					
May 31	Balance	√			4 5 0 0

(b) (Continued)

Unearned Service Revenue   No. 209

Date	Explanation	Ref.	Debit	Credit	Balance
2					
May 31	Balance	√			2 0 0 0

Salaries and Wages Payable   No. 212

Date	Explanation	Ref.	Debit	Credit	Balance

Owner's Capital   No. 301

Date	Explanation	Ref.	Debit	Credit	Balance
2012					
May 31	Balance	√			1 7 7 0 0

Service Revenue   No. 400

Date	Explanation	Ref.	Debit	Credit	Balance
2012					
May 31	Balance	√			7 5 0 0

Supplies Expense   No. 631

Date	Explanation	Ref.	Debit	Credit	Balance

Depreciation Expense   No. 717

Date	Explanation	Ref.	Debit	Credit	Balance

(b) (Continued)

Insurance Expense   No. 722

Date	Explanation	Ref.	Debit	Credit	Balance

Salaries and Wages Expense   No. 726

Date	Explanation	Ref.	Debit	Credit	Balance
2012					
May 31	Balance	√			3 4 0 0

Rent Expense   No. 729

Date	Explanation	Ref.	Debit	Credit	Balance
2012					
May 31	Balance	√			9 0 0

Utilities Expense   No. 736

Date	Explanation	Ref.	Debit	Credit	Balance

(c)

	Omiyale Consulting Adjusted Trial Balance May 31, 2012	Debit	Credit	
1	Cash			1
2	Accounts Rdeceivable			2
3	Prepaid Insurance			3
4	Supplies			4
5	Equipment			5
6	Accumulated Depreciation - Equipment			6
7	Accounts Payable			7
8	Salaries and Wages Payable			8
9	Unearned Service Revenue			9
10	Owner's Capital			10
11	Service Revenue			11
12	Salaries and Wages Expense			12
13	Rent Expense			13
14	Depreciation Expense			14
15	Insurance Expense			15
16	Utilities Expense			16
17	Supplies and Wages Expense			17
18	Totals			18

(a)   General Journal   J1

	Date	Account Titles	Ref.	Debit	Credit	
1	May 31					1
2						2
3						3
4	31					4
5						5
6						6
7	31					7
8						8
9						9
10	31					10
11						11
12						12
13	31					13
14						14
15						15
16	31					16
17						17
18						18
19	31					19
20						20
21						21
22						22
23						23
24						24
25						25
26						26

(b)

Cash   No. 101

Date	Explanation	Ref.	Debit	Credit	Balance
May 31	Balance	√			3 5 0 0

Supplies   No. 126

Date	Explanation	Ref.	Debit	Credit	Balance
May 31	Balance	√			2 0 8 0

(b)

Prepaid Insurance   No. 130

Date	Explanation	Ref.	Debit	Credit	Balance
May 31	Balance	√			2 4 0 0

Land   No. 140

Date	Explanation	Ref.	Debit	Credit	Balance
May 31	Balance	√			1 2 0 0 0

Buildings   No. 141

Date	Explanation	Ref.	Debit	Credit	Balance
May 31	Balance	√			6 0 0 0 0

Accumulated Depreciation - Buildings   No. 142

Date	Explanation	Ref.	Debit	Credit	Balance

Equipment   No. 149

Date	Explanation	Ref.	Debit	Credit	Balance
May 31	Balance	√			1 5 0 0 0

Accumulated Depreciation - Equipment   No. 150

Date	Explanation	Ref.	Debit	Credit	Balance

Accounts Payable   No. 201

Date	Explanation	Ref.	Debit	Credit	Balance
May 31	Balance	√			4 8 0 0

Unearned Rent Revenue   No. 209

Date	Explanation	Ref.	Debit	Credit	Balance
May 31	Balance	√			3 3 0 0

Salaries and Wages Payable   No. 212

Date	Explanation	Ref.	Debit	Credit	Balance

Interest Payable   No. 230

Date	Explanation	Ref.	Debit	Credit	Balance

(b) (Continued)

Mortgage Payable   No. 275

Date	Explanation	Ref.	Debit	Credit	Balance
May 31	Balance	√			4 0 0 0 0

Owner's Capital   No. 301

Date	Explanation	Ref.	Debit	Credit	Balance
May 31	Balance	√			4 1 3 8 0

Rent Revenue   No. 429

Date	Explanation	Ref.	Debit	Credit	Balance
May 31	Balance	√			1 0 3 0 0

Advertising Expense   No. 610

Date	Explanation	Ref.	Debit	Credit	Balance
May 31	Balance	√			6 0 0

Depreciation Expense   No. 619

Date	Explanation	Ref.	Debit	Credit	Balance

Supplies Expense   No. 631

Date	Explanation	Ref.	Debit	Credit	Balance

Interest Expense   No. 718

Date	Explanation	Ref.	Debit	Credit	Balance

Insurance Expense   No. 722

Date	Explanation	Ref.	Debit	Credit	Balance

Salaries and Wages Expense   No. 726

Date	Explanation	Ref.	Debit	Credit	Balance
May 31	Balance	√			3 3 0 0

(b) (Continued)

Utilities Expense   No. 732

Date	Explanation	Ref.	Debit	Credit	Balance
May 31	Balance	√			9 0 0

(c)

	Bear Motel Adjusted Trial Balance May 31, 2012	Debit	Credit	
1	Cash			1
2	Supplies			2
3	Prepaid Insurance			3
4	Land			4
5	Buildings			5
6	Accum. Depreciation - Buildings			6
7	Equipment			7
8	Accum. Depreciation - Equipment			8
9	Accounts Payable			9
10	Unearned Rent Revenue			10
11	Salaries and Wages Payable			11
12	Interest Payable			12
13	Mortgage Payable			13
14	Owner's Capital			14
15	Rent Revenue			15
16	Advertising Expense			16
17	Depreciation Expense			17
18	Supplies Expense			18
19	Interest Expense			19
20	Insurance Expense			20
21	Salaries and Wages Expense			21
22	Utilities Expense			22
23	Totals			23
24				24
25				25
26				26
27				27

(d)

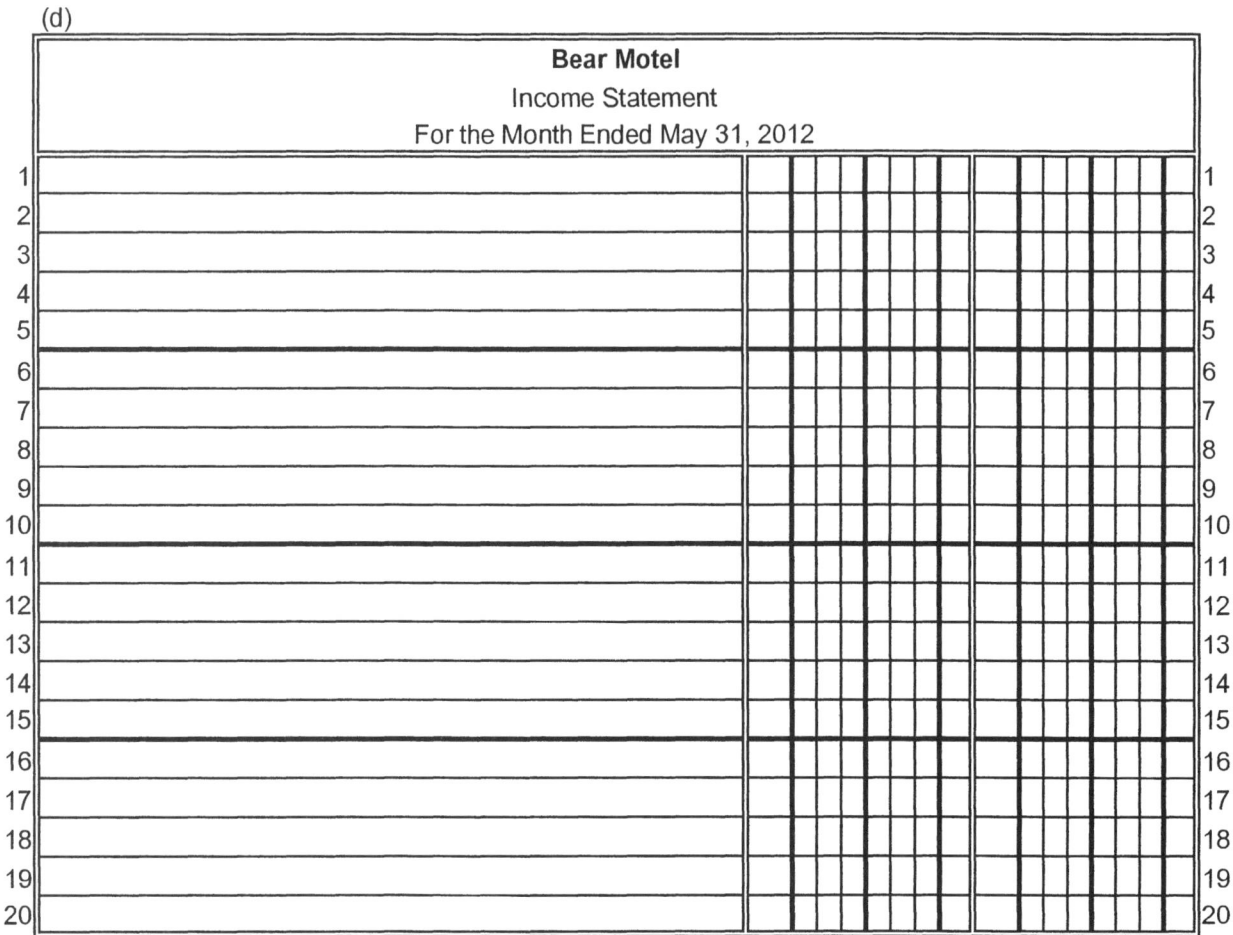

Bear Motel

Income Statement

For the Month Ended May 31, 2012

Bear Motel

Owner's Equity Statement

For the Month Ended May 31, 2012

(d) (Continued)

Bear Motel
Balance Sheet
May 31, 2012

	Assets				
1					
2					
3					
4					
5					
6					
7					
8					
9					
10					
11					
12					
13					
14					
15					
16	Liabilities and Owner's Equity				
17					
18					
19					
20					
21					
22					
23					
24					
25					
26					
27					
28					
29					
30					
31					
32					
33					
34					
35					
36					
37					
38					
39					
40					

(a)

	Date	Accounts Titles	Debit	Credit	
1	Sept. 30				1
2					2
3					3
4	30				4
5					5
6					6
7	30				7
8					8
9					9
10	30				10
11					11
12					12
13	30				13
14					14
15					15
16	30				16
17					17
18					18
19	30				19
20					20
21					21

(b)

Peterman Co.

Income Statement

For the Quarter Ended September 30, 2012

1	Revenues:			1
2				2
3				3
4				4
5	Expenses:			5
6				6
7				7
8				8
9				9
10				10
11				11
12				12
13				13
14				14

(b) (Continued)

Peterman Co.
Owner's Equity Statement
For the Quarter Ended September 30, 2012

Peterman Co.
Balance Sheet
September 30, 2012

Assets

Liabilities and Owner's Equity

(c)

General Journal

	Date	Accounts Titles	Debit	Credit	
1	1.				1
2	Dec. 31				2
3					3
4					4
5					5
6	2.				6
7	Dec. 31				7
8					8
9					9
10					10
11	3.				11
12	Dec. 31				12
13					13
14					14
15					15
16	4.				16
17	Dec. 31				17
18					18
19					19
20					20
21					21
22					22
23					23
24					24
25					25
26					26
27					27
28					28
29					29
30					30
31					31
32					32
33					33
34					34
35					35
36					36
37					37
38					38
39					39
40					40

(a), (c) and (e)

Cash   No. 101

Date	Explanation	Ref.	Debit	Credit	Balance
Nov. 1	Balance	√			2 4 0 0

Accounts Receivable   No. 112

Date	Explanation	Ref.	Debit	Credit	Balance
Nov. 1	Balance	√			4 2 5 0

Supplies   No. 126

Date	Explanation	Ref.	Debit	Credit	Balance
Nov. 1	Balance	√			1 8 0 0

Equipment   No. 153

Date	Explanation	Ref.	Debit	Credit	Balance
Nov. 1	Balance	√			1 2 0 0 0

Accumulated Depreciation - Equipment   No. 154

Date	Explanation	Ref.	Debit	Credit	Balance
Nov. 1	Balance	√			2 0 0 0

Accounts Payable   No. 201

Date	Explanation	Ref.	Debit	Credit	Balance
Nov. 1	Balance	√			2 6 0 0

(a), (c) and (e) (Continued)

Unearned Service Revenue   No. 209

Date	Explanation	Ref.	Debit	Credit	Balance
Nov. 1	Balance	√			1 2 0 0

Salaries and Wages Payable   No. 212

Date	Explanation	Ref.	Debit	Credit	Balance
Nov. 1	Balance	√			7 0 0

Owner's Capital   No. 301

Date	Explanation	Ref.	Debit	Credit	Balance
Nov. 1	Balance	√			1 3 9 5 0

Service Revenue   No. 407

Date	Explanation	Ref.	Debit	Credit	Balance

Depreciation Expense   No. 615

Date	Explanation	Ref.	Debit	Credit	Balance

Supplies Expense   No. 631

Date	Explanation	Ref.	Debit	Credit	Balance

Salaries and Wages Expense   No. 726

Date	Explanation	Ref.	Debit	Credit	Balance

Rent Expense   No. 729

Date	Explanation	Ref.	Debit	Credit	Balance

(b)   General Journal   J1

	Date	Account Titles	Ref	Debit	Credit	
1	Nov. 8					1
2						2
3						3
4						4
5	10					5
6						6
7						7
8	12					8
9						9
10						10
11	15					11
12						12
13						13
14	17					14
15						15
16						16
17	20					17
18						18
19						19
20	22					20
21						21
22						22
23	25					23
24						24
25						25
26	27					26
27						27
28						28
29	29					29
30						30
31						31
32						32
33						33
34						34
35						35

(d) & (f)

Robinson Equipment Repair
Trial Balances
November 30, 2012

	Before Adjustment		After Adjustment	
	Dr.	Cr.	Dr.	Cr.
1 Cash				
2 Accounts Receivable				
3 Supplies				
4 Equipment				
5 Accumulated Depreciation - Equipment				
6 Accounts Payable				
7 Unearned Service Revenue				
8 Salaries and Wages Payable				
9 Owner's Capital				
10 Service Revenue				
11 Depreciation Expense				
12 Supplies Expense				
13 Salaries and Wages Expense				
14 Rent Expense				
15 Totals				
16				
17				
18				
19				
20				

(e)

General Journal   J1

Date	Account Titles	Ref	Debit	Credit
1.				
Nov. 30				
2.				
Nov. 30				
3.				
Nov. 30				
4.				
Nov. 30				

(g)

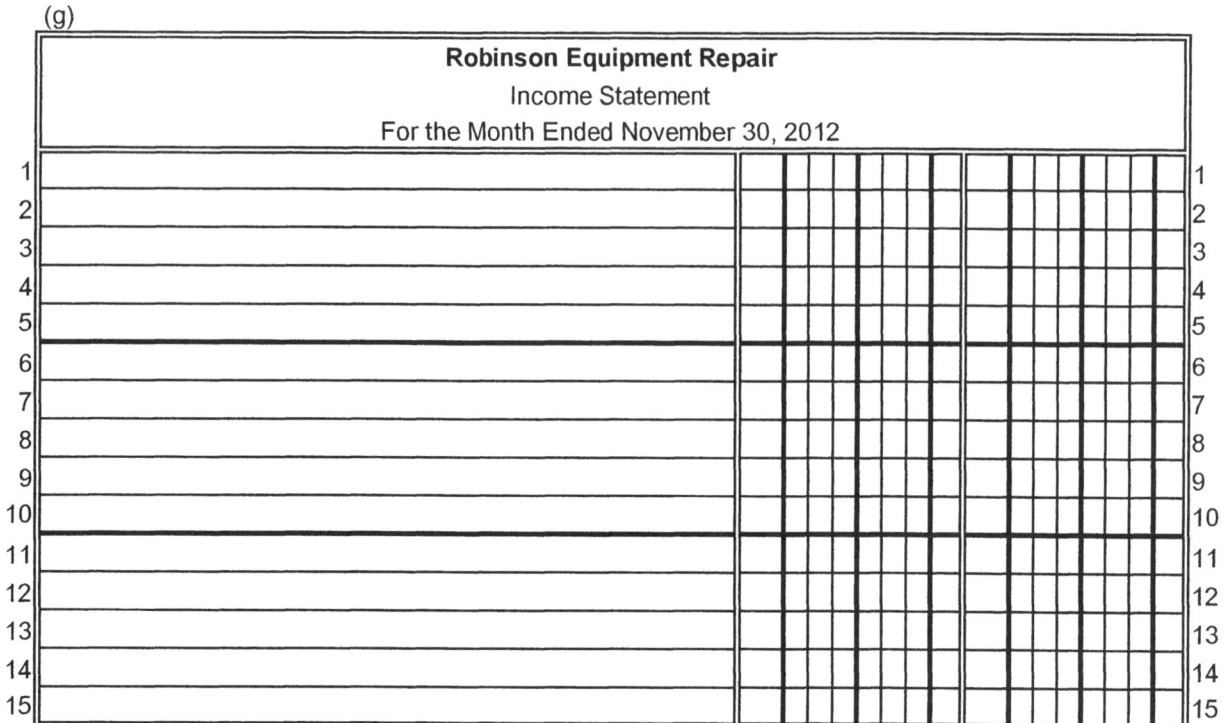

Robinson Equipment Repair

Income Statement

For the Month Ended November 30, 2012

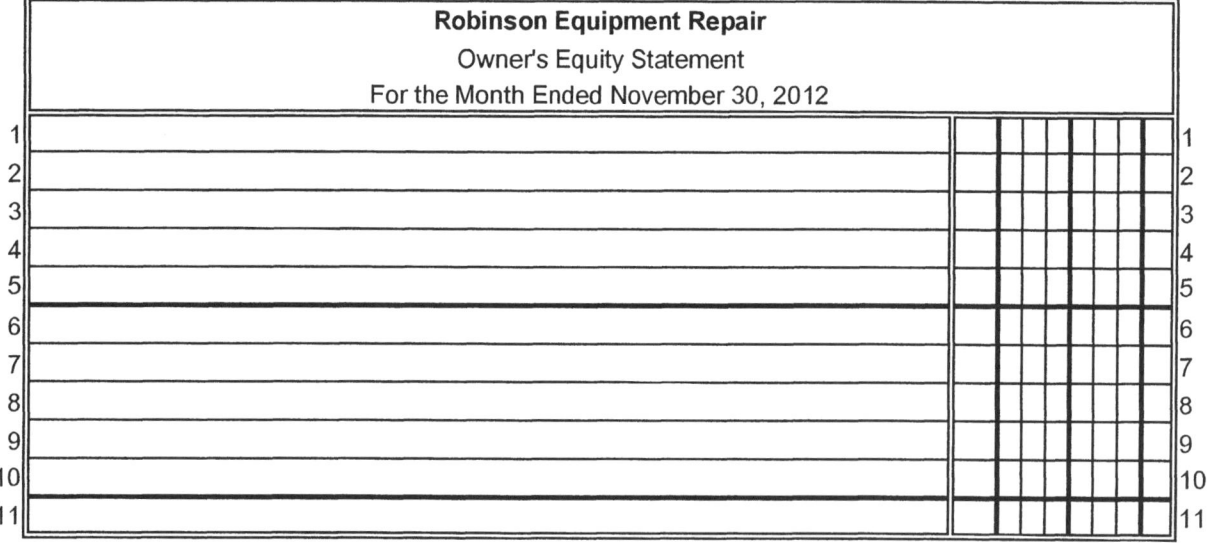

Robinson Equipment Repair

Owner's Equity Statement

For the Month Ended November 30, 2012

(g) (Continued)

Robinson Equipment Repair

Balance Sheet

November 30, 2012

	Assets																	
1																		1
2																		2
3																		3
4																		4
5																		5
6																		6
7																		7
8																		8
9																		9
10																		10
11	Liabilities and Owner's Equity																	11
12																		12
13																		13
14																		14
15																		15
16																		16
17																		17
18																		18
19																		19
20																		20
21																		21
22																		22

	PepsiCo	Coca-Cola	
1 Increase (decrease) from 2008 to 2009 in:			1
2			2
3			3
4 (a) Property, plant, and equipment, net			4
5			5
6			6
7			7
8 (b) Selling, general, and administrative expenses			8
9			9
10			10
11			11
12 (c) Long-term debt (obligations)			12
13			13
14			14
15			15
16 (d) Net income			16
17			17
18			18
19			19
20 (e) Cash and cash equivalents			20
21			21
22			22
23			23
24			24
25			25
26			26
27			27
28			28
29			29
30			30
31			31
32			32
33			33
34			34
35			35
36			36
37			37
38			38
39			39

(a)

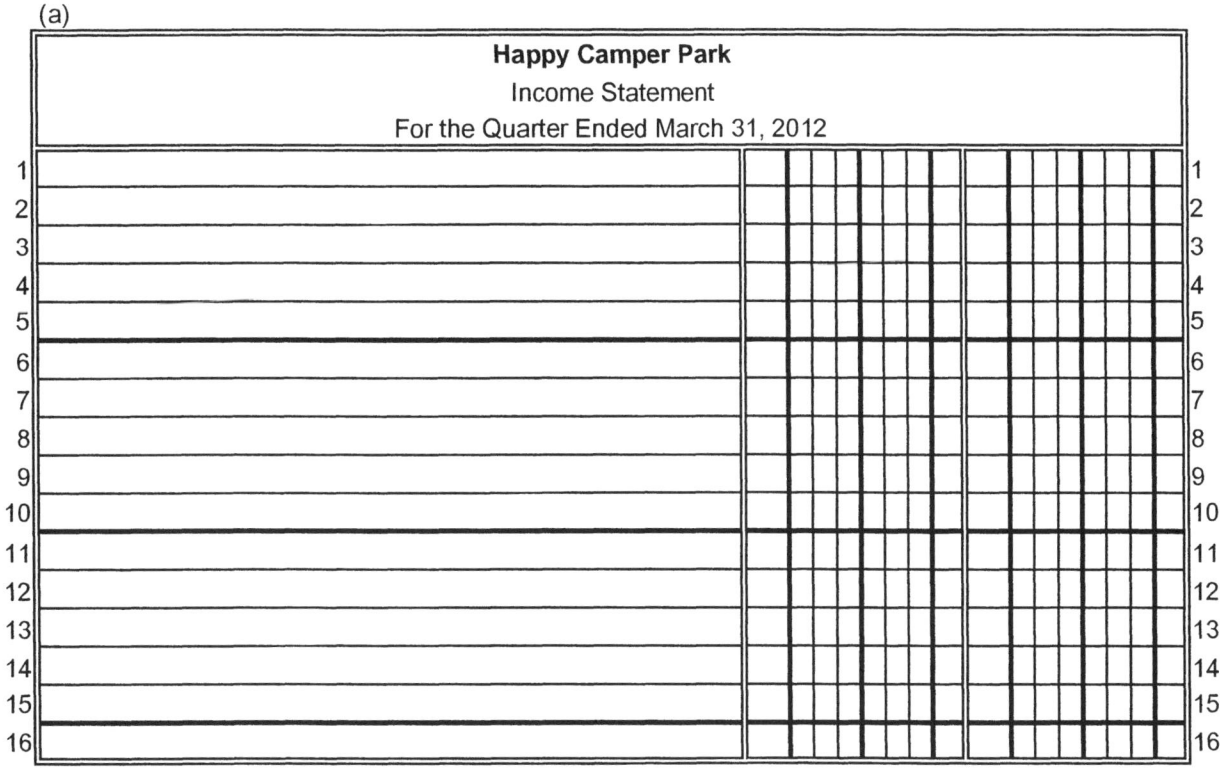

Happy Camper Park

Income Statement

For the Quarter Ended March 31, 2012

(b)

	Date	Account Titles	Debit	Credit	
1	**BE4-2** is on the next page				1
2					2
3	**BE4-4**				3
4	Date	Account Titles	Debit	Credit	4
5	Dec. 31				5
6					6
7					7
8	31				8
9					9
10					10
11					11
12	31				12
13					13
14					14
15	31				15
16					16
17					17
18					18
19					19
20					20
21					21
22					22
23					23
24					24
25					25
26					26
27					27
28					28
29					29
30					30

Brief Exercise 4-2

Saddler Company

See Appendix

BE4-5

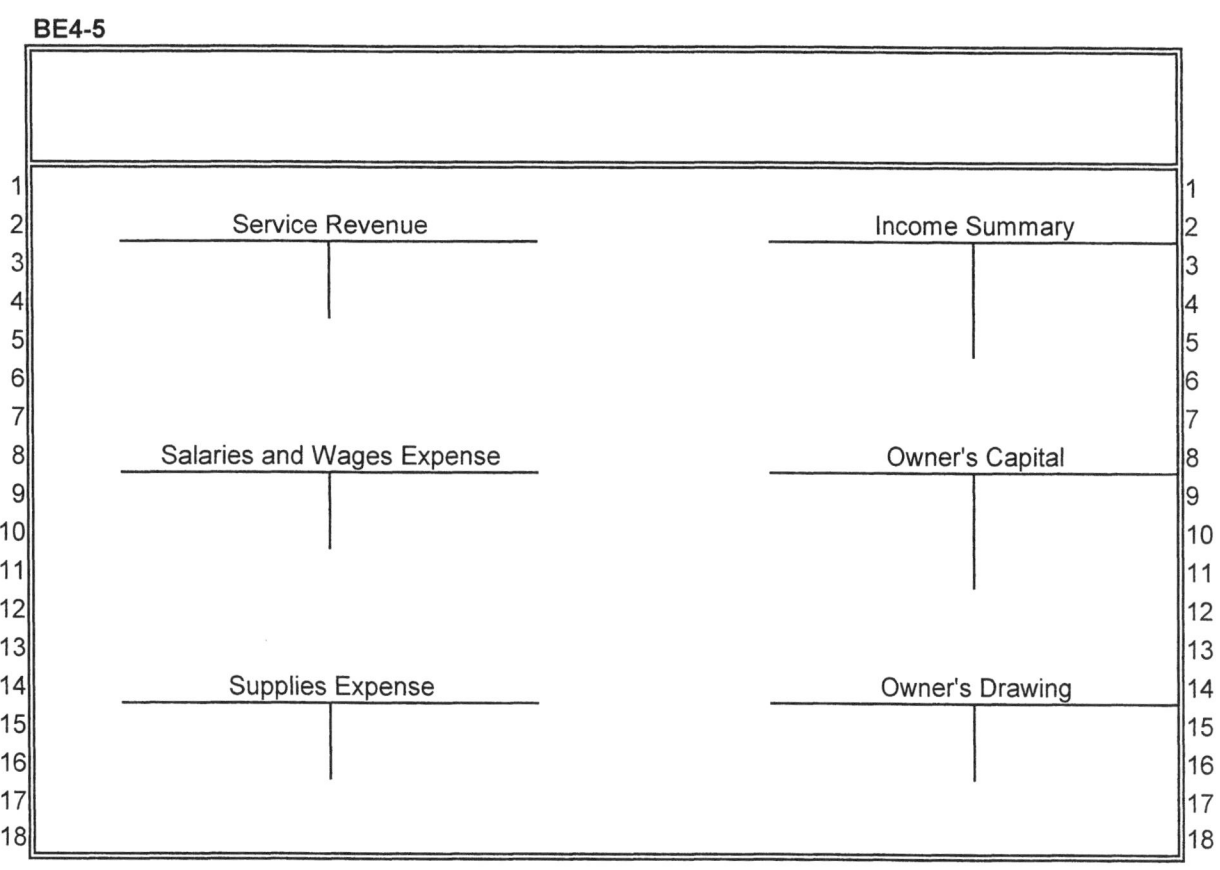

1		1
2	Service Revenue	Income Summary	2
3		3
4		4
5		5
6		6
7		7
8	Salaries and Wages Expense	Owner's Capital	8
9		9
10		10
11		11
12		12
13		13
14	Supplies Expense	Owner's Drawing	14
15		15
16		16
17		17
18		18

BE4-6

	Date	Account Titles	Debit	Credit	
1	July 31				1
2					2
3					3
4	31				4
5					5
6					6

Service Revenue

Date	Explanation	Ref.	Debit	Credit	Balance

Salaries and Wages Expense

Date	Explanation	Ref.	Debit	Credit	Balance

Maintenenace and Repairs Expense

Date	Explanation	Ref.	Debit	Credit	Balance

BE4-9

		Account Titles	Debit	Credit	
1	1.				1
2					2
3					3
4	2.				4
5					5
6					6

BE4-10

Shaw Company
Partial Balance Sheet

Current assets

*BE4-12

Date	Account Titles	Debit	Credit
Nov. 1			

DO IT! 4-2

	Date	Account Titles	Debit	Credit	
1	Dec. 31				1
2					2
3					3
4	Dec. 31				4
5					5
6					6
7					7

DO IT! 4-3

8			8
9	**Taylor Company**		9
10	Partial Balance Sheet		10
11	December 31, 2012		11
12			12
13			13
14			14
15			15
16			16
17			17
18			18
19			19
20			20
21			21
22			22
23			23
24			24
25			25
26			26
27			27
28			28
29			29
30			30
31			31
32			32
33			33
34			34
35			35
36			36
37			37
38			38
39			39
40			40

Exercise 4-1

Tinoisamoa Company

See Appendix

Pisa Company
(Partial) Worksheet
For the Month Ended April 30, 2012

Account Titles	Adjusted Trial Balance Dr.	Adjusted Trial Balance Cr.	Income Statement Dr.	Income Statement Cr.	Balance Sheet Dr.	Balance Sheet Cr.
1 Cash	10000					
2 Accounts Receivable	7840					
3 Prepaid Rent	2280					
4 Equipment	23050					
5 Accum. Depr. - Equipment		4921				
6 Notes Payable		5700				
7 Accounts Payable		4920				
8 Owner's Capital		27960				
9 Owner's Drawings	3650					
10 Service Revenue		15590				
11 Salaries and Wages Expense	10840					
12 Rent Expense	760					
13 Depreciation Expense	671					
14 Interest Expense	57					
15 Interest Payable		57				
16 Totals	59148	59148				
17 Net Income						
18 Totals						
19						
20						

Pisa Company

Income Statement

For the Month Ended April 30, 2012

1		
2		
3		
4		
5		
6		
7		
8		
9		
10		
11		
12		
13		
14		
15		
16		
17		
18		

Pisa Company

Owner's Equity Statement

For the Month Ended April 30, 2012

1	
2	
3	
4	
5	
6	

	Pisa Company			
	Balance Sheet			
	April 30, 2012			
1	Assets			1
2				2
3				3
4				4
5				5
6				6
7				7
8				8
9				9
10				10
11				11
12				12
13	Liabilities and Owner's Equity			13
14				14
15				15
16				16
17				17
18				18
19				19
20				20
21				21
22				22
23				23
24				24
25				25
26				26

(a)

	Date	Account Titles	Debit	Credit	
1	Apr. 30				1
2					2
3					3
4	30				4
5					5
6					6
7					7
8					8
9					9
10	30				10
11					11
12					12
13	30				13
14					14
15					15

(b)

INCOME SUMMARY	OWNER'S CAPITAL

(c)

Pisa Company

Post-Closing Trial Balance

April 30, 2012

		Debit	Credit	
1				1
2				2
3				3
4				4
5				5
6				6
7				7
8				8
9				9
10				10
11				11

(a)

	Account Titles	Debit	Credit	
1				1
2				2
3				3
4				4
5				5
6				6
7				7
8				8
9				9
10				10
11				11
12				12

(b)

		Income Statement		Balance Sheet		
		Debit	Credit	Debit	Credit	
1	Accounts Receivable					1
2	Prepaid Insurance					2
3	Accum. Depreciation					3
4	Salaries and Wages					4
5	Payable					5
6	Service Revenue					6
7	Salaries and Wages					7
8	Expense					8
9	Insurance Expense					9
	Depr. Expense					

(a)

	Account Titles	Trial Balance Debit	Trial Balance Credit	Adjustments Debit	Adjustments Credit	Adjusted Trial Balance Debit	Adjusted Trial Balance Credit
1	Accounts Receivable					34000	
2	Prepaid Insurance	26000				20000	
3	Supplies	7000					
4	Accumulated Depreciation		12000				
5	Salaries and Wages Payable						5600
6	Service Revenue		88000				97000
7	Insurance Expense						
8	Depreciation Expense					10000	
9	Supplies Expense					4500	
10	Salaries and Wages Expense					49000	

(b)

	Account Titles	Debit	Credit
1			
2			
3			
4			
5			
6			
7			
8			
9			
10			
11			
12			
13			
14			

(a)

	Account Titles	Debit	Credit	
1				1
2				2
3				3
4				4
5				5
6				6
7				7
8				8
9				9
10				10
11				11
12				12
13				13
14				14
15				15

(b)

Willow Turenne Company
Post-Closing Trial Balance
For the Month Ended June 30, 2012

	Account Titles	Debit	Credit	
1				1
2				2
3				3
4				4
5				5
6				6
7				7
8				8
9				9
10				10

(a)

General Journal   J15

	Date	Account Titles	Ref.	Debit	Credit	
1	July 31					1
2						2
3						3
4						4
5	31					5
6						6
7						7
8						8
9						9
10	31					10
11						11
12						12
13	31					13
14						14

(b)

Owner's Capital   No. 301

Date	Explanation	Ref.	Debit	Credit	Balance

Income Summary   No. 350

Date	Explanation	Ref.	Debit	Credit	Balance

(c)

Turner Company
Post-Closing Trial Balance
July 31, 2012

		Debit	Credit	
1				1
2				2
3				3
4				4
5				5
6				6
7				7
8				8

(a)

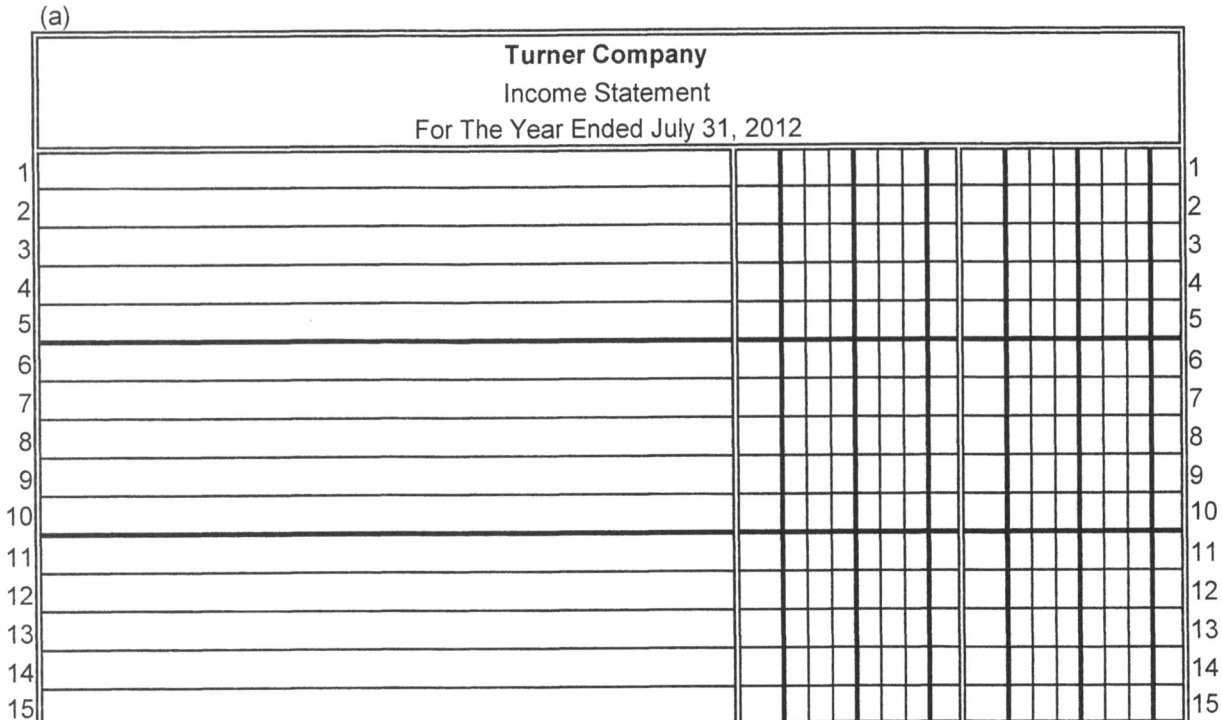

Turner Company
Income Statement
For The Year Ended July 31, 2012

Turner Company
Owner's Equity Statement
For the Year Ended July 31, 2012

(b)

Turner Company				
Balance Sheet				
July 31, 2012				
Assets				
Liabilities and Owner's Equity				

E4-11

	Date	Account Titles	Debit	Credit	
1	(a)				1
2	June 30				2
3					3
4					4
5	30				5
6					6
7					7
8					8
9					9
10	30				10
11					11
12					12
13	30				13
14					14

(b)

INCOME SUMMARY

E4-13

	Item	Account Titles	Debit	Credit	
1	1.				1
2					2
3					3
4	2.				4
5					5
6					6
7					7
8	3.				8
9					9
10					10

Item	Account Titles	Debit	Credit
1 (a)			
2 1.			
3			
4			
5			
6			
7			
8 2.			
9			
10			
11			
12			
13			
14 3.			
15			
16			
17			
18			
19			
20 (b)			
21 1.			
22			
23			
24 2.			
25			
26			
27			
28 3.			
29			
30			
31			
32			
33			
34			
35			
36			
37			
38			
39			
40			

(a)

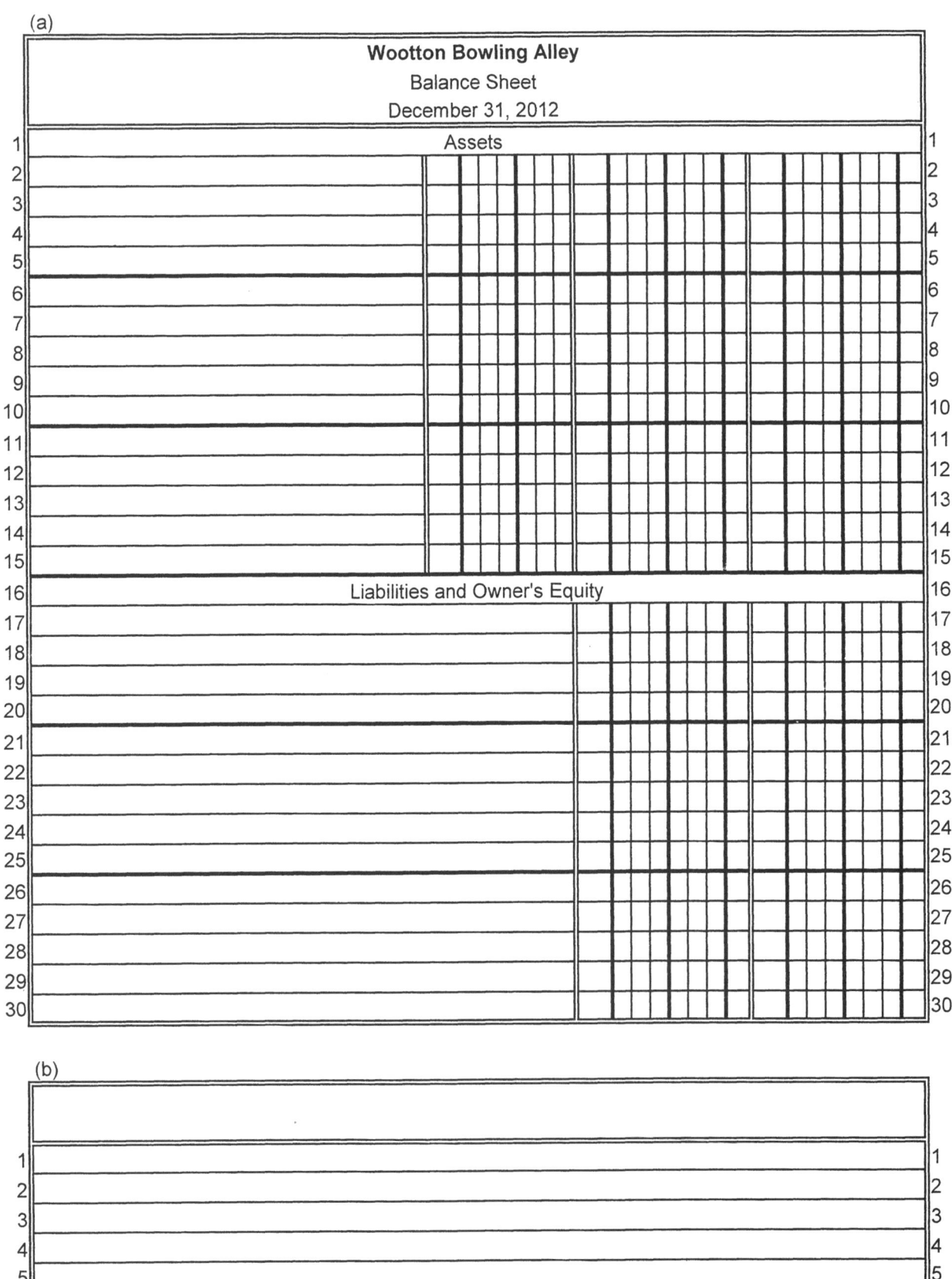

Wootton Bowling Alley
Balance Sheet
December 31, 2012

Assets

Liabilities and Owner's Equity

(b)

M. Wright Company				
Balance Sheet				
December 31, 2012				
(in thousands)				

	Assets			
1				
2				
3				
4				
5				
6				
7				
8				
9				
10				
11				
12				
13				
14				
15				
16	Liabilities and Owner's Equity			
17				
18				
19				
20				
21				
22				
23				
24				
25				
26				
27				
28				
29				
30				

(a)

Major Company		
Income Statement		
For The Year Ended July 31, 2012		
Revenues:		
Expenses:		

Major Company		
Owner's Equity Statement		
For the Year Ended July 31, 2012		

(b)

	Major Company		
	Balance Sheet		
	July 31, 2012		
1	Assets		
2			
3			
4			
5			
6			
7			
8			
9			
10			
11			
12			
13	Liabilities and Owner's Equity		
14			
15			
16			
17			
18			
19			
20			
21			
22			
23			
24			
25			

	Date	Account Titles	Debit	Credit	
1	(a)				1
2	Dec. 31				2
3					3
4					4
5	Jan. 6				5
6					6
7					7
8					8
9	(b)				9
10	Dec. 31				10
11					11
12					12
13	Jan. 1				13
14					14
15					15
16	6				16
17					17
18					18
19					19
20					20

(a) & (b)

	Date	Account Titles	Debit	Credit	
1	Dec. 31				1
2					2
3					3
4					4
5	31				5
6					6
7					7
8					8
9	Jan. 1				9
10					10
11					11
12	1				12
13					13
14					14
15					15

(c) & (e)

ACCOUNTS RECEIVABLE

Dec 31 Bal   19,500

SERVICE REVENUE

Dec 31 Bal   87,500

INTEREST PAYABLE

INTEREST EXPENSE

Dec 31 Bal   6,300

(d)

	Date	Account Titles		Debit	Credit	
31	Date	Account Titles		Debit	Credit	31
32		(1)				32
33	Jan. 10					33
34						34
35						35
36		(2)				36
37	15					37
38						38
39						39
40						40

Problem 4-1A

Omer Asik, P.I.

See Appendix

(b)

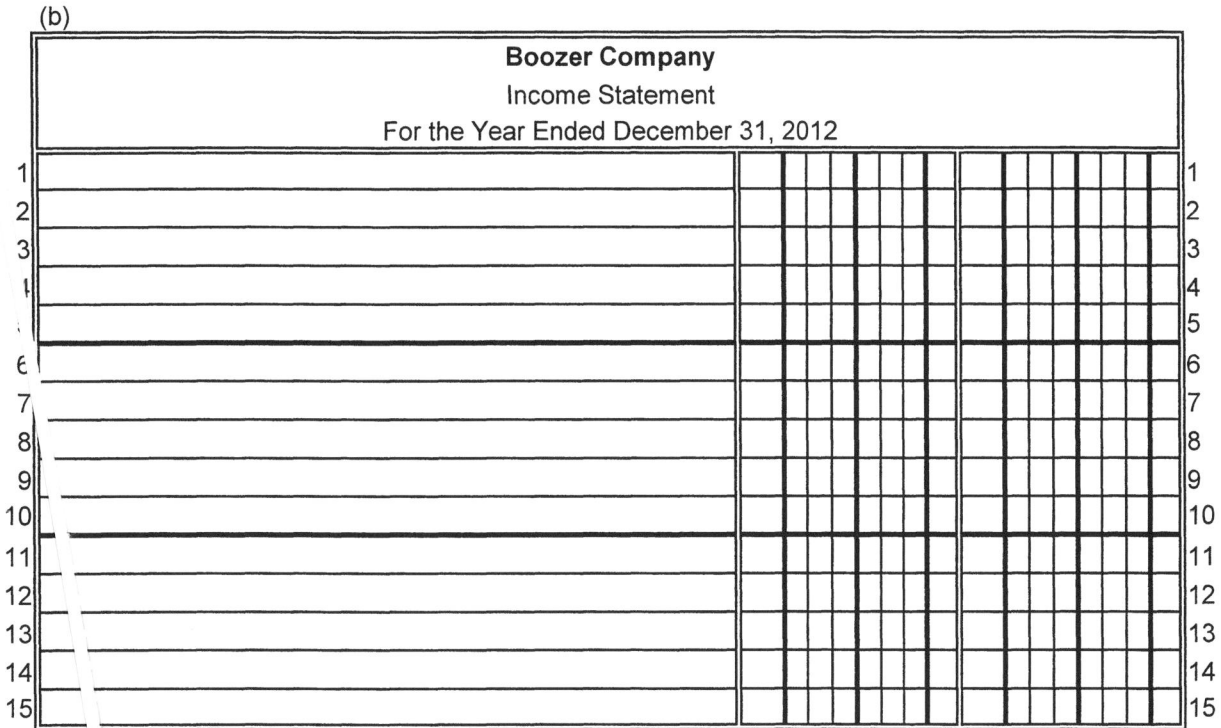

Boozer Company

Income Statement

For the Year Ended December 31, 2012

1		
2		
3		
4		
5		
6		
7		
8		
9		
10		
11		
12		
13		
14		
15		

Boozer Company

Owner's Equity Statement

For the Year Ended December 31, 2012

1	
2	
3	
4	
5	
6	
7	
8	
9	
10	

(b) (Continued)

Boozer Company
Balance Sheet
December 31, 2012

	Assets						
1							1
2							2
3							3
4							4
5							5
6							6
7							7
8							8
9							9
10							10
11							11
12							12
13							13
14							14
15							15
16	Liabilities and Owner's Equity						16
17							17
18							18
19							19
20							20
21							21
22							22
23							23
24							24
25							25
26							26
27							27
28							28
29							29
30							30
31							31
32							32
33							33

(c)

General Journal   J14

	Date	Account Titles	Ref.	Debit	Credit	
1	Dec. 31					1
2						2
3						3
4	31					4
5						5
6						6
7						7
8						8
9						9
10						10
11						11
12	31					12
13						13
14						14
15	31					15
16						16
17						17
18						18

(d)

Owner's Capital   No. 301

Date	Explanation	Ref.	Debit	Credit	Balance
Dec 31	Balance	√			2 6 0 0 0

Owner's Drawings   No. 306

Date	Explanation	Ref.	Debit	Credit	Balance
Dec 31	Balance	√			1 2 0 0 0

Income Summary   No. 350

Date	Explanation	Ref.	Debit	Credit	Balance

(d) (Continued)

Service Revenue   No. 400

Date	Explanation	Ref.	Debit	Credit	Balance
Dec 31	Balance	√			8 7 8 0 0

Advertising Expense   No. 610

Date	Explanation	Ref.	Debit	Credit	Balance
Dec 31	Balance	√			1 0 0 0 0

Supplies Expense   No. 631

Date	Explanation	Ref.	Debit	Credit	Balance
Dec 31	Balance	√			3 7 0 0

Depreciation Expense   No. 711

Date	Explanation	Ref.	Debit	Credit	Balance
Dec 31	Balance	√			8 0 0 0

Insurance Expense   No. 722

Date	Explanation	Ref.	Debit	Credit	Balance
Dec 31	Balance	√			4 0 0 0

Salaries and Wages Expense   No. 726

Date	Explanation	Ref.	Debit	Credit	Balance
Dec 31	Balance	√			3 9 0 0 0

Interest Expense   No. 905

Date	Explanation	Ref.	Debit	Credit	Balance
Dec 31	Balance	√			1 0 0 0

(e)

Boozer Company Post-Closing Trial Balance December 31, 2012	Debit	Credit
1		
2		
3		
4		
5		
6		
7		
8		
9		
10		
11		
12		
13		
14		
15		
16		
17		
18		
19		
20		

Section

Date   Carlos Company

(a)

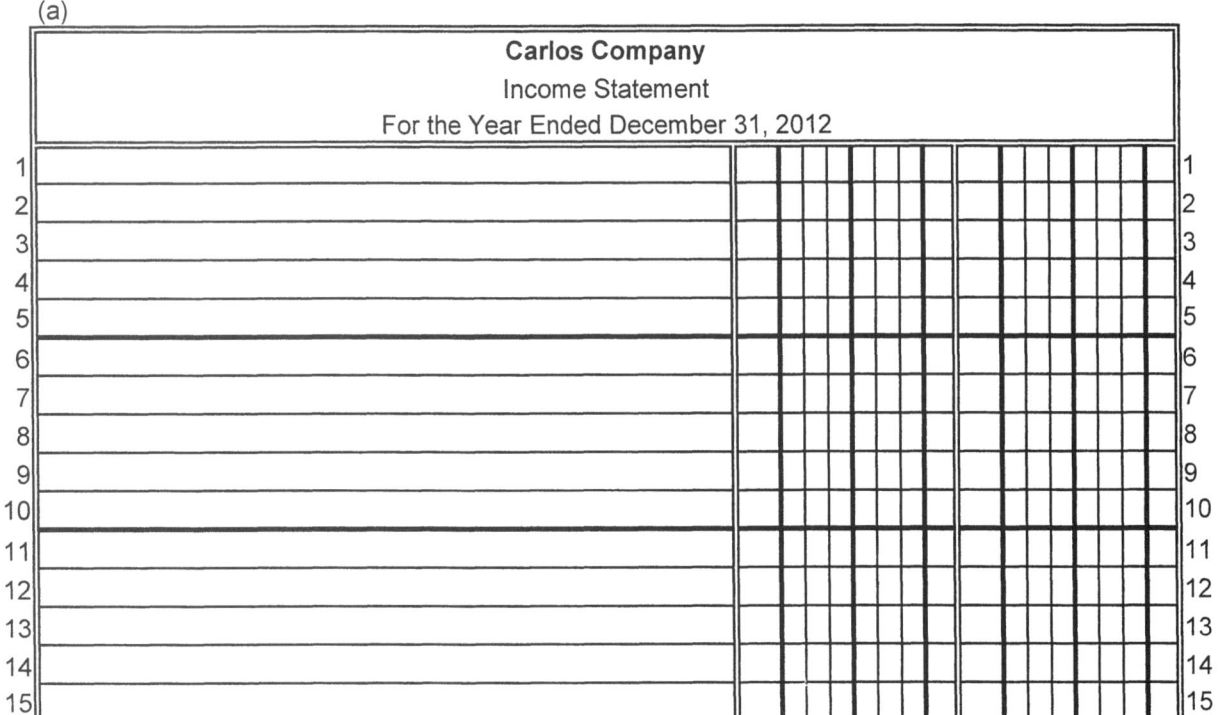

Carlos Company
Income Statement
For the Year Ended December 31, 2012

Carlos Company
Owner's Equity Statement
For the Year Ended December 31, 2012

(a) (Continued)

	Carlos Company								
	Balance Sheet								
	December 31, 2012								
1	Assets								1
2									2
3									3
4									4
5									5
6									6
7									7
8									8
9									9
10									10
11									11
12									12
13	Liabilities and Owner's Equity								13
14									14
15									15
16									16
17									17
18									18
19									19
20									20
21									21
22									22
23									23
24									24

(b)   General Journal

	Date	Accounts Titles	Ref.	Debit	Credit	
1		Closing Entries				1
2	Dec. 31					2
3						3
4						4
5	31					5
6						6
7						7
8						8
9						9
10						10
11						11
12	31					12
13						13
14						14
15	31					15
16						16
17						17
18						18
19						19
20						20
21						21
22						22
23						23
24						24
25						25

Section

Date   Carlos Company

(c)

Owner's Capital No. 301		Maintenance and Repairs Expense No. 622
	12/31 Bal 34,000	12/31 Bal 4,400

Depreciation Expense No. 711

12/31 Bal 2,800

Owner's Drawings No.306
12/31 Bal 7,200

Insurance Expense No. 722

12/31 Bal 1,200

Income Summary No. 350

Salaries and Wages Expense No. 726

12/31 Bal 35,200

Service Revenue No. 400

12/31 Bal 46,000

Utilities Expense No. 732

12/31 Bal 4,000

(d)

Carlos Company
Post-Closing Trial Balance
December 31, 2012

	Debit	Credit
1		
2		
3		
4		
5		
6		
7		
8		
9		
10		

Problem 4-4A

Noah Amusement Park

See Appendix

(b)

Noah Amusement Park
Balance Sheet
September 30, 2012

Assets

Liabilities and Owner's Equity

(c) & (d)

	Date	Accounts Titles	Debit	Credit	
1	(c)	Adjusting Entries			1
2	Sept. 30				2
3					3
4					4
5	30				5
6					6
7					7
8	30				8
9					9
10					10
11	30				11
12					12
13					13
14	30				14
15					15
16					16
17	30				17
18					18
19					19
20	(d)	Closing Entries			20
21	Sept. 30				21
22					22
23					23
24	30				24
25					25
26					26
27					27
28					28
29					29
30					30
31					31
32					32
33					33
34					34
35	30				35
36					36
37					37
38	30				38
39					39
40					40

(e)

Noah Amusement Park Post-Closing Trial Balance September 30, 2012	Debit	Credit
1		
2		
3		
4		
5		
6		
7		
8		
9		
10		
11		
12		
13		
14		
15		
16		
17		
18		
19		
20		
21		
22		
23		
24		
25		
26		
27		
28		
29		
30		

(a)   General Journal   J1

	Date	Accounts Titles	Ref.	Debit	Credit	
1	Mar. 1					1
2						2
3						3
4	1					4
5						5
6						6
7						7
8	3					8
9						9
10						10
11	5					11
12						12
13						13
14	14					14
15						15
16						16
17	18					17
18						18
19						19
20	20					20
21						21
22						22
23	21					23
24						24
25						25
26	28					26
27						27
28						28
29	31					29
30						30
31						31
32	31					32
33						33
34						34
35						35
36						36
37						37
38						38
39						39
40						40

Problem 4-5A

Devine's Carpet Cleaners

See Appendix

(a), (e) and (f)

Cash   No. 101

Date	Explanation	Ref.	Debit	Credit	Balance

Accounts Receivable   No. 112

Date	Explanation	Ref.	Debit	Credit	Balance

Supplies   No. 128

Date	Explanation	Ref.	Debit	Credit	Balance

Prepaid Insurance   No. 130

Date	Explanation	Ref.	Debit	Credit	Balance

Equipment   No. 157

Date	Explanation	Ref.	Debit	Credit	Balance

(a), (e) and (f) (Continued)

Accumulated Depreciation - Equipment   No. 158

Date	Explanation	Ref.	Debit	Credit	Balance

Accounts Payable   No. 201

Date	Explanation	Ref.	Debit	Credit	Balance

Salaries and Wages   No. 212

Date	Explanation	Ref.	Debit	Credit	Balance
			Debit	Credit	Balance

Owner's Capital   No. 301

Date	Explanation	Ref.	Debit	Credit	Balance

Owner's Drawings   No. 306

Date	Explanation	Ref.	Debit	Credit	Balance

Income Summary   No. 350

Date	Explanation	Ref.	Debit	Credit	Balance

Service Revenue   No. 400

Date	Explanation	Ref.	Debit	Credit	Balance

(a), (e) and (f) (Continued)

Gasoline Expense   No. 633

Date	Explanation	Ref.	Debit	Credit	Balance

Supplies Expense   No. 634

Date	Explanation	Ref.	Debit	Credit	Balance

Depreciation Expense   No. 711

Date	Explanation	Ref.	Debit	Credit	Balance

Insurance Expense   No. 722

Date	Explanation	Ref.	Debit	Credit	Balance

Salaries and Wages Expense   No. 726

Date	Explanation	Ref.	Debit	Credit	Balance

(d)

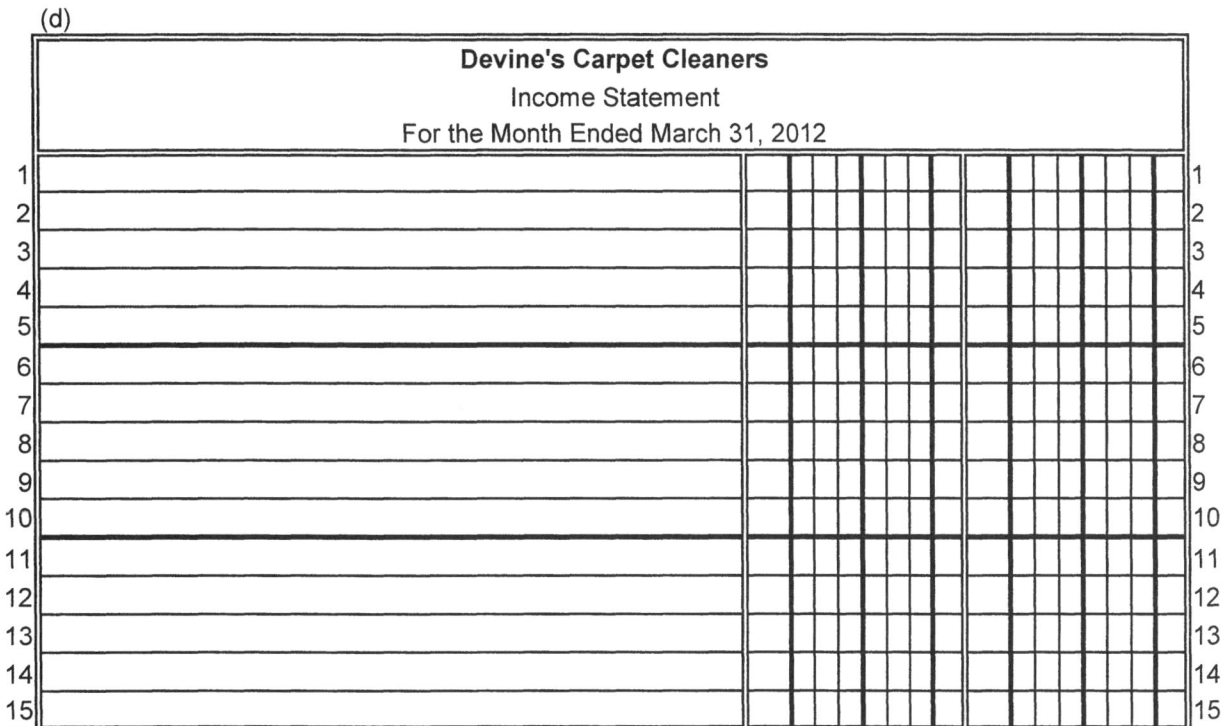

Devine's Carpet Cleaners
Income Statement
For the Month Ended March 31, 2012

Devine's Carpet Cleaners
Owner's Equity Statement
For the Month Ended March 31, 2012

(d) (Continued)

Devine's Carpet Cleaners

Balance Sheet

March 31, 2012

Assets				
Liabilities and Owner's Equity				

(e)

General Journal

J2

	Date	Accounts Titles	Ref.	Debit	Credit	
1		Adjusting Entries				1
2	Mar. 31					2
3						3
4						4
5	31					5
6						6
7						7
8	31					8
9						9
10						10
11	31					11
12						12
13						13
14	31					14
15						15
16						16

(f)

General Journal

J3

	Date	Account Titles	Ref.	Debit	Credit	
1		Closing Entries				1
2	Mar. 31					2
3						3
4						4
5	31					5
6						6
7						7
8						8
9						9
10						10
11						11
12	31					12
13						13
14						14
15	31					15
16						16
17						17
18						18
19						19

(g)

Devine's Carpet Cleaners Post-Closing Trial Balance March 31, 2012	Debit	Credit	
			1
			2
			3
			4
			5
			6
			7
			8
			9
			10
			11
			12

Problem 4-6A

Acie Cable

See Appendix

Section

(b)

Acie Cable

Trial Balance

April 30, 2012

	Debit	Credit
1 Cash		
2 Accounts Receivable		
3 Supplies		
4 Equipment		
5 Accumulated Depreciation - Equipment		
6 Accounts Payable		
7 Salaries and Wages Payable		
8 Unearned Service Revenue		
9 Owner's Capital		
11 Service Revenue		
12 Salaries and Wages Expense		
13 Advertising Expense		
14 Miscellaneous Expense		
15 Depreciation Expense		
16 Maintenance and Repairs Expense		
17		
18		
19		
20		
21		
22		
23		
24		
25		
26		
27		
28		
29		
30		

Problem 4-1B

Gibson Roofing

See Appendix

(b)

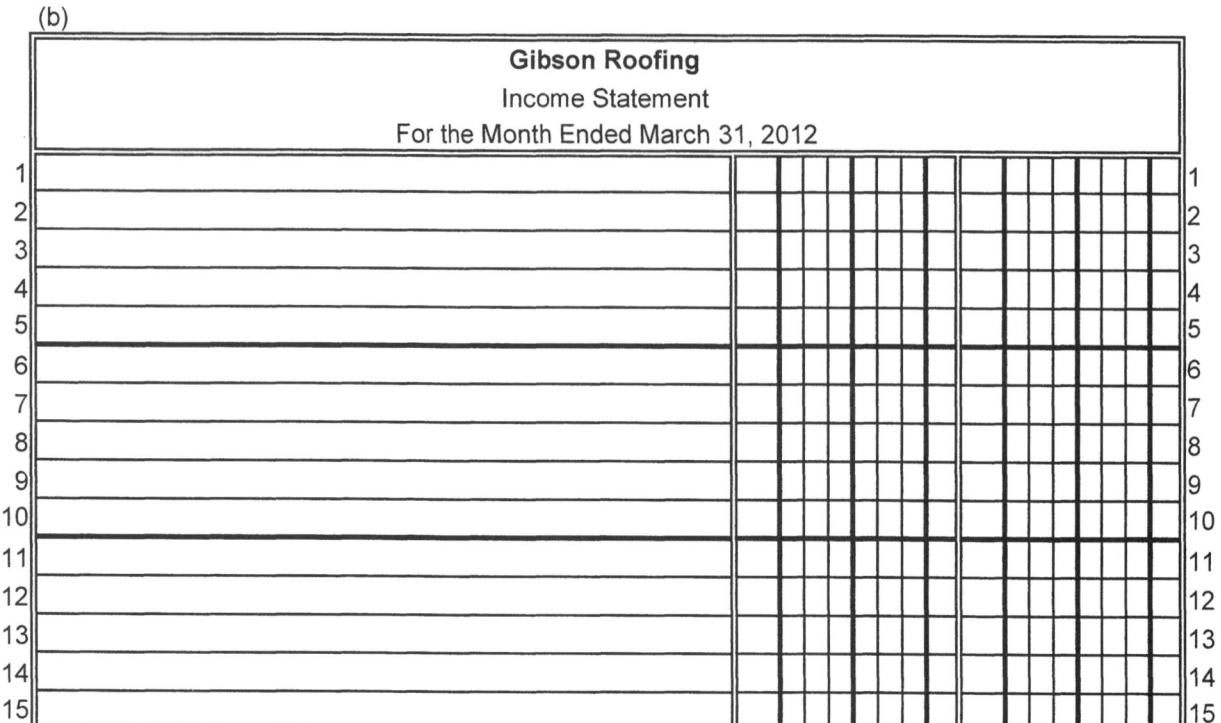

Gibson Roofing

Income Statement

For the Month Ended March 31, 2012

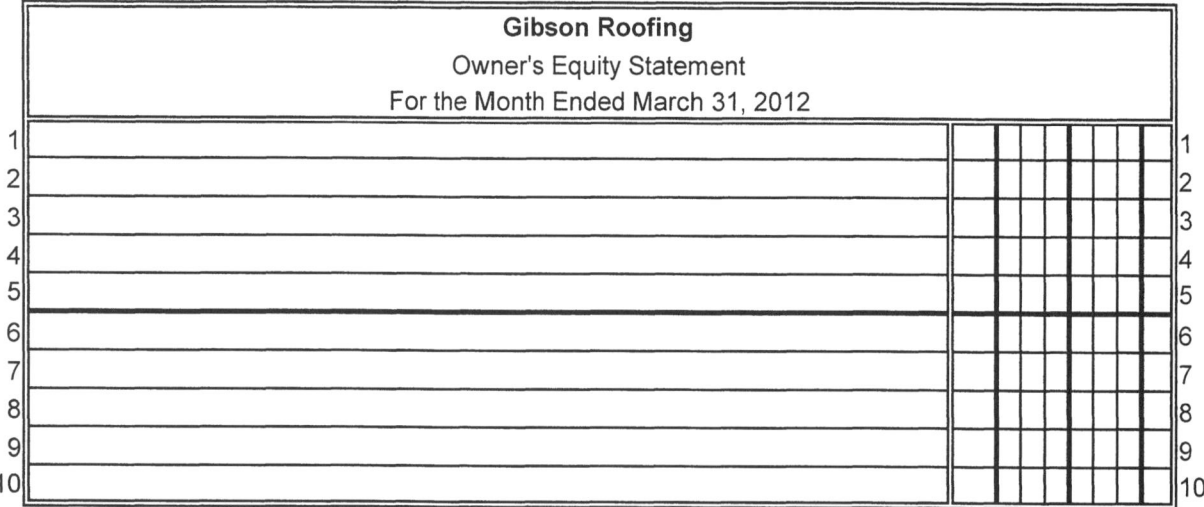

Gibson Roofing

Owner's Equity Statement

For the Month Ended March 31, 2012

(b) (Continued)

Gibson Roofing
Balance Sheet
March 31, 2012

	Assets			
1				
2				
3				
4				
5				
6				
7				
8				
9				
10				
11				
12				
13				
14				
15				
16	Liabilities and Owner's Equity			
17				
18				
19				
20				
21				
22				
23				
24				
25				
26				
27				
28				
29				
30				

(c)   General Journal

	Date	Account Titles	Debit	Credit	
1		Adjusting Entries			1
2	Mar. 31				2
3					3
4					4
5	31				5
6					6
7					7
8	31				8
9					9
10					10
11	31				11
12					12
13					13
14					14
15					15

(d)   General Journal

	Date	Account Titles	Debit	Credit	
1		Closing Entries			1
2	Mar. 31				2
3					3
4					4
5	31				5
6					6
7					7
8					8
9					9
10					10
11	31				11
12					12
13					13
14	31				14
15					15
16					16

Name

Section

Date

(a)

Taj Company
Partial Worksheet
For the Year Ended December 31, 2012

No.	Account Titles	Adjusted Trial Balance Dr.	Adjusted Trial Balance Cr.	Income Statement Dr.	Income Statement Cr.	Balance Sheet Dr.	Balance Sheet Cr.	
1	101 Cash	8100						1
2	112 Accounts Receivable	10800						2
3	126 Supplies	1500						3
4	130 Prepaid Insurance	2000						4
5	151 Equipment	24000						5
6	152 Accum. Depr. - Equip.		5600					6
7	200 Notes Payable		15000					7
8	201 Accounts Payable		6100					8
9	212 Salaries & Wages Pay.		2400					9
10	230 Interest Payable		600					10
11	301 Owner's Capital		15800					11
12	306 Owner's Drawings	7000						12
13	400 Service Revenue		61000					13
14	610 Advertising Expense	8400						14
15	631 Supplies Expense	4000						15
16	711 Depreciation Expense	5600						16
17	722 Insurance Expense	3500						17
18	726 Salaries & Wages Exp.	31000						18
19	905 Interest Expense	600						19
20	Totals	106500	106500					20
21	Net Income							21
22	Totals							22
23								23

(b)

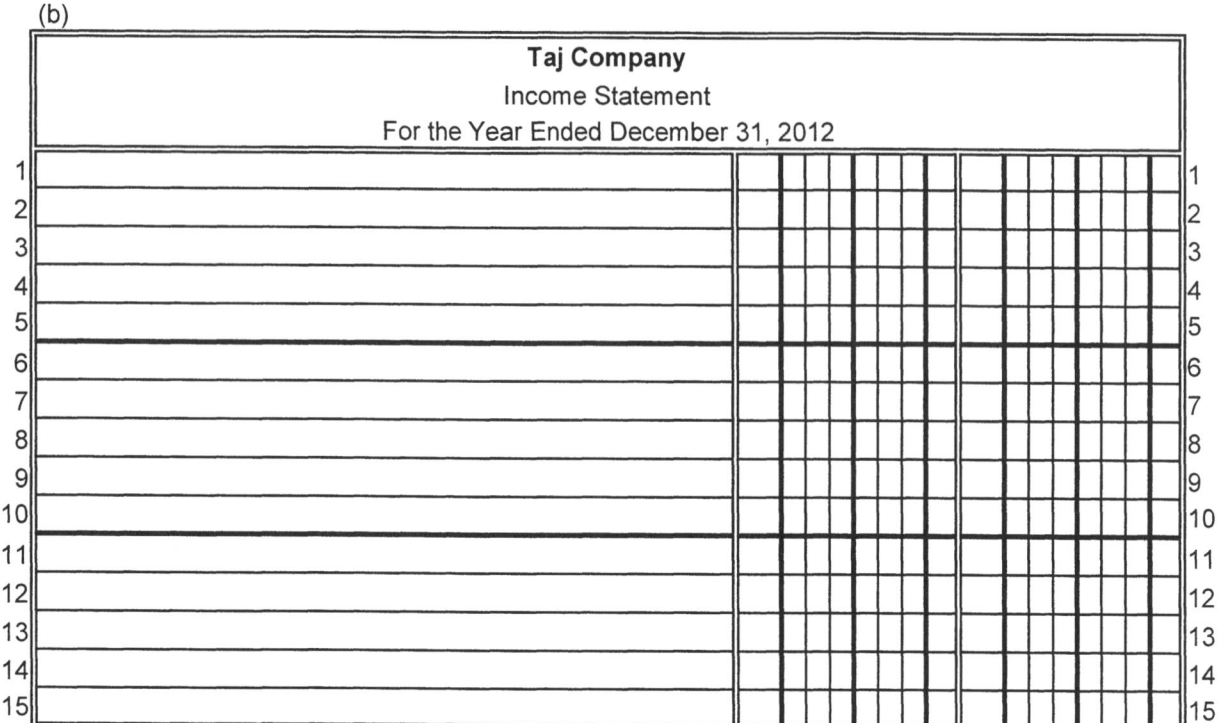

Taj Company

Income Statement

For the Year Ended December 31, 2012

Taj Company

Owner's Equity Statement

For the Year Ended December 31, 2012

(b) (Continued)

Taj Company		
Balance Sheet		
December 31, 2012		
Assets		
Liabilities and Owner's Equity		

(c)

General Journal   J14

	Date	Account Titles	Ref.	Debit	Credit	
1	Dec. 31					1
2						2
3						3
4	31					4
5						5
6						6
7						7
8						8
9						9
10						10
11						11
12	31					12
13						13
14						14
15	31					15
16						16
17						17
18						18

(d)

Owner's Capital   No.301

Date	Explanation	Ref.	Debit	Credit	Balance
Jan 1	Balance	√			1 3 0 0 0

Owner's Drawings   No. 306

Date	Explanation	Ref.	Debit	Credit	Balance
Dec 31	Balance	√			7 0 0 0

Income Summary   No. 350

Date	Explanation	Ref.	Debit	Credit	Balance

(d) (Continued)

Service Revenue   No. 400

Date	Explanation	Ref.	Debit	Credit	Balance
Dec 31	Balance	√			6 1 0 0 0

Advertising Expense   No. 610

Date	Explanation	Ref.	Debit	Credit	Balance
Dec 31	Balance	√			8 4 0 0

Supplies Expense   No. 631

Date	Explanation	Ref.	Debit	Credit	Balance
Dec 31	Balance	√			4 0 0 0

Depreciation Expense   No. 711

Date	Explanation	Ref.	Debit	Credit	Balance
Dec 31	Balance	√			5 6 0 0

Insurance Expense   No. 722

Date	Explanation	Ref.	Debit	Credit	Balance
Dec 31	Balance	√			3 5 0 0

Salaries and Wages Expense   No. 726

Date	Explanation	Ref.	Debit	Credit	Balance
Dec 31	Balance	√			2 8 0 0 0

Interest Expense   No. 905

Date	Explanation	Ref.	Debit	Credit	Balance
Dec 31	Balance	√			6 0 0

(e)

Taj Company Post-Closing Trial Balance December 31, 2012	Debit	Credit
1		
2		
3		
4		
5		
6		
7		
8		
9		
10		
11		
12		
13		
14		
15		
16		
17		
18		
19		
20		

Section

(a)

Korver Company
Income Statement
For the Year Ended December 31, 2012

1			
2			
3			
4			
5			
6			
7			
8			
9			
10			
11			
12			
13			
14			
15			

Korver Company
Owner's Equity Statement
For the Year Ended December 31, 2012

1	
2	
3	
4	
5	
6	
7	
8	
9	
10	

(a) (Continued)

Korver Company

Balance Sheet

December 31, 2012

Assets						
Liabilities and Owner's Equity						

(b)   General Journal

	Date	Accounts Titles	Ref.	Debit	Credit	
1		Closing Entries				1
2	Dec. 31					2
3						3
4						4
5	31					5
6						6
7						7
8						8
9						9
10						10
11						11
12	31					12
13						13
14						14
15	31					15
16						16
17						17
18						18
19						19
20						20
21						21
22						22
23						23
24						24
25						25

(c)

Owner's Capital No. 301		Maint. & Repairs Expense No. 622
	1/1 Bal 19,000	12/31 Bal 1,600
		Depreciation Expense No. 711
		12/31 Bal 3,100
Owner's Drawings No.306		
12/31 Bal 11,000		**Insurance Expense No. 722**
		12/31 Bal 1,800
Income Summary No. 350		
		Salaries & Wages Expense No. 726
		12/31 Bal 30,000
		Utilities Expense No. 732
Service Revenue No. 400		12/31 Bal 1,400
	12/31 Bal 60,000	

(d)

Korver Company		
Post-Closing Trial Balance		
December 31, 2012		
	Debit	Credit
1		
2		
3		
4		
5		
6		
7		
8		
9		
10		

Problem 4-4B

Law Management Services

See Appendix

(b)

	Law Management Services																		
	Balance Sheet																		
	December 31, 2012																		
1	Assets																		
2																			
3																			
4																			
5																			
6																			
7																			
8																			
9																			
10																			
11																			
12																			
13																			
14																			
15																			
16																			
17																			
18																			
19	Liabilities and Owner's Equity																		
20																			
21																			
22																			
23																			
24																			
25																			
26																			
27																			
28																			
29																			
30																			
31																			
32																			
33																			
34																			
35																			
36																			
37																			
38																			
39																			
40																			

	Date	Accounts Titles	Debit	Credit	
1	(c)	Adjusting Entries			1
2	Dec. 31				2
3					3
4					4
5	31				5
6					6
7					7
8	31				8
9					9
10					10
11	31				11
12					12
13					13
14	31				14
15					15
16					16
17					17
18					18
19	(d)	Closing Entries			19
20	Dec. 31				20
21					21
22					22
23					23
24	31				24
25					25
26					26
27					27
28					28
29					29
30					30
31					31
32					32
33	31				33
34					34
35					35
36	31				36
37					37
38					38
39					39
40					40

(e)

Law Management Services	Debit	Credit
Post-Closing Trial Balance		
December 31, 2012		
1		
2		
3		
4		
5		
6		
7		
8		
9		
10		
11		
12		
13		
14		
15		
16		
17		
18		
19		
20		
21		
22		
23		
24		
25		
26		
27		
28		
29		
30		

(a)

General Journal   J1

	Date	Accounts Titles	Ref.	Debit	Credit	
1	July 1					1
2						2
3						3
4	1					4
5						5
6						6
7						7
8	3					8
9						9
10						10
11	5					11
12						12
13						13
14	12					14
15						15
16						16
17	18					17
18						18
19						19
20	20					20
21						21
22						22
23	21					23
24						24
25						25
26	25					26
27						27
28						28
29	31					29
30						30
31						31
32	31					32
33						33
34						34
35						35
36						36
37						37
38						38
39						39

Problem 4-5B

Pargo's Cleaning Service

See Appendix

(a), (e) and (f)

Cash   No. 101

Date	Explanation	Ref.	Debit	Credit	Balance

Accounts Receivable   No. 112

Date	Explanation	Ref.	Debit	Credit	Balance

Supplies   No. 128

Date	Explanation	Ref.	Debit	Credit	Balance

Prepaid Insurance   No. 130

Date	Explanation	Ref.	Debit	Credit	Balance

Equipment   No. 157

Date	Explanation	Ref.	Debit	Credit	Balance

(a), (e) and (f) (Continued)

Accumulated Depreciation - Equipment　　　No. 158

Date	Explanation	Ref.	Debit	Credit	Balance

Accounts Payable　　　No. 201

Date	Explanation	Ref.	Debit	Credit	Balance

Salaries and Wages Payable　　　No. 212

Date	Explanation	Ref.	Debit	Credit	Balance

Owner's Capital　　　No. 301

Date	Explanation	Ref.	Debit	Credit	Balance

Owner's Drawings　　　No. 306

Date	Explanation	Ref.	Debit	Credit	Balance

Income Summary　　　No. 350

Date	Explanation	Ref.	Debit	Credit	Balance

Service Revenue　　　No. 400

Date	Explanation	Ref.	Debit	Credit	Balance

(a), (e) and (f) (Continued)

Gasoline Expense   No. 633

Date	Explanation	Ref.	Debit	Credit	Balance

Supplies Expense   No. 634

Date	Explanation	Ref.	Debit	Credit	Balance

Depreciation Expense   No. 711

Date	Explanation	Ref.	Debit	Credit	Balance

Insurance Expense   No. 722

Date	Explanation	Ref.	Debit	Credit	Balance

Salaries and Wages Expense   No. 726

Date	Explanation	Ref.	Debit	Credit	Balance

(d)

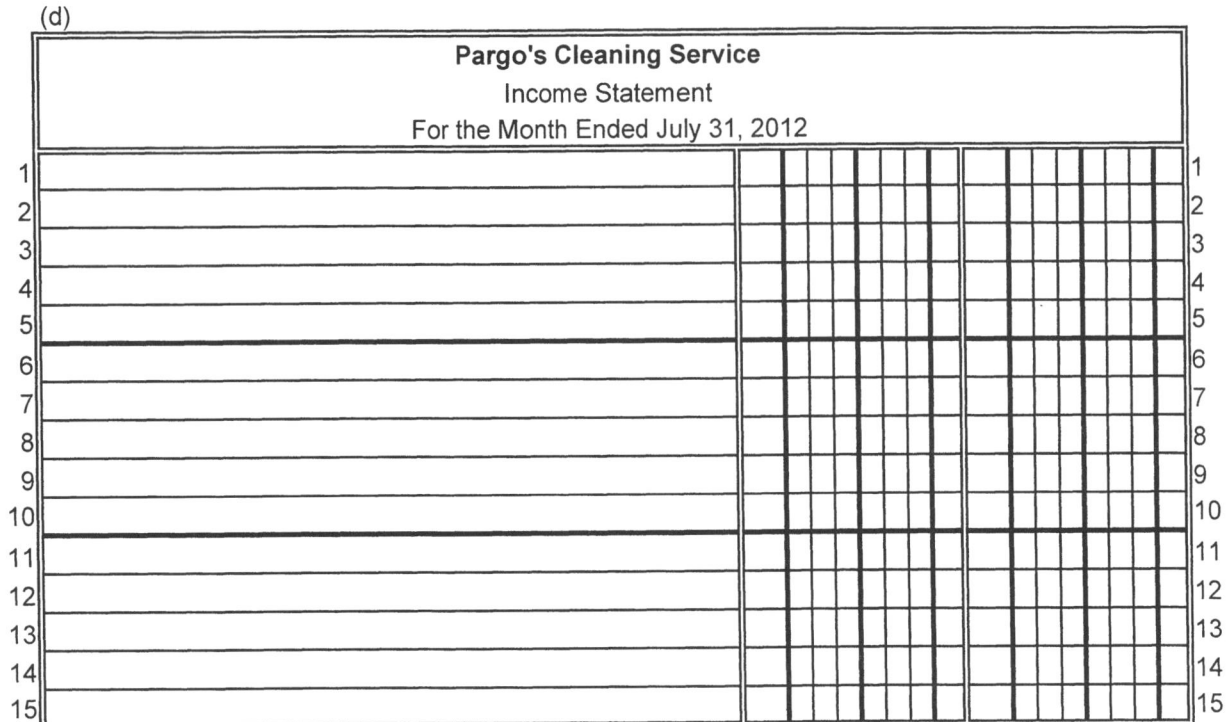

Pargo's Cleaning Service
Income Statement
For the Month Ended July 31, 2012

Pargo's Cleaning Service
Owner's Equity Statement
For the Month Ended July 31, 2012

(d) (Continued)

Pargo's Cleaning Service

Balance Sheet

July 31, 2012

Assets						
Liabilities and Owner's Equity						

(e)   General Journal   J2

	Date	Accounts Titles	Ref.	Debit	Credit	
1		Adjusting Entries				1
2	July 31					2
3						3
4						4
5	31					5
6						6
7						7
8	31					8
9						9
10						10
11	31					11
12						12
13						13
14	31					14
15						15
16						16

(f)   General Journal   J3

	Date	Account Titles	Ref.	Debit	Credit	
1		Closing Entries				1
2	July 31					2
3						3
4						4
5	31					5
6						6
7						7
8						8
9						9
10						10
11						11
12	31					12
13						13
14						14
15	31					15
16						16
17						17
18						18
19						19

(g)

Pargo's Cleaning Service		
Post-Closing Trial Balance		
July 31, 2012		
	Debit	Credit

(a) General Journal J1

	Date	Accounts Titles	Ref.	Debit	Credit	
1	July 1					1
2						2
3						3
4	1					4
5						5
6						6
7						7
8	3					8
9						9
10						10
11	5					11
12						12
13						13
14	12					14
15						15
16						16
17	18					17
18						18
19						19
20	20					20
21						21
22						22
23	21					23
24						24
25						25
26	25					26
27						27
28						28
29	31					29
30						30
31						31
32	31					32
33						33
34						34
35						35
36						36
37						37
38						38
39						39
40						40

Comprehensive Problem Ch 2 - 4

Julie's Maids Cleaning Service

See Appendix

(a), (e) and (f)

Cash   No. 101

Date	Explanation	Ref.	Debit	Credit	Balance

Accounts Receivable   No. 112

Date	Explanation	Ref.	Debit	Credit	Balance

Supplies   No. 128

Date	Explanation	Ref.	Debit	Credit	Balance

Prepaid Insurance   No. 130

Date	Explanation	Ref.	Debit	Credit	Balance

Equipment   No. 157

Date	Explanation	Ref.	Debit	Credit	Balance

Accumulated Depreciation - Equipment   No. 158

Date	Explanation	Ref.	Debit	Credit	Balance

(a), (e) and (f) (Continued)

Accounts Payable   No. 201

Date	Explanation	Ref.	Debit	Credit	Balance

Salaries and Wages Payable   No. 212

Date	Explanation	Ref.	Debit	Credit	Balance

Owner's Capital   No. 301

Date	Explanation	Ref.	Debit	Credit	Balance

Owner's Drawings   No. 306

Date	Explanation	Ref.	Debit	Credit	Balance

Income Summary   No. 350

Date	Explanation	Ref.	Debit	Credit	Balance

Service Revenue   No. 400

Date	Explanation	Ref.	Debit	Credit	Balance

(a), (e) and (f) (Continued)

Gasoline Expense   No. 633

Date	Explanation	Ref.	Debit	Credit	Balance

Supplies Expense   No. 634

Date	Explanation	Ref.	Debit	Credit	Balance

Depreciation Expense   No. 711

Date	Explanation	Ref.	Debit	Credit	Balance

Insurance Expense   No. 722

Date	Explanation	Ref.	Debit	Credit	Balance

Salaries and Wages   No. 726

Date	Explanation	Ref.	Debit	Credit	Balance

(d)

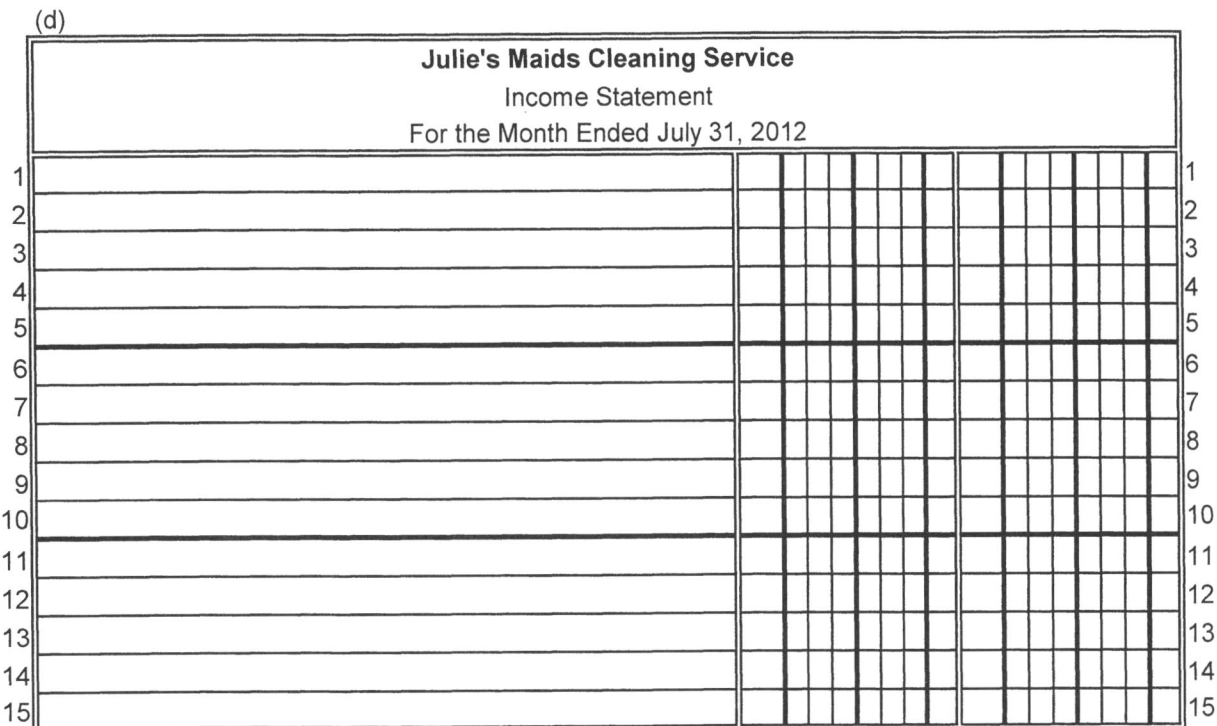

Julie's Maids Cleaning Service

Income Statement

For the Month Ended July 31, 2012

Julie's Maids Cleaning Service

Statement of Owner's Equity

For the Month Ended July 31, 2012

(d) (Continued)

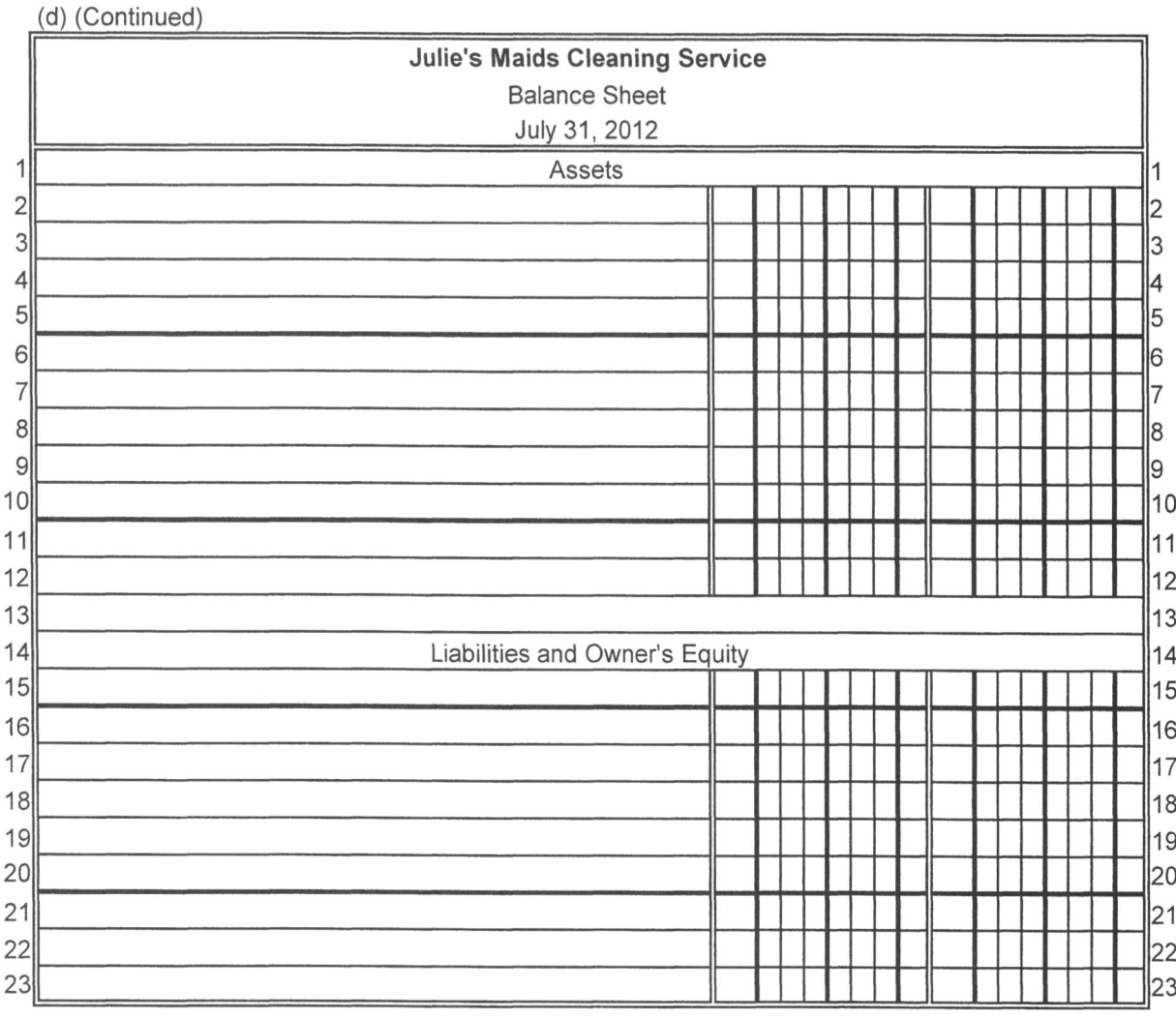

Julie's Maids Cleaning Service

Balance Sheet

July 31, 2012

Assets

Liabilities and Owner's Equity

(g)

Julie's Maids Cleaning Service

Post-Closing Trial Balance

July 31, 2012

	Debit	Credit

General Journal   J2

	Date	Accounts Titles	Ref.	Debit	Credit	
1	(e)	Adjusting Entries				1
2	July 31					2
3						3
4						4
5	31					5
6						6
7						7
8	31					8
9						9
10						10
11	31					11
12						12
13						13
14	31					14
15						15
16						16

General Journal   J3

	Date	Account Titles	Ref.	Debit	Credit	
1	(f)	Closing Entries				1
2	July 31					2
3						3
4						4
5	31					5
6						6
7						7
8						8
9						9
10						10
11						11
12	31					12
13						13
14						14
15	31					15
16						16
17						17
18						18
19						19
20						20

	PepsiCo	Coca-Cola
(a) (in millions)		
1. Total current assets		
2. Net property, plant, and equipment		
3. Total current liabilities		
4. Total stockholders' (shareholders') equity		

(b)

(a)

	Whitegloves Janitorial Service				
	Balance Sheet				
	December 31, 2012				

Assets

Liabilities and Owner's Equity

Whitegloves Janitorial Service				
Capital Account Detail				
December 31, 2012				

1	Capital account balance as reported				
2					
3					
4					
5					
6					
7					
8					
9					
10					
11					
12					
13					
14					
15					
16					
17					
18					
19					
20					
21					
22	(b)				
23					
24					
25					
26					
27					
28					
29					
30					
31					
32					
33					
34					
35					
36					
37					
38					
39					
40					

Name

Section

Date

1	Assets						1
2							2
3							3
4							4
5							5
6							6
7							7
8							8
9							9
10							10
11							11
12							12
13							13
14							14
15							15
16	Liabilities and Owner's Equity						16
17							17
18							18
19							19
20							20
21							21
22							22
23							23
24							24
25							25
26							26
27							27
28							28
29							29
30							30
31							31
32							32
33							33
34							34
35							35
36							36
37							37
38							38
39							39
40							40

IFRS4-3

Diaz Company

Partial Statement of Financial Position

1 | Current assets:

IFRS4-4

Zurich Company

Partial Statement of Financial Position

December 31, 2012

IFRS4-5

Karr Bowling Alley
Statement of Financial Position
December 31, 2012
Assets

Equity and Liabilities

IFRS4-6

BE5-1

		Sales	Cost of Goods Sold	Gross Profit	Operating Expenses	Net Income	
1							1
2	(a)	$ 75000		$ 30000		$ 10800	2
3							3
4	(b)	108000	70000			29500	4
5							5
6	(c)		83900	79600	39500		6
7							7
8							8
9							9

	BE5-2	Account Titles	Debit	Credit	
10		Account Titles	Debit	Credit	10
11	Brad Company				11
12					12
13					13
14					14
15					15
16	Murray Company				16
17					17
18					18
19					19
20					20
21					21
22					22
23					23

	BE5-3	Account Titles	Debit	Credit	
24		Account Titles	Debit	Credit	24
25	(a)				25
26					26
27					27
28					28
29					29
30					30
31	(b)				31
32					32
33					33
34					34
35					35
36					36
37	(c)				37
38					38
39					39
40					40

BE5-4

	Account Titles	Debit	Credit	
1	(a)			1
2				2
3				3
4	(b)			4
5				5
6				6
7	(c)			7
8				8
9				9
10				10

BE5-5

	Account Titles	Debit	Credit	
12				12
13				13
14				14
15				15

BE5-6

	Account Titles	Debit	Credit	
18				18
19				19
20				20
21				21
22				22
23				23
24				24
25				25

BE5-7

27	**Myers Company**		27
28	Income Statement (Partial)		28
29	For the Month Ended October 31, 2012		29
30			30
31			31
32			32
33			33
34			34
35			35
36			36
37			37
38			38
39			39
40			40

BE5-10

		Debit	Credit
1			
2			
3			
4			
5			
6			
7			
8			
9			
10			

*BE5-11

		Debit	Credit
11			
12			
13			
14			
15			
16			
17			
18			
19			
20			

*BE5-12

	Account Titles	Debit	Credit
21			
22 (a)			
23			
24			
25 (b)			
26			
27			
28 (c)			
29			
30			
31			
32			
33			
34			
35			
36			
37			
38			
39			
40			

DO IT! 5-1

	Date	Account Titles	Debit	Credit	
1	Oct. 5				1
2					2
3					3
4					4
5	Oct. 8				5
6					6
7					7
8					8

DO IT! 5-2

	Date	Account Titles	Debit	Credit	
9					9
10	Date	Account Titles	Debit	Credit	10
11	Oct. 5				11
12					12
13					13
14					14
15					15
16					16
17					17
18					18
19	Oct. 8				19
20					20
21					21
22					22
23					23
24					24
25					25
26					26
27					27
28					28
29					29
30					30
31					31
32					32
33					33
34					34
35					35
36					36
37					37
38					38
39					39
40					40

Name

Section

Date   Ogilvy's Boutique

	Date	Account Titles	Debit	Credit	
1	Dec. 31				1
2					2
3					3
4					4
5					5
6					6
7					7
8					8
9					9
10					10
11					11
12					12
13					13
14					14
15					15
16					16
17					17
18					18
19					19
20					20
21					21
22					22
23					23
24					24
25					25
26					26
27					27
28					28
29					29
30					30
31					31
32					32
33					33
34					34
35					35
36					36
37					37
38					38
39					39
40					40

E5-2   General Journal

	Date	Account Titles	Debit	Credit	
1	(a)				1
2	Apr. 5				2
3					3
4					4
5	6				5
6					6
7					7
8	7				8
9					9
10					10
11	8				11
12					12
13					13
14	15				14
15					15
16					16
17					17
18	(b)				18
19	May 4				19
20					20
21					21

E5-3

	Date	Account Titles	Debit	Credit	
1	Sept. 6				1
2					2
3					3
4	9				4
5					5
6					6
7	10				7
8					8
9					9
10	12				10
11					11
12					12
13					13
14					14

E5-3 (Continued)   General Journal

	Date	Account Titles	Debit	Credit	
1	Sept. 14				1
2					2
3					3
4					4
5					5
6	20				6
7					7
8					8
9					9
10					10
11					11
12					12

E5-4

	Date	Account Titles	Debit	Credit	
1	(a)				1
2	June 10				2
3					3
4					4
5	11				5
6					6
7					7
8	12				8
9					9
10					10
11	19				11
12					12
13					13
14					14
15	(b)				15
16	June 10				16
17					17
18					18
19					19
20					20
21					21
22					22
23					23

E5-4 (Continued)   General Journal

	Date	Account Titles	Debit	Credit	
1	June 12				1
2					2
3					3
4					4
5					5
6	19				6
7					7
8					8
9					9
10					10

E5-5

	Date	Account Titles	Debit	Credit	
1	(a)				1
2	Dec. 3				2
3					3
4					4
5					5
6					6
7					7
8	8				8
9					9
10					10
11	13				11
12					12
13					13
14					14
15					15
16					16
17	(b)				17
18	Jan. 2				18
19					19
20					20
21					21
22					22
23					23
24					24
25					25

E5-6 (a)

Garcia Company
Income Statement (Partial)
For the Year Ended October 31, 2012

1		
2		
3		
4		
5		
6		

(b)

	Date	Account Titles	Debit	Credit
1	Oct. 31			
2				
3				
4	31			
5				
6				
7				

E5-7

	Account Titles	Debit	Credit
1	(a)		
2			
3			
4	(b)		
5			
6			
7			
8			
9			
10			
11			
12			
13			
14			
15			
16			
17			

		Account Titles	Debit	Credit	
1	(a)				1
2					2
3					3
4	(b)				4
5					5
6					6
7					7
8					8
9					9
10					10
11					11
12					12
13					13
14					14
15					15
16					16
17					17
18					18
19					19
20					20
21					21
22					22
23					23
24					24
25					25
26					26
27					27
28					28
29					29
30					30
31					31
32					32
33					33
34					34
35					35
36					36
37					37
38					38
39					39
40					40

(a)

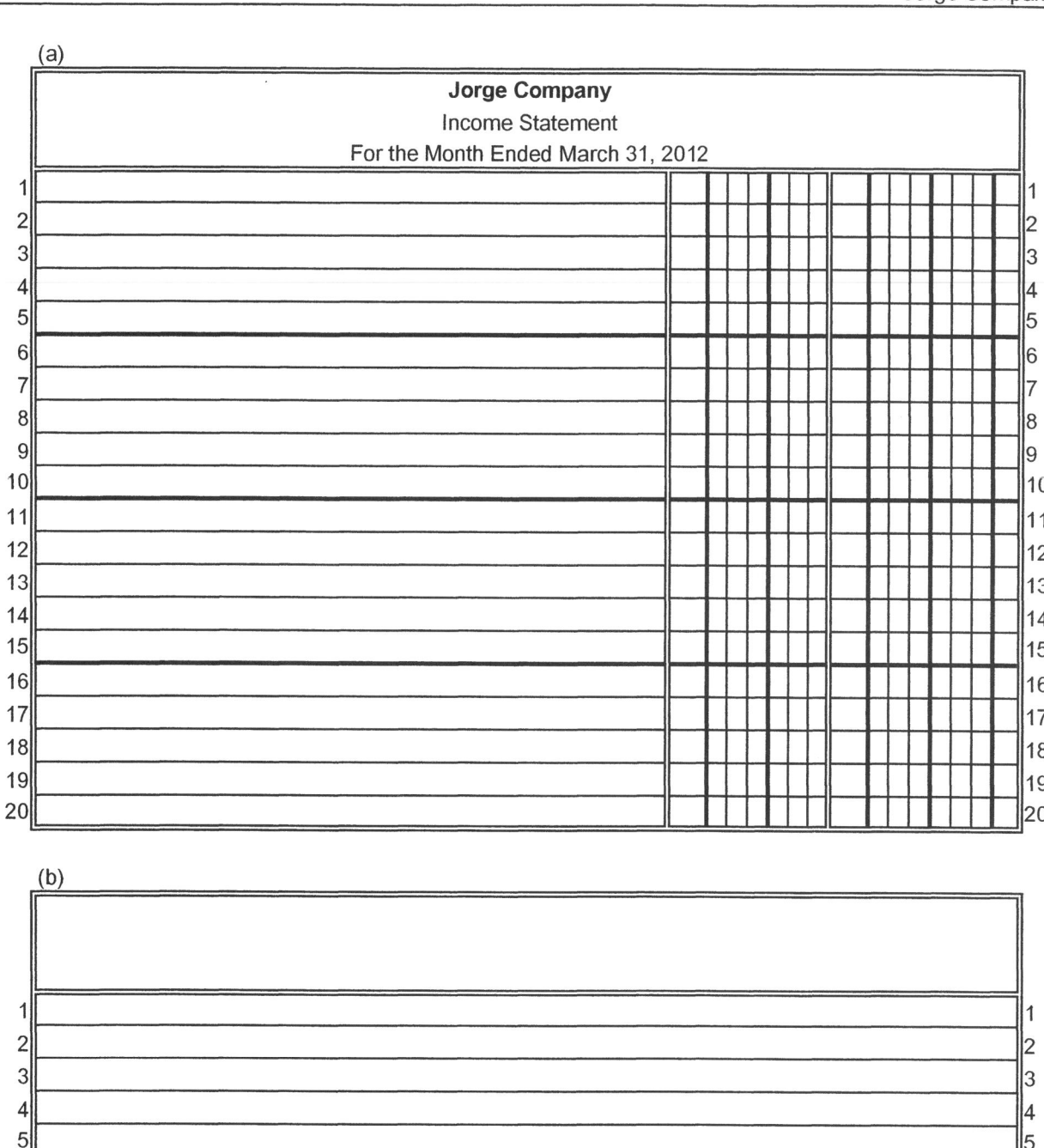

Jorge Company
Income Statement
For the Month Ended March 31, 2012

(b)

(a)

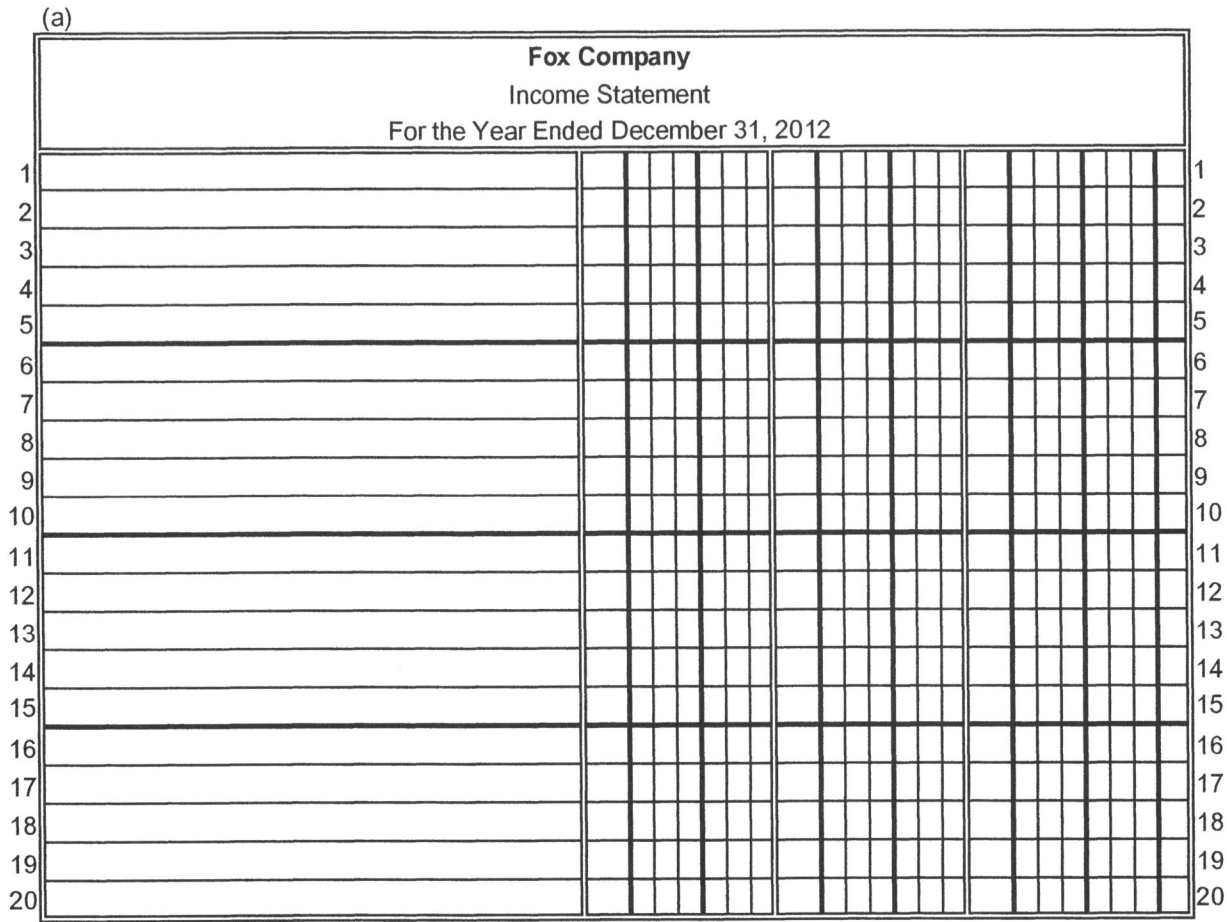

Fox Company

Income Statement

For the Year Ended December 31, 2012

(b)

Fox Company

Income Statement

For the Year Ended December 31, 2012

E5-11

		Account Titles	Debit	Credit	
1	1.				1
2					2
3					3
4	2.				4
5					5
6					6
7					7
8					8
9	3.				9
10					10
11					11
12	4.				12
13					13
14					14
15					15

E5-13

		Dae Company	Kim Company	
	(a)			
1				1
2	Sales	$ 90 0 0 0	$	2
3				3
4	Sales Returns		5 0 0 0	4
5				5
6	Net Sales	8 7 0 0 0	1 0 2 0 0 0	6
7				7
8	Cost of Goods Sold	5 6 0 0 0		8
9				9
10	Gross Profit		4 1 5 0 0	10
11				11
12	Operating Expenses	1 5 0 0 0		12
13				13
14	Net Income	$	$ 1 5 0 0 0	14
15				15
16	(b)　　Gross profit rate			16
17				17
18				18
19				19
20				20

		Holloway Cosmetics			Jin Grocery			Kwon Wholesalers			
1	Sales	$	9 0 0 0 0		$			$	1 2 2 0 0 0			1
2	Sales returns and allowances					5 0 0 0			1 2 0 0 0			2
3	Net sales		8 6 0 0 0			9 5 0 0 0						3
4	Cost of goods sold		5 6 0 0 0									4
5	Gross profit					3 8 0 0 0			2 4 0 0 0			5
6	Operating expenses		1 5 0 0 0						1 8 0 0 0			6
7	Income from operations											7
8	Other expenses and losses		4 0 0 0			7 0 0 0						8
9	Net income	$			$	1 1 0 0 0		$	5 0 0 0			9
10												10
11												11
12												12
13												13
14												14
15												15

*E5-15

		1
1		1
2		2
3		3
4		4
5		5
6		6
7		7
8		8
9		9
10		10
11		11
12		12
13		13
14		14
15		15

*E5-17

		B	F	L	R	
1	Beginning inventory	$ 150	$ 70	$ 1000	$	1
2						2
3	Purchases	1620	1060		43590	3
4						4
5	Purchase returns and					5
6	allowances	40		290		6
7						7
8	Net purchases		1030	6210	41090	8
9						9
10	Freight-in	110			2240	10
11						11
12	Cost of goods purchased		1280	7940		12
13						13
14	Cost of goods available for sale	1840	1350		49530	14
15						15
16	Ending inventory	310		1450	6230	16
17						17
18	Cost of goods sold		1230	7490	43300	18
19						19
20						20

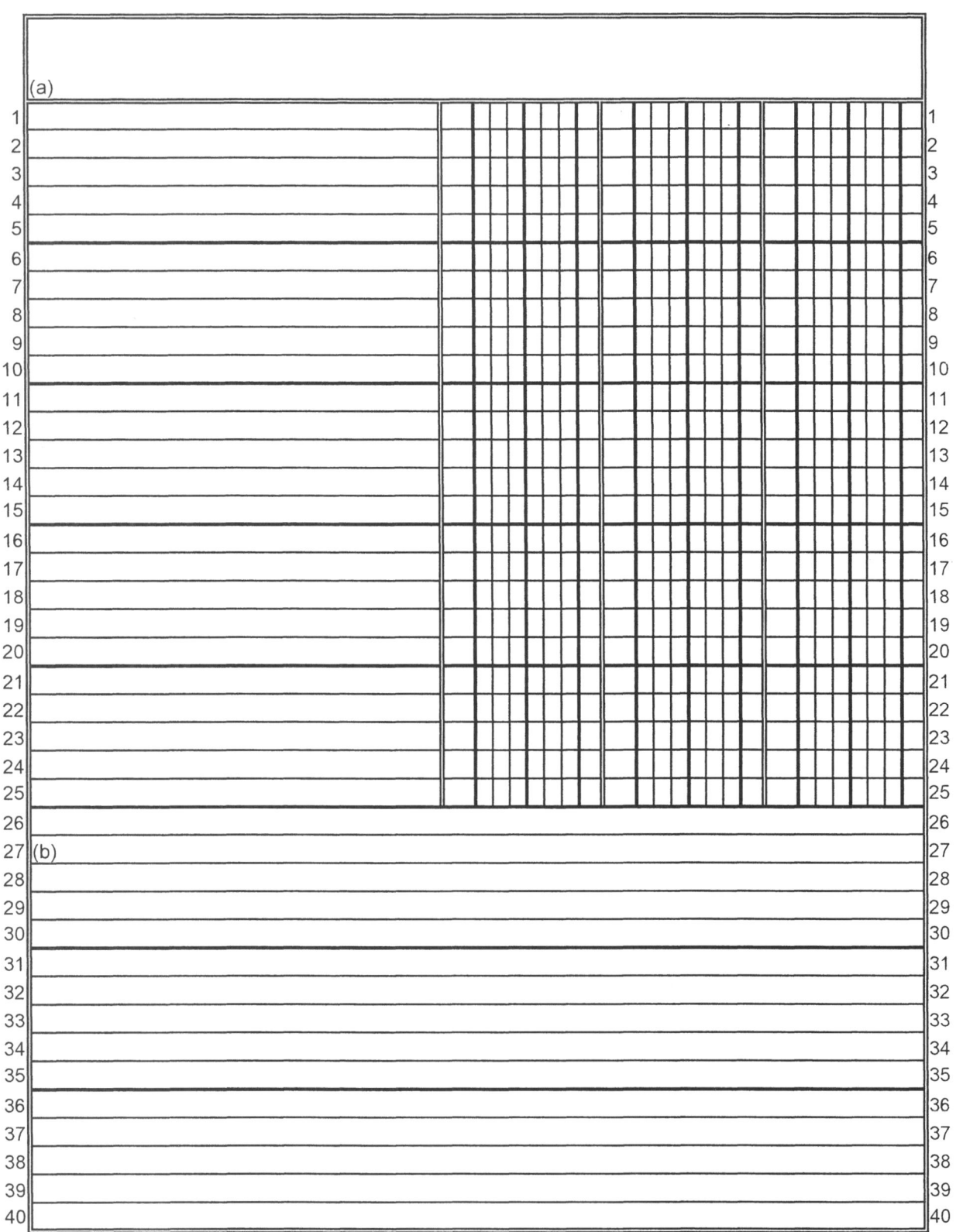

	Date	Account Titles	Debit	Credit	
1	(a)				1
2	Apr. 5				2
3					3
4					4
5	6				5
6					6
7					7
8	7				8
9					9
10					10
11	8				11
12					12
13					13
14	15				14
15					15
16					16
17					17
18					18
19	(b)				19
20	May 4				20
21					21
22					22
23					23
24					24
25					25

	Date	Account Titles	Debit	Credit	
1	(a)				1
2	Apr. 5				2
3					3
4					4
5	6				5
6					6
7					7
8	7				8
9					9
10					10
11	8				11
12					12
13					13
14	15				14
15					15
16					16
17					17
18					18
19	(b)				19
20	May 4				20
21					21
22					22
23					23
24					24
25					25

Dawson Company
Worksheet (Partial)
For the Period Ended May 31, 2012

	Account Titles	Adjusted Trial Balance Dr.	Adjusted Trial Balance Cr.	Income Statement Dr.	Income Statement Cr.	Balance Sheet Dr.	Balance Sheet Cr.	
1	Cash	11 0 0 0						1
2	Inventory	7 6 0 0 0						2
3	Sales Revenue		4 8 0 0 0 0					3
4	Sales Returns and Allowances	1 0 0 0 0						4
5	Sales Discounts	9 0 0 0						5
6	Cost of Goods Sold	3 0 0 0 0 0						6
7								7
8								8
9								9
10								10
11								11
12								12
13								13
14								14
15								15

Exercise 5-21

Linus Company

See Appendix

Section

General Journal

	Date	Account Titles	Debit	Credit	
1	July 1				1
2					2
3					3
4	3				4
5					5
6					6
7					7
8					8
9					9
10	9				10
11					11
12					12
13					13
14	12				14
15					15
16					16
17					17
18	17				18
19					19
20					20
21					21
22					22
23					23
24	18				24
25					25
26					26
27					27
28					28
29					29
30	20				30
31					31
32					32
33	21				33
34					34
35					35
36					36
37					37
38					38
39					39
40					40

General Journal

	Date	Account Titles	Debit	Credit	
1	July 22				1
2					2
3					3
4					4
5					5
6					6
7	30				7
8					8
9					9
10	31				10
11					11
12					12
13					13
14					14
15					15
16					16
17					17
18					18
19					19
20					20
21					21
22					22
23					23
24					24
25					25
26					26
27					27
28					28
29					29
30					30
31					31
32					32
33					33
34					34
35					35
36					36
37					37
38					38
39					39
40					40

(a)   General Journal   J1

	Date	Account Titles	Ref.	Debit	Credit	
1	Apr. 2					1
2						2
3						3
4	4					4
5						5
6						6
7						7
8						8
9						9
10	5					10
11						11
12						12
13	6					13
14						14
15						15
16	11					16
17						17
18						18
19						19
20	13					20
21						21
22						22
23						23
24	14					24
25						25
26						26
27	16					27
28						28
29						29
30	18					30
31						31
32						32
33	20					33
34						34
35						35
36	23					36
37						37
38						38
39						39
40						40

(a) (Continued)   J1

	Date	Account Titles	Ref.	Debit	Credit	
1	Apr. 26					1
2						2
3						3
4	27					4
5						5
6						6
7						7
8	29					8
9						9
10						10
11						11
12						12
13						13
14	30					14
15						15
16						16
17						17
18						18
19						19

(b)

Cash   No. 101

Date	Explanation	Ref.	Debit	Credit	Balance
Apr. 1	Balance	√			9 0 0 0

Accounts Receivable   No. 112

Date	Explanation	Ref.	Debit	Credit	Balance

(b) (Continued)

Inventory   No. 120

Date	Explanation	Ref.	Debit	Credit	Balance

Accounts Payable   No. 201

Date	Explanation	Ref.	Debit	Credit	Balance

Owner's Capital   No. 301

Date	Explanation	Ref.	Debit	Credit	Balance
Apr. 1	Balance	√			9 0 0 0

Sales Revenue   No. 401

Date	Explanation	Ref.	Debit	Credit	Balance

Sales Returns and Allowances   No. 412

Date	Explanation	Ref.	Debit	Credit	Balance

(b) (Continued)

Sales Discounts   No. 414

Date	Explanation	Ref.	Debit	Credit	Balance

Cost of Goods Sold   No. 505

Date	Explanation	Ref.	Debit	Credit	Balance

Freight-out   No. 644

Date	Explanation	Ref.	Debit	Credit	Balance

(c)

Pace Distributing Company
Income Statement (Partial)
For the Month Ended April 30, 2012

1		
2		
3		
4		
5		
6		
7		
8		
9		
10		

(a)

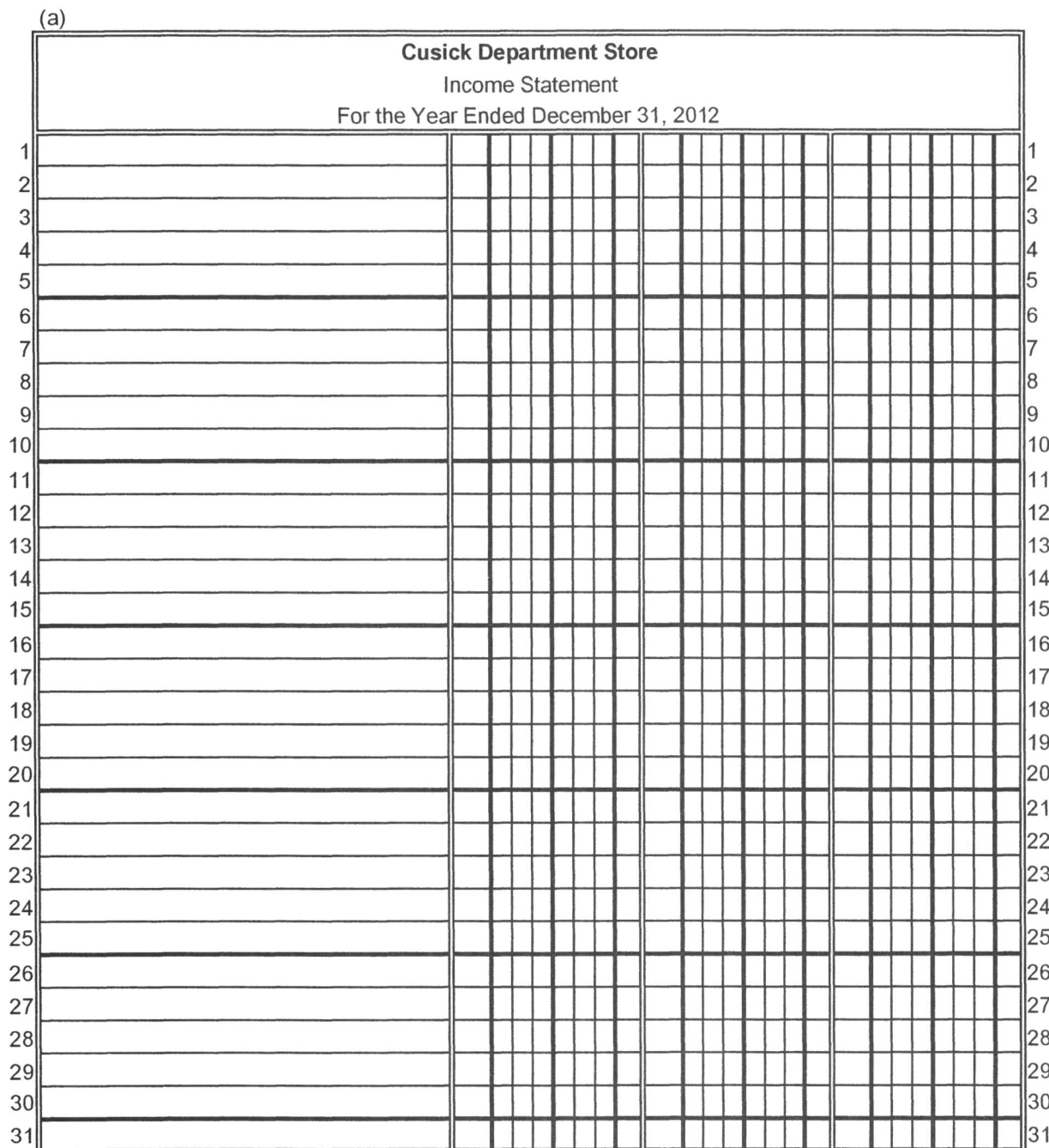

Cusick Department Store
Income Statement
For the Year Ended December 31, 2012

Cusick Department Store
Owner's Equity Statement
For the Year Ended December 31, 2012

(a) (Continued)

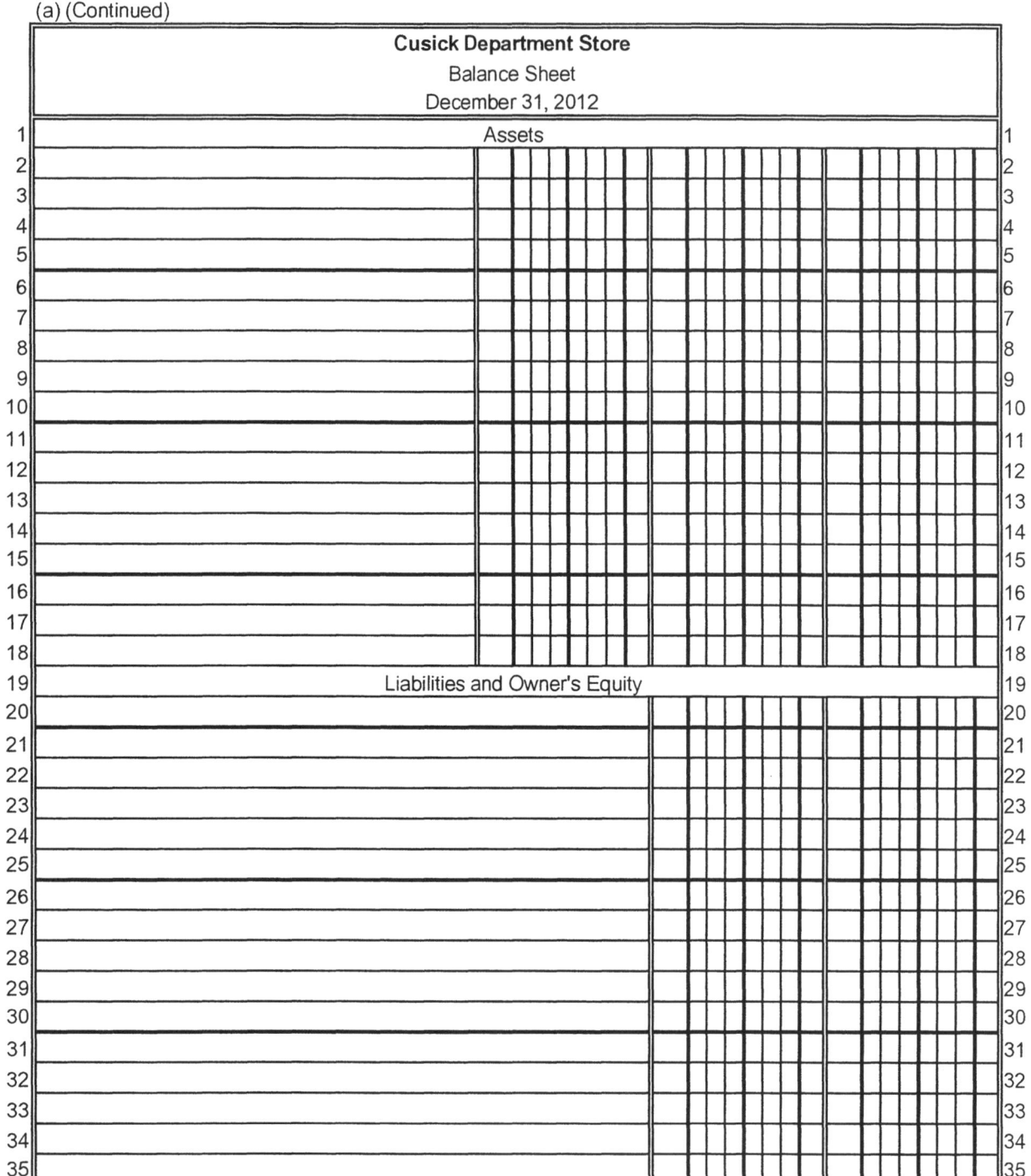

Cusick Department Store
Balance Sheet
December 31, 2012

Assets

Liabilities and Owner's Equity

(b)   General Journal

	Date	Account Titles	Debit	Credit	
1		Adjusting Entries			1
2	Dec. 31				2
3					3
4					4
5	31				5
6					6
7					7
8	31				8
9					9
10					10
11	31				11
12					12
13					13
14	31				14
15					15
16					16
17	31				17
18					18
19					19
20	31				20
21					21
22					22
23					23
24					24
25					25

(c)   General Journal

	Date	Account Titles	Debit	Credit	
1		Closing Entries			1
2	Dec. 31				2
3					3
4					4
5					5
6	31				6
7					7
8					8
9					9
10					10
11					11
12					12
13					13
14					14
15					15
16					16
17					17
18					18
19	31				19
20					20
21					21
22	31				22
23					23
24					24
25					25
26					26
27					27
28					28
29					29
30					30
31					31
32					32
33					33
34					34
35					35

(a)   General Journal   J1

Date	Account Titles	Ref.	Debit	Credit	
1 Apr. 4					1
2					2
3					3
4 6					4
5					5
6					6
7 8					7
8					8
9					9
10					10
11					11
12					12
13 10					13
14					14
15					15
16 11					16
17					17
18					18
19 13					19
20					20
21					21
22					22
23 14					23
24					24
25					25
26 15					26
27					27
28					28
29 17					29
30					30
31					31
32 18					32
33					33
34					34
35					35
36					36
37					37
38					38
39					39
40					40
41					41

(a) (Continued)   General Journal   J1

	Date	Account Titles	Ref.	Debit	Credit	
1	Apr. 20					1
2						2
3						3
4	21					4
5						5
6						6
7						7
8	27					8
9						9
10						10
11	30					11
12						12
13						13
14						14
15						15
16						16
17						17
18						18
19						19
20						20
21						21
22						22
23						23
24						24
25						25
26						26
27						27
28						28
29						29
30						30
31						31
32						32
33						33
34						34
35						35
36						36
37						37
38						38
39						39
40						40

(b)

Cash   No. 101

Date	Explanation	Ref.	Debit	Credit	Balance
Apr 1	Balance	√			2 5 0 0

Accounts Receivable   No. 112

Date	Explanation	Ref.	Debit	Credit	Balance

Inventory   No. 120

Date	Explanation	Ref.	Debit	Credit	Balance
Apr 1	Balance	√			1 7 0 0

Accounts Payable   No. 201

Date	Explanation	Ref.	Debit	Credit	Balance

(b) (Continued)

Owner's Capital   No. 301

Date	Explanation	Ref.	Debit	Credit	Balance
Apr 1	Balance	√			4 2 0 0

Sales Revenue   No. 401

Date	Explanation	Ref.	Debit	Credit	Balance

Sales Returns and Allowances   No. 412

Date	Explanation	Ref.	Debit	Credit	Balance

Cost of Goods Sold   No. 505

Date	Explanation	Ref.	Debit	Credit	Balance

(c)

Juliet's Tennis Shop
Trial Balance
April 30, 2012

	Debit	Credit
1		
2		
3		
4		
5		
6		
7		
8		
9		
10		

Rutherford Department Store
Income Statement (Partial)
For the Year Ended December 31, 2012

1				
2				
3				
4				
5				
6				
7				
8				
9				
10				
11				
12				
13				
14				
15				
16				
17				
18				
19				
20				
21				
22				
23				
24				
25				
26				
27				
28				
29				
30				
31				
32				
33				
34				
35				

(a)	2008	2009	2010
1 Cost of goods sold:			
2			
3			
4			
5			
6			
7			
8 (b)			
9 Sales revenue			
10			
11			
12			
13 (c)			
14 Beginning accounts payable			
15			
16			
17			
18			
19 (d)			
20 Gross profit rate			
21			
22			
23			
24			
25			
26			
27			
28			
29			
30			

(a)   General Journal

	Date	Account Titles	Debit	Credit	
1	Apr. 4				1
2					2
3					3
4	6				4
5					5
6					6
7	8				7
8					8
9					9
10	10				10
11					11
12					12
13	11				13
14					14
15					15
16	13				16
17					17
18					18
19					19
20	14				20
21					21
22					22
23	15				23
24					24
25					25
26	17				26
27					27
28					28
29	18				29
30					30

(a) (Continued)   General Journal

	Date	Account Titles	Debit	Credit
1	Apr. 20			
2				
3				
4	21			
5				
6				
7				
8	27			
9				
10				
11	30			
12				
13				
14				
15				
16				
17				
18				
19				
20				
21				
22				
23				
24				
25				
26				
27				
28				
29				
30				

(b)

Cash			Sales
4/1 Bal.	2,500		Returns and Allowances

			Purchases

Accounts Receivable			

			Purchase
			Returns and Allowances

Inventory			
4/1/ Bal.	1,700		

			Purchase Discount

Accounts Payable			

			Freight-in

Owner's Capital			
		4/1/ Bal.	4,200

Sales			

Name _____

Section _____

Date _____

Alpert Tennis Shop

(c)

Alpert Tennis Shop

Trial Balance

April 30, 2012

	Debit	Credit
1			1
2			2
3			3
4			4
5			5
6			6
7			7
8			8
9			9
10			10
11			11
12			12
13			13

Alpert Tennis Shop

Income Statement (Partial)

For the Month Ended April 30, 2012

1						1
2						2
3						3
4						4
5						5
6						6
7						7
8						8
9						9
10						10
11						11
12						12
13						13
14						14
15						15
16						16
17						17
18						18
19						19
20						20
21						21
22						22

Problem 5-8A

Mr. Eko Fashion Center

See Appendix

(b)

	Mr. Eko Fashion Center				
	Income Statement				
	For the Year Ended November 30, 2012				

(b) (Continued)

Mr. Eko Fashion Center
Owner's Equity Statement
For the Year Ended November 30, 2012

1			
2			
3			
4			
5			

Mr. Eko Fashion Center
Balance Sheet
November 30, 2012

	Assets		
1			
2			
3			
4			
5			
6			
7			
8			
9			
10			
11			
12			
13			
14			
15			
16			
17	Liabilities and Owner's Equity		
18			
19			
20			
21			
22			
23			
24			
25			
26			
27			
28			
29			
30			

(c)

General Journal

Date	Account Titles	Debit	Credit
	Adjusting Entries		
Nov. 30			
30			
30			
30			
30			

(d)

Date	Account Titles	Debit	Credit
	Closing Entries		
Nov. 30			
30			
30			
30			

(e)

Mr. Eko Fashion Center		
Post-Closing Trial Balance		
November 30, 2012		
1		
2		
3		
4		
5		
6		
7		
8		
9		
10		
11		
12		
13		
14		
15		
16		

General Journal

	Date	Account Titles	Debit	Credit	
1	June 1				1
2					2
3					3
4	3				4
5					5
6					6
7					7
8					8
9					9
10	6				10
11					11
12					12
13	9				13
14					14
15					15
16					16
17	15				17
18					18
19					19
20	17				20
21					21
22					22
23					23
24					24
25					25
26	20				26
27					27
28					28
29	24				29
30					30
31					31
32					32
33	26				33
34					34
35					35
36					36
37					37
38					38
39					39
40					40

General Journal

	Date	Account Titles	Debit	Credit	
1	June 28				1
2					2
3					3
4					4
5					5
6					6
7	30				7
8					8
9					9
10					10
11					11
12					12
13					13
14					14
15					15
16					16
17					17
18					18
19					19
20					20
21					21
22					22
23					23
24					24
25					25
26					26
27					27
28					28
29					29
30					30
31					31
32					32
33					33
34					34
35					35
36					36
37					37
38					38
39					39
40					40

(a)

	Date	Account Titles	Ref.	Debit	Credit	
			General Journal		J1	
1	May 1					1
2						2
3						3
4	2					4
5						5
6						6
7						7
8						8
9						9
10	5					10
11						11
12						12
13	9					13
14						14
15						15
16						16
17	10					17
18						18
19						19
20						20
21	11					21
22						22
23						23
24	12					24
25						25
26						26
27	15					27
28						28
29						29
30	17					30
31						31
32						32
33	19					33
34						34
35						35
36	24					36
37						37
38						38
39						39
40						40

(a) (Continued)   J1

	Date	Account Titles	Ref.	Debit	Credit	
1	May 25					1
2						2
3						3
4	27					4
5						5
6						6
7						7
8						8
9	29					9
10						10
11						11
12						12
13						13
14						14
15	31					15
16						16
17						17
18						18
19						19
20						20

(b)

Cash   No. 101

Date	Explanation	Ref.	Debit	Credit	Balance
May 1	Balance	√			5 0 0 0

Accounts Receivable   No. 112

Date	Explanation	Ref.	Debit	Credit	Balance

(b) (Continued)

Inventory   No. 120

Date	Explanation	Ref.	Debit	Credit	Balance

Supplies   No. 126

Date	Explanation	Ref.	Debit	Credit	Balance

Accounts Payable   No. 201

Date	Explanation	Ref.	Debit	Credit	Balance

Owner's Capital   No. 301

Date	Explanation	Ref.	Debit	Credit	Balance
May 1	Balance	√			5 0 0 0

Sales   No. 401

Date	Explanation	Ref.	Debit	Credit	Balance

(b) (Continued)

Sales Returns and Allowances   No. 412

Date	Explanation	Ref.	Debit	Credit	Balance

Sales Discounts   No. 414

Date	Explanation	Ref.	Debit	Credit	Balance

Cost of Goods Sold   No. 505

Date	Explanation	Ref.	Debit	Credit	Balance

(c)

	Boone Hardware Store		
	Income Statement (Partial)		
	For the Month Ended May 31, 2012		
1				1
2				2
3				3
4				4
5				5
6				6
7				7
8				8
9				9
10				10

(a)

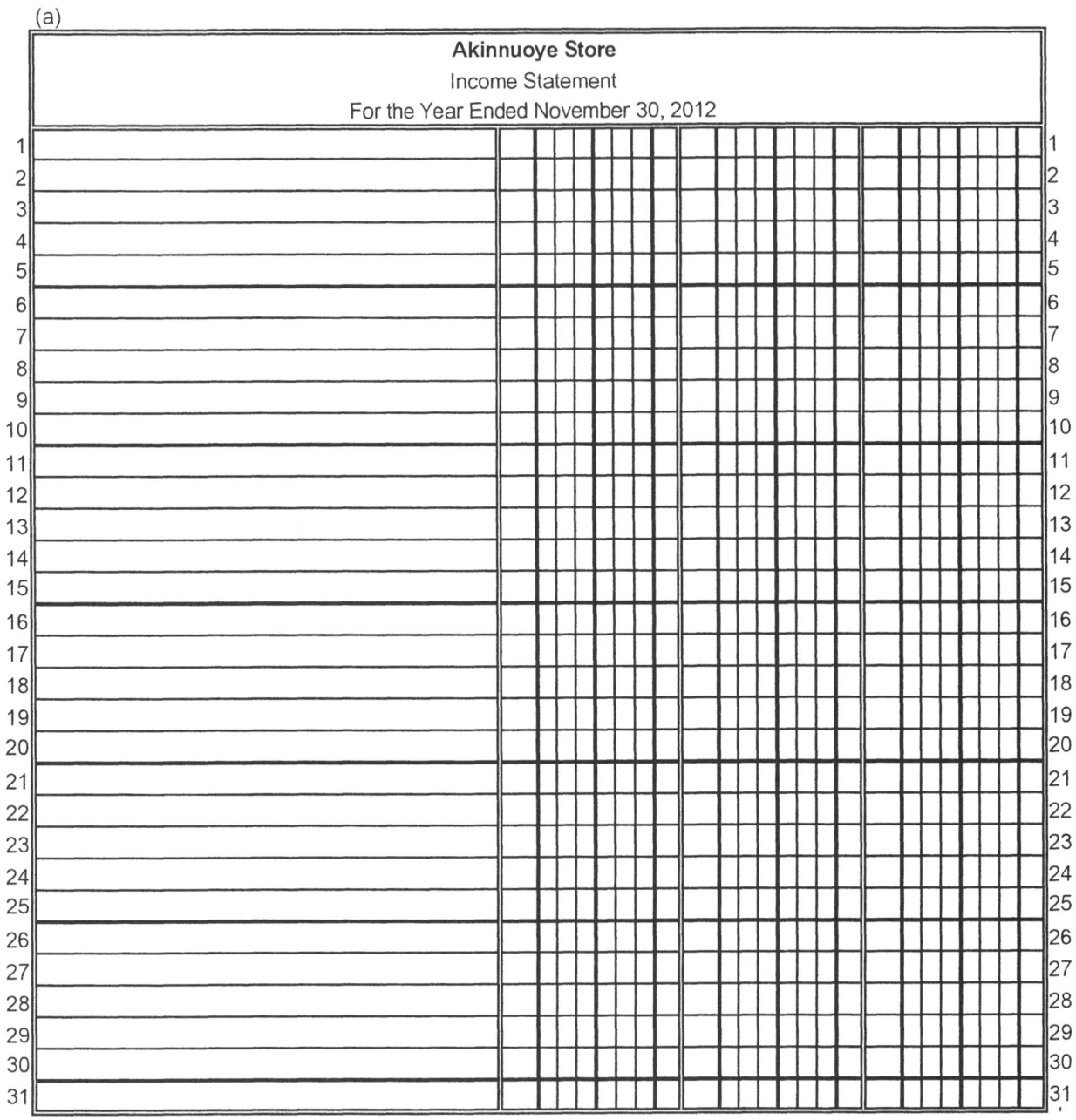

Akinnuoye Store

Income Statement

For the Year Ended November 30, 2012

Akinnuoye Store

Owner's Equity Statement

For the Year Ended November 30, 2012

(a) (Continued)

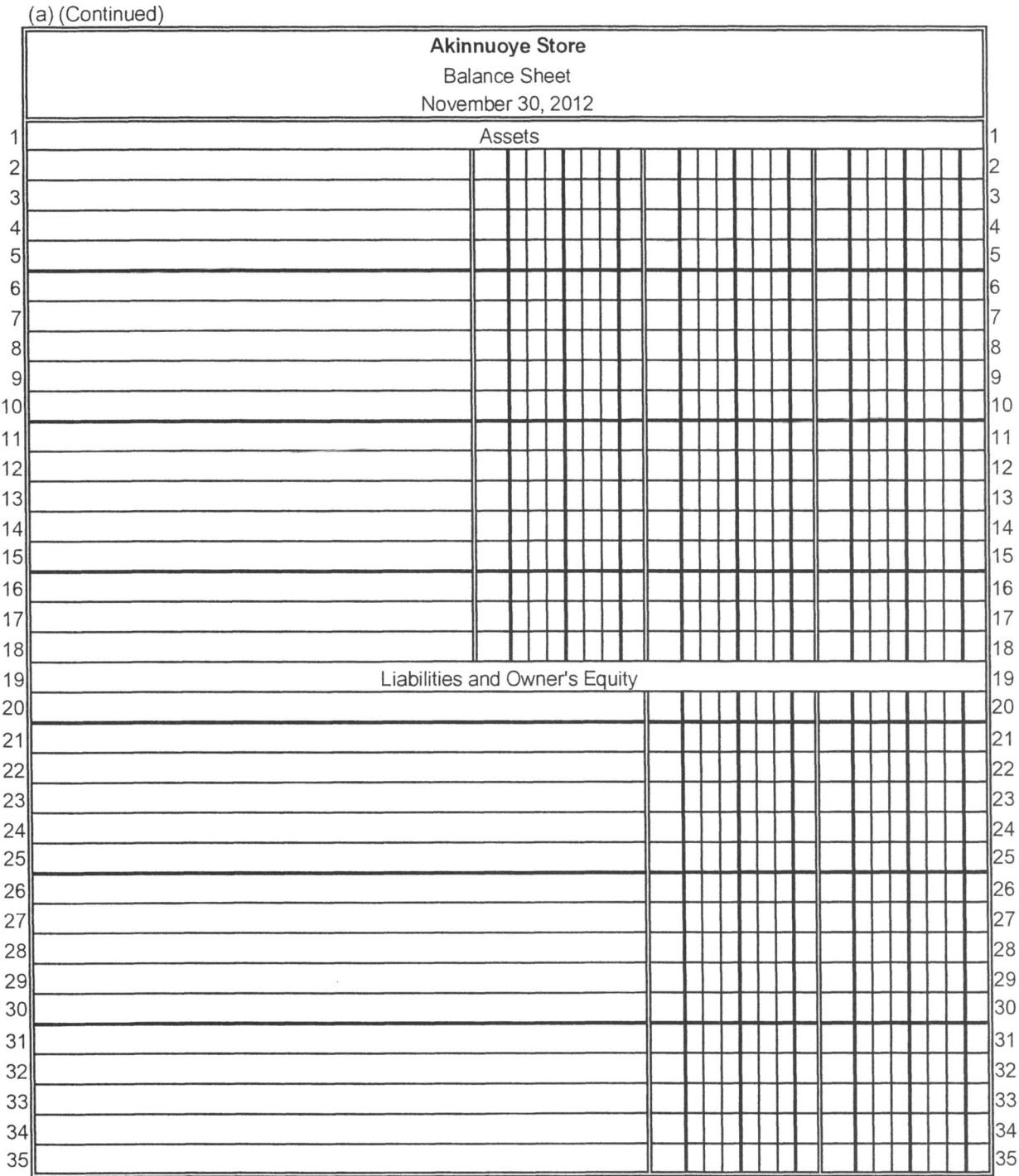

Akinnuoye Store
Balance Sheet
November 30, 2012

Assets

Liabilities and Owner's Equity

(b)   General Journal

	Date	Account Titles	Debit	Credit	
1		Adjusting Entries			1
2	Nov. 30				2
3					3
4					4
5	30				5
6					6
7					7
8	30				8
9					9
10					10
11	30				11
12					12
13					13
14	30				14
15					15
16					16
17					17
18					18
19					19
20					20
21					21
22					22
23					23
24					24
25					25

(c)

General Journal

Date	Account Titles	Debit	Credit
	Closing Entries		
Nov. 30			
30			
30			
30			

(a) General Journal J1

	Date	Account Titles	Ref.	Debit	Credit	
1	Apr. 5					1
2						2
3						3
4	7					4
5						5
6						6
7	9					7
8						8
9						9
10	10					10
11						11
12						12
13						13
14						14
15						15
16	12					16
17						17
18						18
19	14					19
20						20
21						21
22						22
23	17					23
24						24
25						25
26	20					26
27						27
28						28
29						29
30						30
31						31
32	21					32
33						33
34						34
35						35
36	27					36
37						37
38						38
39	30					39
40						40
41						41

(b)

Cash   No. 101

Date	Explanation	Ref.	Debit	Credit	Balance
Apr 1	Balance	√			1 8 0 0

Accounts Receivable   No. 112

Date	Explanation	Ref.	Debit	Credit	Balance

Inventory   No. 120

Date	Explanation	Ref.	Debit	Credit	Balance
Apr 1	Balance	√			2 5 0 0

Accounts Payable   No. 201

Date	Explanation	Ref.	Debit	Credit	Balance

(b) (Continued)

Owner's Capital   No. 301

Date	Explanation	Ref.	Debit	Credit	Balance
Apr 1	Balance	√			4 3 0 0

Sales Revenue   No. 401

Date	Explanation	Ref.	Debit	Credit	Balance

Sales Returns and Allowances   No. 412

Date	Explanation	Ref.	Debit	Credit	Balance

Cost of Goods Sold   No. 505

Date	Explanation	Ref.	Debit	Credit	Balance

(c)

Ben's Discorama Trial Balance April 30, 2012	Debit	Credit
1		
2		
3		
4		
5		
6		
7		
8		
9		
10		

Cortez Department Store
Income Statement (Partial)
For the Year Ended November 30, 2012

(a)

		2009	2010	2011	2012	
1	**Income Statement Data**					1
2	Sales		$ 55000	$	$ 47000	2
3	Cost of goods sold			13800	14300	3
4	Gross profit		38300	35200		4
5	Operating expenses		34900		28600	5
6	Net income		$	$ 2500	$	6
7						7
8	**Balance Sheet Data**					8
9	Merchandise inventory	$ 7200		$ 8100		9
10	Accounts payable	3200	3600	2500		10
11						11
12	**Additional Information**					12
13	Purchases of merchandise					13
14	inventory on account		14200		13200	14
15	Cash payments to suppliers				13600	15
16						16
17						17
18						18
19						19
20						20

(b)

		2008	2009	2010	
1					1
2					2
3					3
4					4
5					5
6					6
7					7
8					8
9		2008	2009	2010	9
10	Gross profit rate				10
11					11
12					12
13	Profit margin ratio				13
14					14
15					15

(a)   General Journal

	Date	Account Titles	Debit	Credit	
1	Apr. 5				1
2					2
3					3
4	7				4
5					5
6					6
7	9				7
8					8
9					9
10	10				10
11					11
12					12
13	12				13
14					14
15					15
16	14				16
17					17
18					18
19					19
20	17				20
21					21
22					22
23	20				23
24					24
25					25
26	21				26
27					27
28					28
29					29
30	27				30
31					31
32					32
33	30				33
34					34
35					35
36					36
37					37
38					38
39					39
40					40

(b)

Cash		Owner's Capital	
4/1 Bal.	3,000		4/1 Bal. 7,000

Sales

Accounts Receivable	

Sales
Returns and Allowances

Inventory	
4/1 Bal.	4,000

Purchases

Accounts Payable

Freight-in

Purchase
Returns and Allowances

Purchase Discounts

(c)

Ilana Pro Shop Trial Balance April 30, 2012	Debit	Credit
1		
2		
3		
4		
5		
6		
7		
8		
9		
10		
11		
12		
13		

(d)

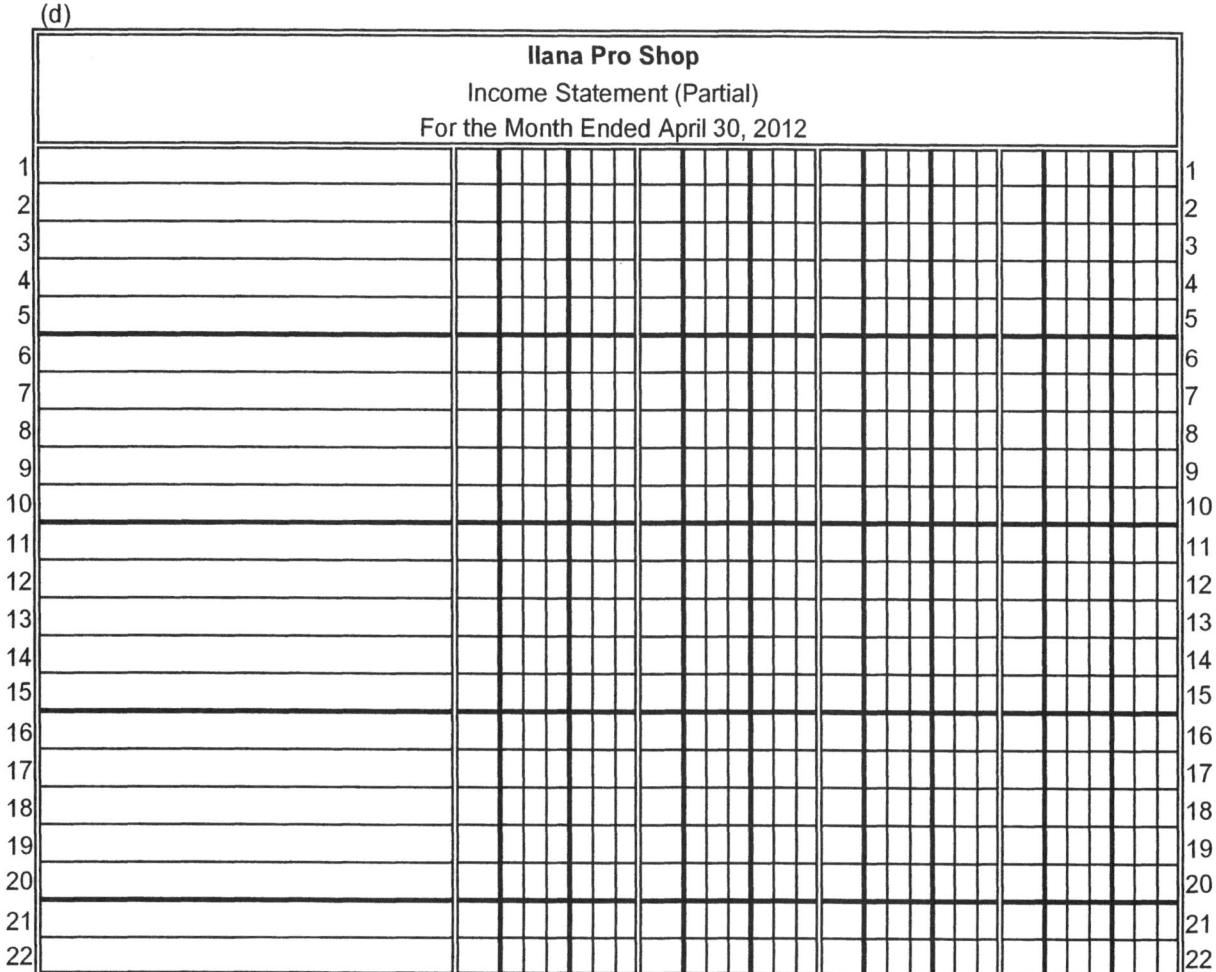

Ilana Pro Shop
Income Statement (Partial)
For the Month Ended April 30, 2012

(a)

General Journal

	Date	Account Titles	Debit	Credit	
1	Dec. 6				1
2					2
3					3
4					4
5	8				5
6					6
7					7
8	10				8
9					9
10					10
11					11
12					12
13					13
14	13				14
15					15
16					16
17	15				17
18					18
19					19
20	18				20
21					21
22					22
23					23
24					24
25					25
26	20				26
27					27
28					28
29	23				29
30					30
31					31
32					32
33	27				33
34					34
35					35
36					36
37					37
38					38
39					39
40					40

(c)   General Journal

	Date	Account Titles	Debit	Credit	
1	Dec 31				1
2					2
3					3
4					4
5					5
6					6
7					7
8					8
9					9
10					10
11					11
12					12
13					13
14					14
15					15
16					16
17					17
18					18
19					19
20					20
21					21
22					22
23					23
24					24
25					25
26					26
27					27
28					28
29					29
30					30
31					31
32					32
33					33
34					34
35					35
36					36
37					37
38					38
39					39
40					40

(b) & (c)

Cash				Accounts Payable	
12/1 Bal	7,200			12/1 Bal	4,500

Accounts Receivable				Salaries and Wages Payable	
12/1 Bal	4,600			12/1 Bal	1,000

Inventory				Owner's Capital	
12/1 Bal	12,000			12/1 Bal	39,300

Supplies				Sales Revenue	
12/1 Bal	1,200				

Sales Discounts

Equipment				Cost of Goods Sold	
12/1 Bal	22,000				

Accumulated Depreciation - Equipment				Depreciation Expense	
		12/1 Bal	2,200		

(b) & (c) (Continued)

Salaries and Wages Expense

Supplies Expense

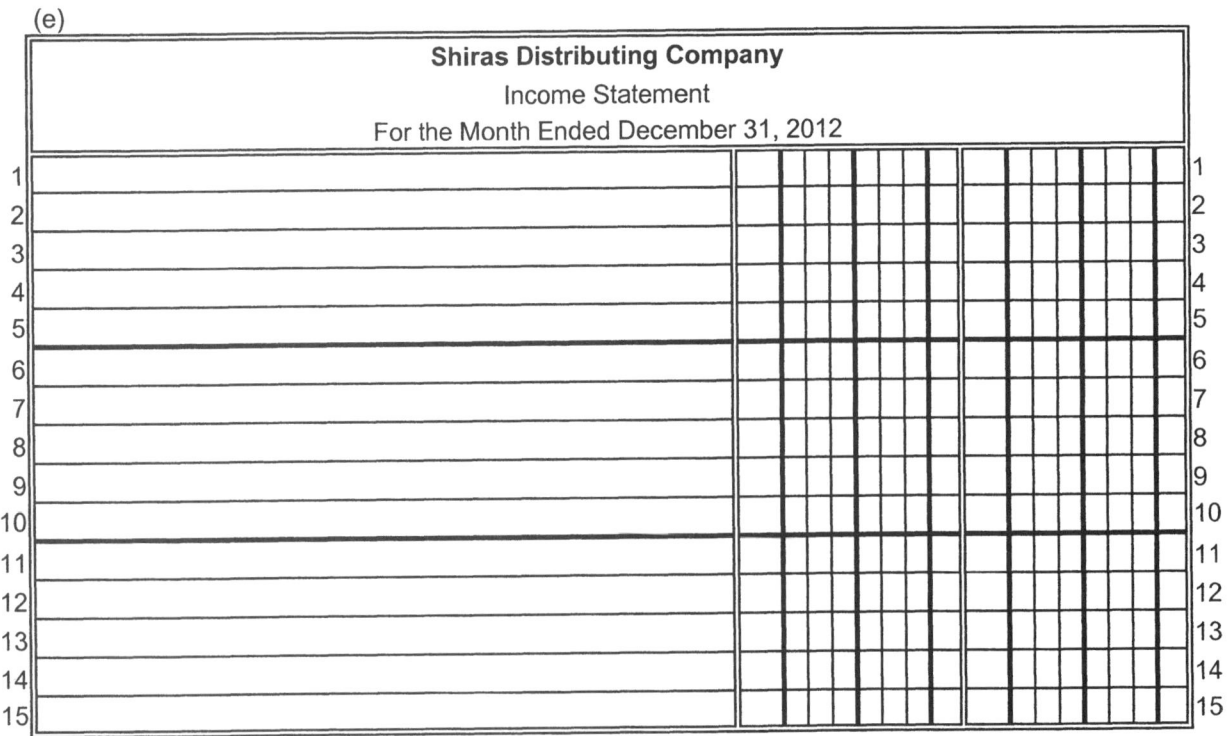

(d)

Shiras Distributing Company

Adjusted Trial Balance

December 31, 2012

	Debit	Credit
1		
2		
3		
4		
5		
6		
7		
8		
9		
10		
11		
12		
13		
14		
15		
16		
17		
18		

(e)

Shiras Distributing Company

Income Statement

For the Month Ended December 31, 2012

1		
2		
3		
4		
5		
6		
7		
8		
9		
10		
11		
12		
13		
14		
15		

(e) (Continued)

Shiras Distributing Company

Owner's Equity Statement

For the Month Ended December 31, 2012

1	1
2	2
3	3
4	4
5	5

Shiras Distributing Company

Balance Sheet

December 31, 2012

Assets	
1	1
2	2
3	3
4	4
5	5
6	6
7	7
8	8
9	9
10	10
11	11
12	12
13	13
Liabilities and Owner's Equity	
15	15
16	16
17	17
18	18
19	19
20	20
21	21
22	22
23	23
24	24
25	25

	2008		2009
1 (a) (1) Percentage change in sales:			
2			
3			
4			
5			
6			
7			
8			
9 (2) Percentage change in net income:			
10			
11			
12			
13			
14			
15			
16			
17			

	2007	2008	2009
18 (b) Gross profit rate:			
19			
20			
21			
22			
23			
24			
25			
26			
27			
28			
29			
30 (c) Percentage of net income to sales:			
31			
32			
33			
34			
35 Comment:			
36			
37			
38			
39			
40			

	PepsiCo		Coca-Cola
(a)			
(1) 2009 Gross profit			
(2) 2009 Gross profit rate			
(3) 2009 Operating Income			
(4) Percentage change in			
operating income, 2008			
to 2009			
(b)			

(a) (1)

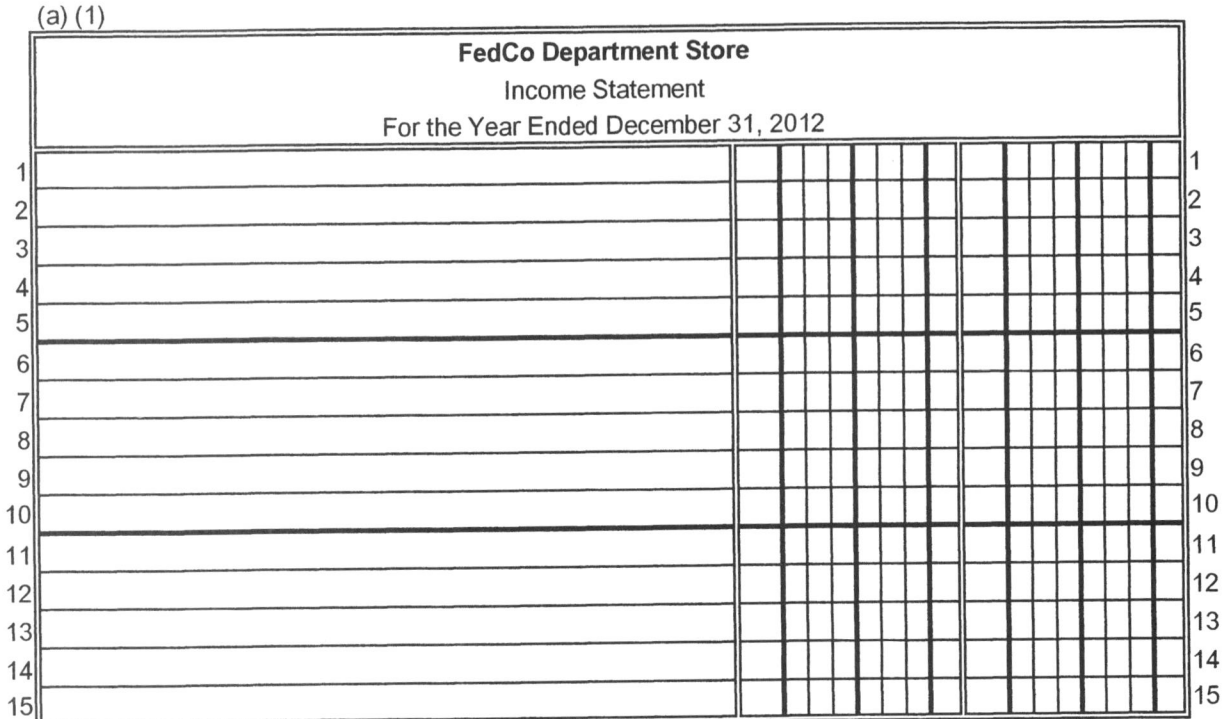

(2)

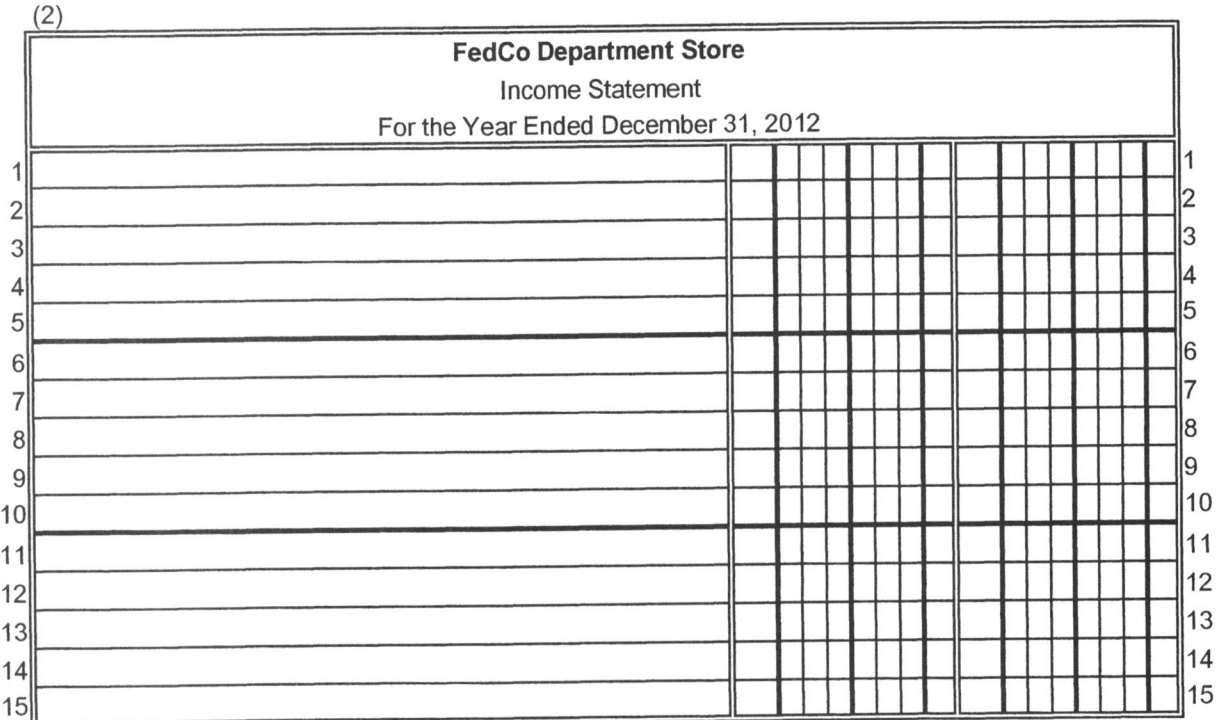

(b)

(c)

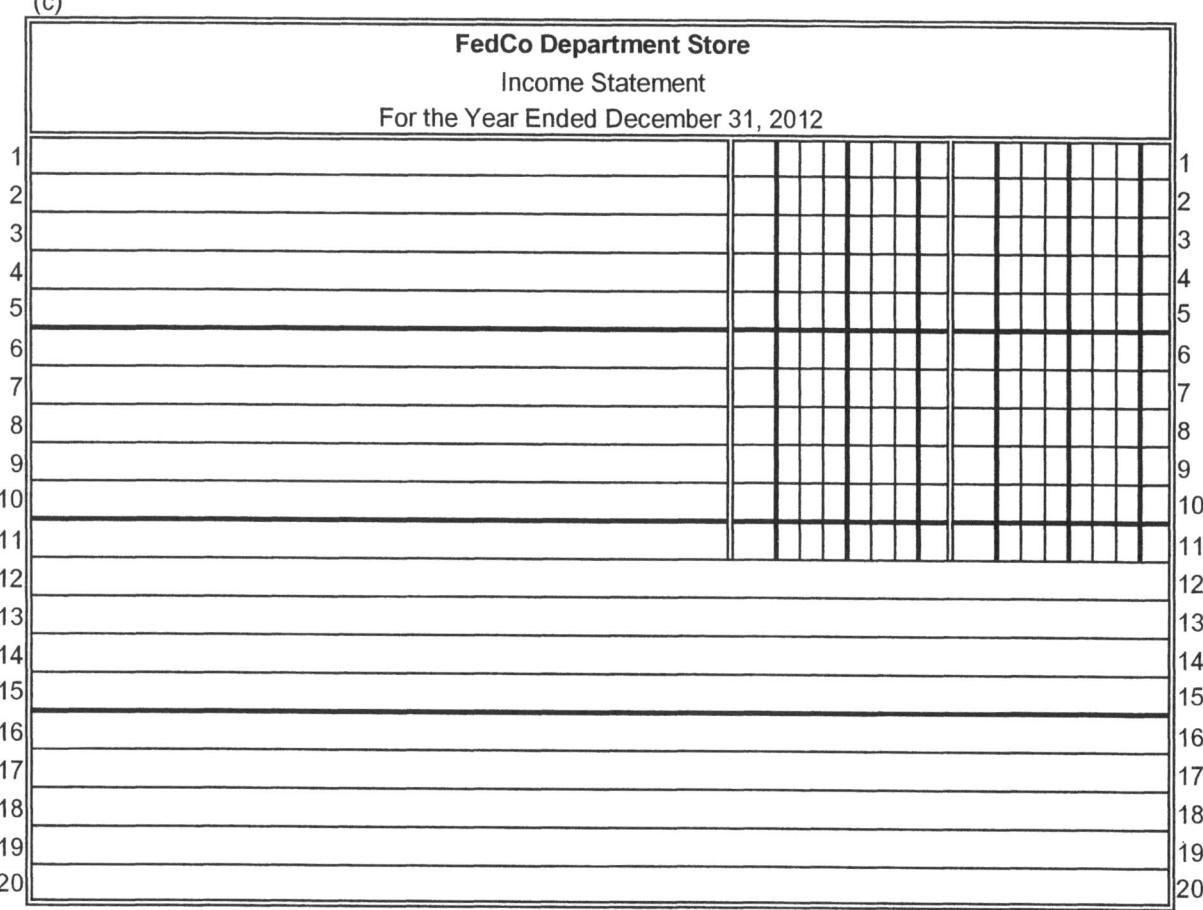

FedCo Department Store

Income Statement

For the Year Ended December 31, 2012

Gribble Company

Comprehensive Income Statement

For the Year Ended 2012

BE6-3

		(a) FIFO			(b) LIFO		
		Units	Unit Cost	Total	Units	Unit Cost	Total
1							
2							
3							
4		Ending inventory			Ending inventory		
5							

BE6-4

					Units	Unit Cost	Total
6							
7							
8							
9							
10							
11							
12		Average cost per unit					
13							
14		Ending inventory					
15							
16							
17							
18							
19							
20							

BE6-6

		LIFO	FIFO	
1	Cost of goods sold under:			1
2	Purchases			2
3				3
4				4
5	Cost of goods available for sale			5
6	Less: Ending inventory			6
7	Cost of goods sold			7
8				8
9				9
10				10
11				11
12				12
13				13
14				14
15				15
16				16

	BE6-7	Cost	Market	LCM	
17					17
18	Inventory categories:				18
19	Cameras				19
20	Camcorders				20
21	DVD players				21
22	Total valuation				22
23					23
24					24
25					25
26					26
27					27
28					28
29					29
30					30
31					31
32					32

*BE6-10

Product E2-D2

(1) FIFO Method

Date	Purchases		Cost of Goods Sold		Balance	
1						
2						
3						
4						
5						
6						
7						
8						
9						

(2) LIFO Method

Date	Purchases		Cost of Goods Sold		Balance	
10						
11						
12						
13						
14						
15						
16						
17						
18						
19						

(3) Average-Cost

Date	Purchases		Cost of Goods Sold		Balance	
20						
21						
22						
23						
24						
25						
26						
27						

*BE6-11

(1)

(2)

	At Cost	At Retail
*BE6-12		

Cost-to-retail ratio:

Estimated cost of ending inventory:

DO IT! 6-1

1	Inventory per physical count	$	3	0	0	0	0	0	1
2									2
3									3
4									4
5									5
6									6
7	**DO IT! 6-2**								7
8	Cost of goods available for sale:								8
9									9
10									10
11									11
12									12
13	Ending inventory (units):								13
14									14
15									15
16									16
17									17
18									18
19	(a) FIFO:								19
20									20
21									21
22									22
23									23
24	(b) LIFO:								24
25									25
26									26
27									27
28									28
29	(c) Average-cost:								29
30									30
31									31
32									32
33									33
34									34
35									35
36									36
37									37
38									38
39									39
40									40

(a) Inventory Item	Cost	Market	Lower of Cost or Market	
1	Small	$ 6 4 0 0 0	$ 7 3 0 0 0	$	1
2	Medium	2 9 0 0 0 0	2 6 0 0 0 0		2
3	Large	1 5 2 0 0 0	1 7 1 0 0 0		3
4					4
5					5
6					6

(b)	2011	2012	
7			7
8	Ending inventory			8
9	Cost of goods sold			9
10	Owner's equity			10

11		11
12		12
13		13
14		14
15		15
16		16
17		17
18		18
19		19
20		20
21		21
22		22
23		23
24		24
25		25
26		26
27		27
28		28
29		29
30		30
31		31
32		32
33		33
34		34
35		35
36		36
37		37
38		38
39		39
40		40

E6-1

		$								
1	Ending Inventory - physical count	$	2	9	7	0	0	0		1
2										2
3										3
4										4
5										5
6										6
7										7
8										8
9										9
10										10
11										11
12										12
13										13

E6-2

14										14
15	Ending inventory - as reported	$	7	4	0	0	0	0		15
16										16
17										17
18										18
19										19
20										20
21										21
22										22
23										23
24										24
25										25
26										26
27										27
28										28
29										29
30										30
31										31
32										32
33										33
34										34
35										35
36										36
37										37
38										38
39										39
40										40

(a)

(b)

(c)

(a)

FIFO			
1			
2			
3			
4			
5			
6			
7			
8			

Proof:

	Date	Units	Unit Cost	Total Cost

LIFO			

Proof:

	Date	Units	Unit Cost	Total Cost

(b)

	FIFO				
1					
2					
3					
4					
5					
6					
7					
8					

Proof:

	Date	Units	Unit Cost	Total Cost

	LIFO		

Proof:

	Date	Units	Unit Cost	Total Cost

(a) (1)	FIFO
(2)	LIFO
(b)	
(c)	

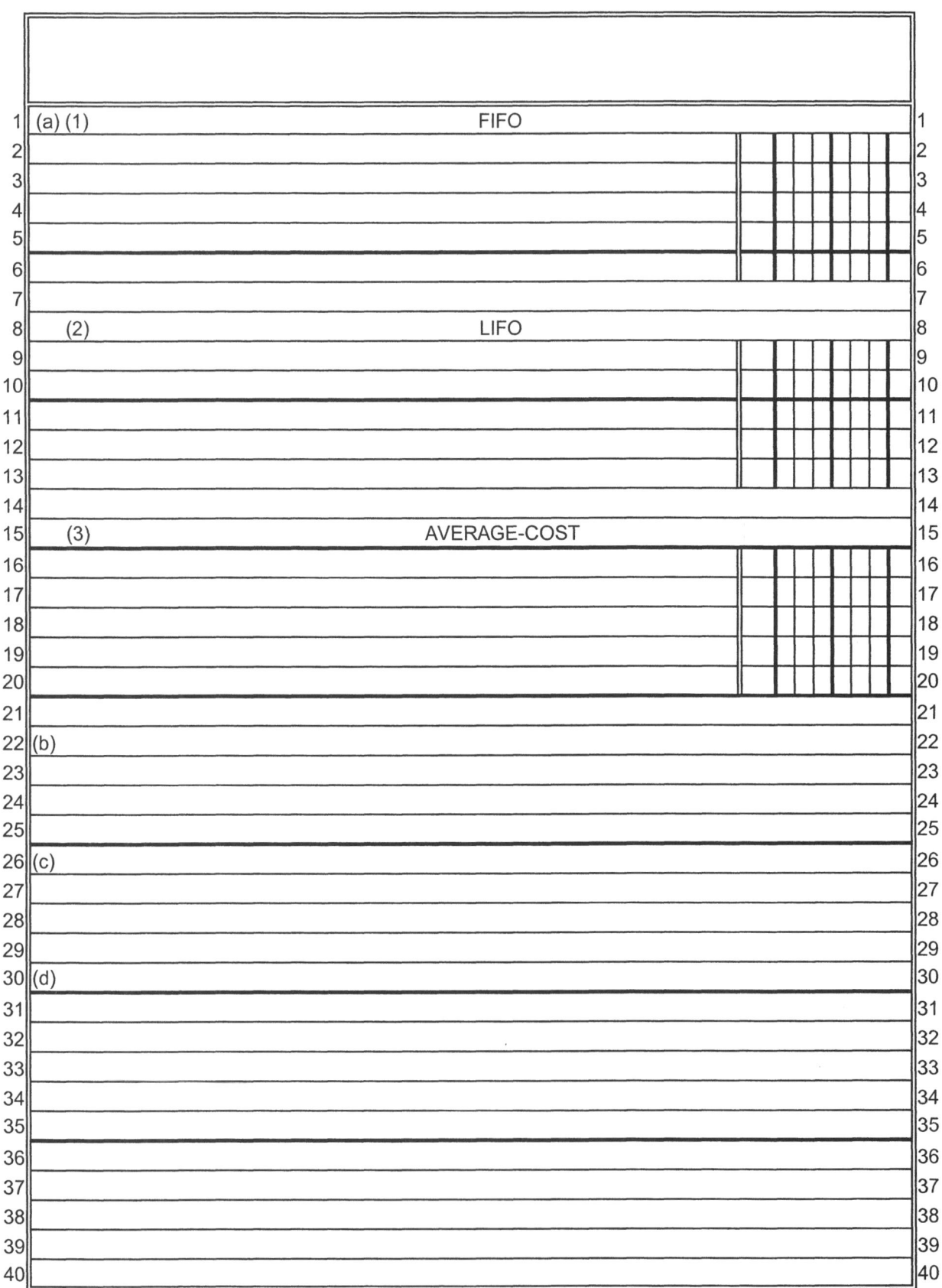

(a) (1)	FIFO	
(2)	LIFO	
(3)	AVERAGE-COST	
(b)		
(c)		
(d)		

E6-8

	Cost of Goods Available for Sale	÷	Total Units Avaialable for Sale	=	Weighted Average Unit Cost	
1	(a)					1
2						2
3	Ending inventory					3
4	Cost of goods sold					4
5						5
6	(b)					6
7						7
8						8
9						9
10	(c)					10
11						11
12						12

E6-9

		Cost	Market	Lower of Cost or Market		
1	Cameras					1
2	Minolta					2
3	Canon					3
4	Total					4
5	Light Meters					5
6	Vivitar					6
7	Kodak					7
8	Total					8
9	Total inventory					9
10						10

E6-10

		Cost	Market	Lower of Cost or Market		
1	Cameras					1
2	DVD players					2
3	Ipods					3
4	Total inventory					4
5						5
6						6
7						7
8						8

	2011	2012	
1 Beginning inventory			
2 Cost of goods purchased			
3 Cost of goods available for sale			
4 Corrected ending inventory			
5 Cost of goods sold			

(a)		2011	2012
1			
2			
3			
4			
5			
6			
7			
8			
9			
10			
11			
12			
(b) 13			
14			
15			
16			
17			
18			
19			
20			
(c) 21			
22			
23			
24			
25			
26			
27			
28			
29			
30			
31			
32			
33			
34			
35			
36			
37			
38			
39			
40			

(1) FIFO

Date	Purchases	Cost of Goods Sold	Balance
Jan. 1			
8			
10			
15			

(2) LIFO

Date	Purchases	Cost of Goods Sold	Balance
Jan. 1			
8			
10			
15			

(3) AVERAGE-COST

Date	Purchases	Cost of Goods Sold	Balance
Jan. 1			
8			
10			
15			

(a)

	Cost of goods available for sale:
1	
2	
3	
4	
5	
6	
7	

FIFO

	Date	Purchases	Cost of goods sold	Balance
8				
9	June 1			
10	12			
11				
12	15			
13				
14				
15	23			
16				
17	27			
18				
19				
20				

	Ending inventory =	Cost of goods sold =
21		
22		

(a) (Continued)

LIFO

Date	Purchases	Cost of goods sold	Balance
June 1			
12			
15			
23			
27			

Ending inventory =

Cost of goods sold =

AVERAGE-COST

Date	Purchases	Cost of goods sold	Balance
June 1			
12			
15			
23			
27			

Ending inventory =

Cost of goods sold =

(b)

(c)

(a)

FIFO

Date	Purchases	Cost of Goods Sold	Balance
9/1			
9/5			
9/12			
9/16			
9/19			
9/26			
9/29			

LIFO

Date	Purchases	Cost of Goods Sold	Balance
9/1			
9/5			
9/12			
9/16			
9/19			
9/26			
9/29			

(a) (Continued)

AVERAGE-COST

	Date	Purchases	Cost of Goods Sold	Balance
1	9/1			
2	9/5			
3	9/12			
4	9/16			
5	9/19			
6	9/26			
7	9/29			
8				
9				
10				
11				
12				
13 (b)			Periodic	Perpetual
14	Ending inventory FIFO			
15				
16	Ending inventory LIFO			
17				
18 (c)				
19				
20				
21				
22				
23				
24				
25				
26				
27				
28				

Name *Exercise 6-18

Section

Date Sanada Company

(a)

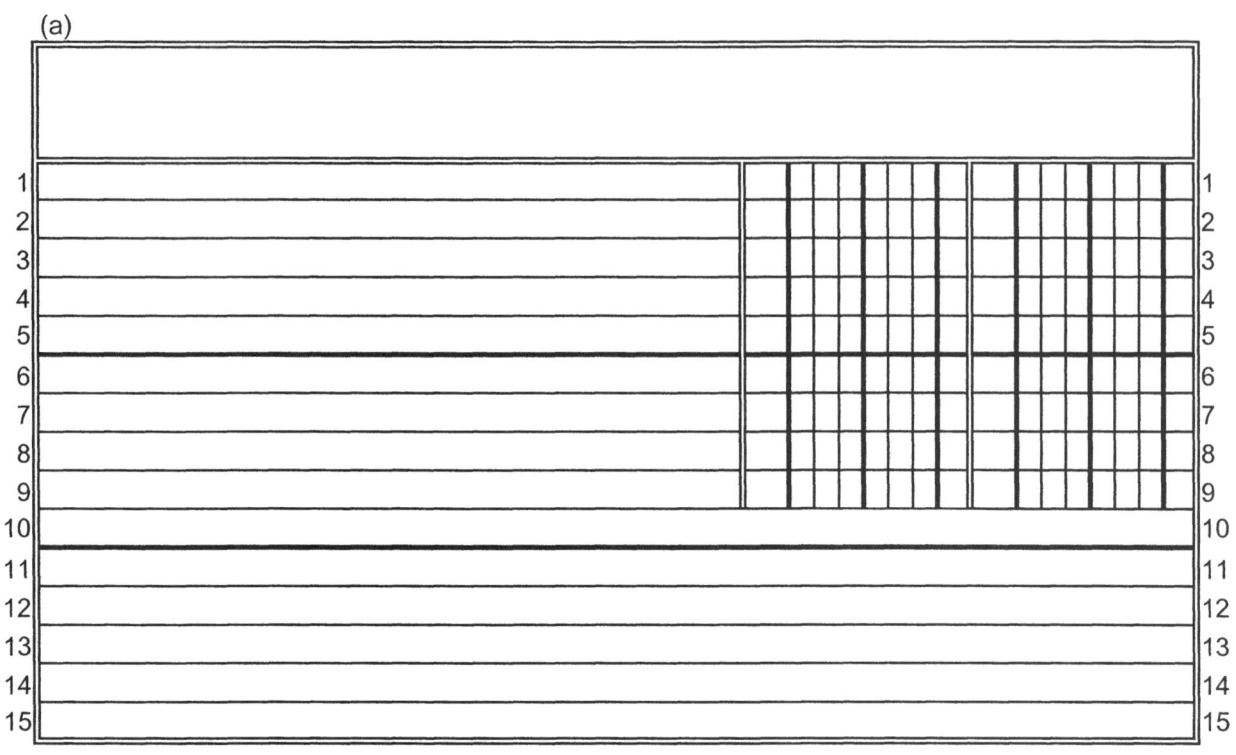

(b)

*E6-19

(a)

(b)

*E6-20

	Women's Department		Men's Department	
	Cost	Retail	Cost	Retail
Beginning inventory				
Goods purchased				
Goods avail. for sale				
Net sales				
Ending inv. at retail				
Cost/retail ratio				
Estimated cost of ending inventory				

(a)

COST OF GOODS AVAILABLE FOR SALE

	Date	Explanation	Units	Unit Cost	Total Cost	
1	March 1					1
2	5					2
3	13					3
4	21					4
5	26					5
6						6
7						7

(b) **FIFO**

(1) Ending Inventory

	Date		Units	Unit Cost	Total Cost	
10	Date		Units	Unit Cost	Total Cost	10
11						11
12						12
13						13
14						14
15						15

(2) Cost of Goods Sold

16	(2) Cost of Goods Sold		16
17			17
18			18
19			19
20			20
21			21

Proof of Cost of Goods Sold

	Date		Units	Unit Cost	Total Cost	
23	Date		Units	Unit Cost	Total Cost	23
24						24
25						25
26						26
27						27
28						28
29						29
30						30
31						31
32						32
33						33
34						34
35						35
36						36
37						37
38						38
39						39
40						40

(b) (Continued)

		LIFO			
(1)		Ending Inventory			
Date		Units	Unit Cost	Total Cost	
1					
2					
3					
4					
5					

	(2)	Cost of Goods Sold		
6				
7				
8				
9				
10				
11				

	Proof of Cost of Goods Sold			
Date		Units	Unit Cost	Total Cost
13				
14				
15				
16				
17				
18				
19				
20				

		Average -Cost			
(1)		Ending Inventory			
Average Cost Per Unit		Units	Unit Cost	Total Cost	
23					
24					
25					

	(2)	Cost of Goods Sold		
26				
27				
28				
29				
30				

(c)

(1)

(2)

(a)

COST OF GOODS AVAILABLE FOR SALE

Date	Explanation	Units	Unit Cost	Total Cost
2/1				
2/20				
5/5				
8/12				
12/8				

(b)   **FIFO**

(1)   Ending Inventory

Date		Units	Unit Cost	Total Cost

(2)   Cost of Goods Sold

Proof of Cost of Goods Sold

Date		Units	Unit Cost	Total Cost

(b) (Continued)

	LIFO			
(1)	Ending Inventory			
Date		Units	Unit Cost	Total Cost

(2)	Cost of Goods Sold	

	Proof of Cost of Goods Sold			
Date		Units	Unit Cost	Total Cost

	Average-Cost			
(1)	Ending Inventory			
Average Cost Per Unit		Units	Unit Cost	Total Cost

(2)	Cost of Goods Sold	

(c)

(1)

(2)

(a)

Reiko Co.

Condensed Income Statements

For the Year Ended December 31, 2012

	FIFO	LIFO

(b)

(a)

Cost of Goods Available For Sale

	Date	Explanation	Units	Unit Cost	Total Cost	
1	Oct. 1					1
2	9					2
3	17					3
4	25					4
5						5

Ending Inventory in Units

6			6
7			7
8			8
9			9
10			10
11			11

Sales Revenue

	Date		Units	Unit Price	Total Sales	
12						12
13	Date		Units	Unit Price	Total Sales	13
14	Oct. 11					14
15	22					15
16	29					16
17						17
18						18

(1)   **LIFO**

(i) Ending Inventory

	Date		Units	Unit Cost	Total Cost	
21	Date		Units	Unit Cost	Total Cost	21
22						22
23						23
24						24
25						25

(ii) Cost of Goods Sold

26		26
27		27
28		28
29		29
30		30
31		31

(iii)   Gross Profit

32		32
33		33
34		34
35		35
36		36

(iv) Gross Profit Rate

37		37
38		38
39		39
40		40

(a) (Continued)

(2) (i)	**FIFO** Ending Inventory				
Date		Units	Unit Cost	Total Cost	1
					2
					3
					4

(ii)	Cost of Goods Sold	

(iii)	Gross Profit	

(iv)	Gross Profit Rate	

(3) **Average-Cost**

Weighted Average Cost Per Unit

(i)	Ending Inventory	

(ii)	Cost of Goods Sold	

(iii)	Gross Profit	

(a) (Continued)

Average-Cost
(iv)   Gross Profit Rate
(b)

(a)

Specific Identification

(1)   To maximize gross profit

Sales Revenue

Date		Units	Unit Price	Sales Revenue
Mar. 5				
25				

Cost of Goods Sold

Date		Units	Unit Cost	Total Cost
Mar. 5				
25				

Sales Revenue

Cost of Goods Sold

Gross profit

(2)   To minimize gross profit

Sales Revenue

Date		Units	Unit Price	Sales Revenue
Mar. 5				
25				

Cost of Goods Sold

Date		Units	Unit Cost	Total Cost
Mar. 5				
25				

Sales Revenue

Cost of Goods Sold

Gross profit

(b)

FIFO

	Cost of Goods Available for Sale			
Date		Units	Unit Cost	Total Cost
Mar. 1				
3				
10				

		Units	Unit Cost	Total Cost
Goods available for sale				
Units sold				
Ending inventory				

Goods available for sale		
Ending inventory		
Cost of goods sold		

Sales revenue		
Cost of goods sold		
Gross profit		

(c)

LIFO

Cost of Goods Available for Sale		
Ending inventory		
Cost of goods sold		

Sales revenue		
Cost of goods sold		
Gross profit		

(d)

(a)

Hillary Inc. Condensed Income Statement For the Year Ended December 31, 2012	FIFO	LIFO
1		
2		
3		
4		
5		
6		
7		
8		
9		
10		
11		
12		
13		
14		

(b)

(a)

1					
2					
3					
4					
5					
6					
7					
8					
9	Sales:				
10					
11	January 6				
12	January 9 return				
13	January 10				
14	January 30				
15					

(a) (Continued)

LIFO

(1) Date	Purchases	Cost of Goods Sold	Balance
Jan. 1			(150 units @ $17) 2550
2			
6			
9			
9			
10			
10			
23			
30			

(i) Cost of goods sold =

(ii) Ending inventory =

(iii) Gross profit =

(a) (Continued)

FIFO

(2) Date	Purchases			Cost of Goods Sold			Balance		
Jan. 1							(150 units @ $17)	2 5 5 0	
2									
6									
9									
9									
10									
10									
23									
30									

(i) Cost of goods sold =

(ii) Ending inventory =

(iii) Gross profit =

(a) (Continued)

Average-Cost

(3) Date	Purchases	Cost of Goods Sold	Balance
Jan. 1			(150 units @ $17) 2 5 5 0
2			
6			
9			
9			
10			
10			
23			
30			

(i) Cost of goods sold =

(ii) Ending inventory =

(iii) Gross profit =

(b)

	LIFO	FIFO	Average-Cost
1			
2			
3			
4			
5			
6			
7			
8			
9			
10			
11			
12			
13			
14			
15			
16			
17			
18			
19			
20			
21			
22			
23			
24			
25			
26			
27			
28			
29			
30			
31			
32			
33			
34			
35			
36			
37			
38			
39			
40			

Farman Appliance Mart

(a)

FIFO

(1)

Date	Purchases	Cost of Goods Sold	Balance
May 1			
4			
8			
12			
15			
20			
25			

Average-Cost

(2)

Date	Purchases	Cost of Goods Sold	Balance
May 1			
4			
8			
12			
15			
20			
25			

(a) (Continued)

LIFO

(3) Date	Purchases	Cost of Goods Sold	Balance
May 1			
4			
8			
12			
15			
20			
25			

(b)

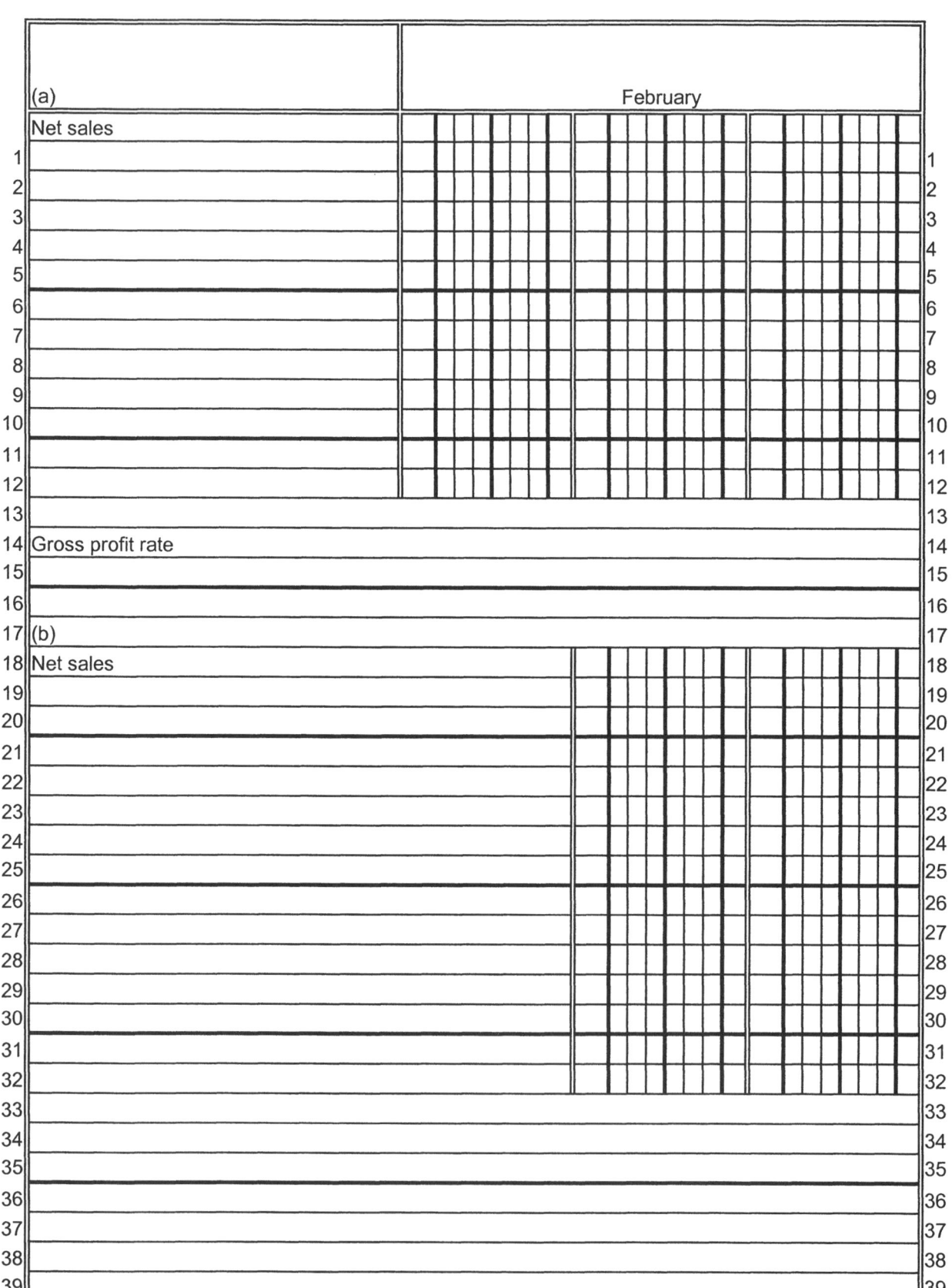

	February
(a)	
Net sales	
Gross profit rate	
(b)	
Net sales	

(a)	Sporting Goods		Jewelry and Cosmetics	
	Cost	Retail	Cost	Retail
Beginning inventory				
Purchases				
Purchase returns				
Purchase discounts				
Freight-in				
Goods available for sale				
Net sales				
Ending inventory at retail				
Cost-to-retail ratio:				
Sporting goods:				
Jewelry and cosmetics:				
Estimated ending inventory at cost:				
Sporting goods:				
Jewelry and cosmetics:				
(b) Sporting goods:				
Jewelry and cosmetics:				

(a)

	COST OF GOODS AVAILABLE FOR SALE			
Date	Explanation	Units	Unit Cost	Total Cost
Oct. 1				
3				
9				
19				
25				

(b)   **FIFO**

(1)   Ending Inventory

Date		Units	Unit Cost	Total Cost

(2)   Cost of Goods Sold

Proof of Cost of Goods Sold

Date		Units	Unit Cost	Total Cost

(b) (Continued)

LIFO

(1)	Ending Inventory			
Date		Units	Unit Cost	Total Cost

(2)	Cost of Goods Sold	

	Proof of Cost of Goods Sold			
Date		Units	Unit Cost	Total Cost

Average-Cost

(1)	Ending Inventory			
Average Cost Per Unit		Units	Unit Cost	Total Cost

(2)	Cost of Goods Sold	

(c)

(1)

(2)

Section

(a)

COST OF GOODS AVAILABLE FOR SALE

	Date	Explanation	Units	Unit Cost	Total Cost	
1	1/1					1
2	3/15					2
3	7/20					3
4	9/4					4
5	12/2					5
6						6
7						7

(b)   **FIFO**

(1)   Ending Inventory

	Date		Units	Unit Cost	Total Cost	
10						10
11						11
12						12
13						13
14						14
15						15

(2)   Cost of Goods Sold

16		16
17		17
18		18
19		19
20		20
21		21

Proof of Cost of Goods Sold

	Date		Units	Unit Cost	Total Cost	
23						23
24						24
25						25
26						26
27						27
28						28
29						29
30						30
31						31
32						32
33						33
34						34
35						35
36						36
37						37
38						38
39						39
40						40

(b) (Continued)

LIFO

(1) Ending Inventory

Date		Units	Unit Cost	Total Cost

(2) Cost of Goods Sold

	Total Cost

Proof of Cost of Goods Sold

Date		Units	Unit Cost	Total Cost

Average-Cost

(1) Ending Inventory

Average Cost Per Unit	Units	Unit Cost	Total Cost

(2) Cost of Goods Sold

	Total Cost

(c)

(1)

(2)

(a)

Perrineau Inc.

Condensed Income Statements

For the Year Ended December 31, 2012

	FIFO	LIFO

(b)

(a)

Cost of Goods Available For Sale

Date	Explanation	Units	Unit Cost	Total Cost
June 1				
4				
18				
18				
28				

Ending Inventory in Units

Sales Revenue

Date		Units	Unit Price	Total Sales
June 10				
11				
25				

(1) **LIFO**

(i) Ending Inventory

Date		Units	Unit Cost	Total Cost

(ii) Cost of Goods Sold

(iii) Gross Profit

(iv) Gross Profit Rate

(a) (Continued)

(2)   **FIFO**

(i)   Ending Inventory

Date		Units	Unit Cost	Total Cost

(ii)   Cost of Goods Sold

(iii)   Gross Profit

(iv)   Gross Profit Rate

(3)   **Moving-Average**

Weighted Average Cost Per Unit

(i)   Ending Inventory

(ii)   Cost of Goods Sold

(iii)   Gross Profit

(a) (Continued)

Average-Cost

(iv)   Gross Profit Rate

(b)

(a)

Dabinpons Inc. Income Statement (Partial) For the Year Ended December, 31, 2012			
	Specific Identification	FIFO	LIFO

Specific identification ending inventory consists of:

	Units	Unit Cost	Total Cost

FIFO ending inventory consists of:

LIFO ending inventory consists of:

(b)

(a)

		Tamara Co.				
		Condensed Income Statement				
		For the Year Ended December 31, 2012				
		FIFO		LIFO		
1						1
2						2
3						3
4						4
5						5
6						6
7						7
8						8
9						9
10						10
11						11
12						12
13						13
14						14
15	(b) (1)					15
16						16
17						17
18						18
19	(2)					19
20						20
21						21
22						22
23	(3)					23
24						24
25						25
26						26
27	(4)					27
28						28
29						29
30	(5)					30
31						31
32						32
33						33
34						34
35						35
36						36
37						37
38						38
39						39

(a)

1					1
2					2
3					3
4					4
5					5
6					6
7					7
8					8
9	Sales:				9
10	January 8				10
11	January 10 return				11
12	January 20				12
13					13
14					14
15					15
16					16
17					17
18					18
19					19
20					20
21					21
22					22
23					23
24					24
25					25
26					26
27					27
28					28
29					29
30					30
31					31
32					32
33					33
34					34
35					35
36					36
37					37
38					38
39					39
40					40

(a) (Continued)

LIFO

(1) Date	Purchases	Cost of Goods Sold	Balance
Jan. 1			(100 units @ $15) 1 5 0 0
5			
8			
10			
15			
16			
20			
25			

(i) Cost of goods sold =

(ii) Ending inventory =

(iii) Gross profit =

(a) (Continued)

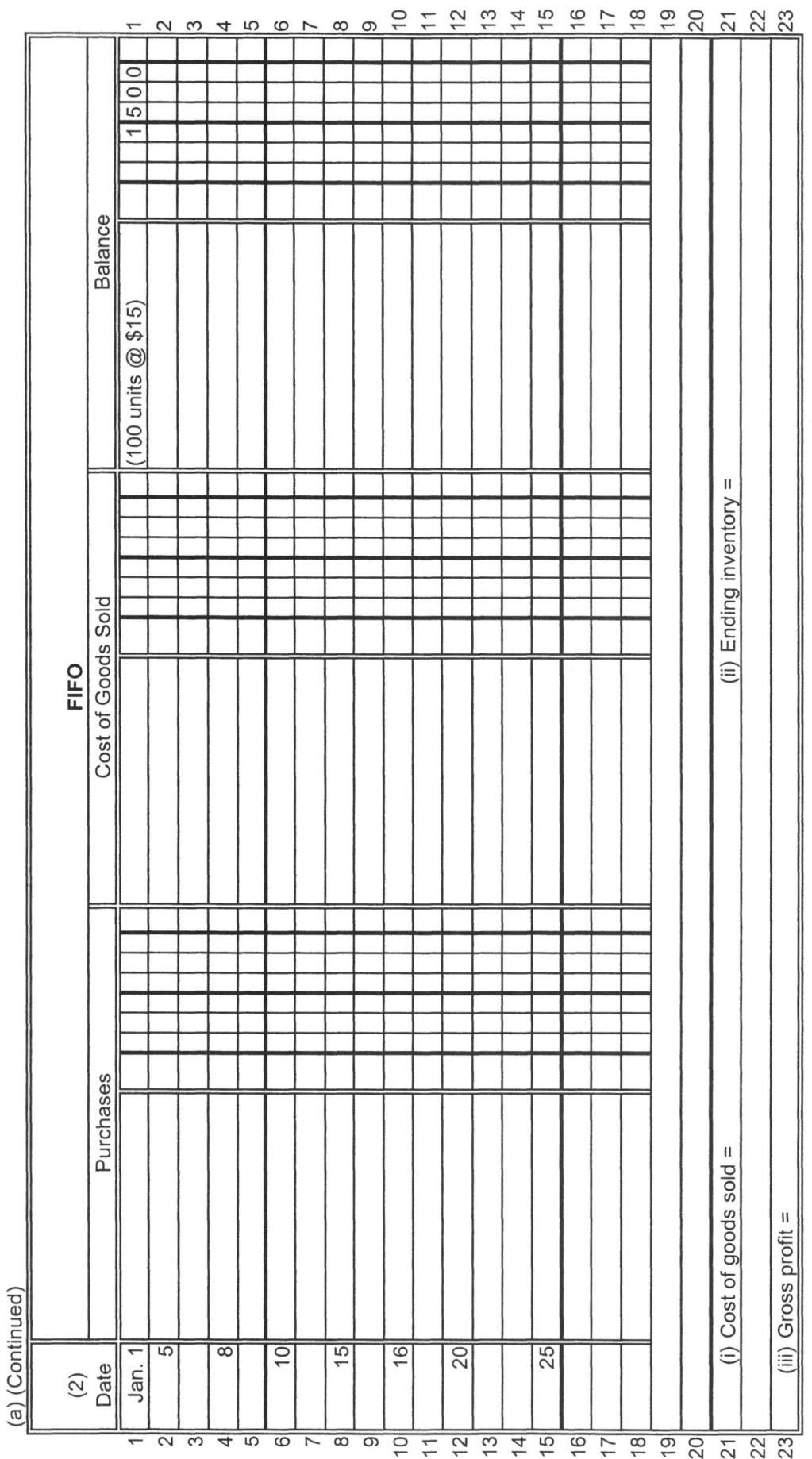

FIFO

(2) Date	Purchases	Cost of Goods Sold	Balance
Jan. 1			(100 units @ $15) 1 5 0 0
5			
8			
10			
15			
16			
20			
25			

(i) Cost of goods sold =

(ii) Ending inventory =

(iii) Gross profit =

(a) (Continued)

(3)

Average-Cost

Date	Purchases	Cost of Goods Sold	Balance
Jan. 1			(100 units @ $15) 1500
5			
8			
10			
15			
16			
20			
25			

(i) Cost of goods sold =

(ii) Ending inventory =

(iii) Gross profit =

(b)

	LIFO	FIFO	Average-Cost
1			
2			
3			
4			
5			
6			
7			
8			
9			
10			
11			
12			
13			
14			
15			
16			
17			
18			
19			
20			
21			
22			
23			
24			
25			
26			
27			
28			
29			
30			
31			
32			
33			
34			
35			
36			
37			
38			
39			
40			

(a)

FIFO

(1) Date	Purchases	Cost of Goods Sold	Balance
July 1			
6			
11			
14			
21			
27			

AVERAGE-COST

(2) Date	Purchases	Cost of Goods Sold	Balance
July 1			
6			
11			
14			
21			
27			

(a) (Continued)

LIFO

(3) Date	Purchases	Cost of Goods Sold	Balance
July 1			
6			
11			
14			
21			
27			

(b)

(a)	November
Net sales	
1	
2	
3	
4	
5	
6	
7	
8	
9	
10	
11	
12	
13	
14 Gross profit rate	
15	
16	
17 (b)	
18 Net sales	
19	
20	
21	
22	
23	
24	
25	
26	
27	
28	
29	
30	
31	
32	
33	
34	
35	
36	
37	
38	
39	

	Hardcovers		Paperbacks	
(a)	Cost	Retail	Cost	Retail
Beginning inventory				
Purchases				
Purchase returns				
Purchase discounts				
Freight-in				
Goods available for sale				
Net sales				
Ending inventory at retail				
Cost-to-retail ratio:				
Hardcovers:				
Paperbacks:				
Estimated ending inventory at cost:				
Hardcovers:				
Paperbacks:				
(b) Hardcovers:				
Paperbacks:				

(a)

	Date	Account Titles	Debit	Credit	
1	Dec. 3				1
2					2
3					3
4	5				4
5					5
6					6
7					7
8					8
9					9
10	7				10
11					11
12					12
13					13
14					14
15					15
16	17				16
17					17
18					18
19	22				19
20					20
21					21
22					22
23					23
24					24
25	31				25
26					26
27					27
28					28
29					29
30					30
31					31
32					32
33					33
34					34
35					35
36					36
37					37
38					38
39					39
40					40

(b)   General Ledger

Cash		Owner's Capital	
Bal. 4,800			Bal. 27,000

Accounts Receivable		Sales Revenue	
Bal. 3,900			

Inventory		Sales Returns & Allowances	
Bal. 1,800			

		Cost of Goods Sold	

Equipment		Depreciation Expense	
Bal. 21,000			

Accumulated Depreciation - Equipment		Salaries and Wages Expense	
	Bal. 1,500		

Accounts Payable	
	Bal. 3,000

Salaries and Wages Payable	

(c)

Ruggiero Company

Adjusted Trial Balance

For the Year Ended December 31, 2012

	Debit	Credit
1		
2		
3		
4		
5		
6		
7		
8		
9		
10		
11		
12		
13		
14		
15		

(d)

Ruggiero Company

Income Statement

For the Month Ending December 31, 2012

1		
2		
3		
4		
5		
6		
7		
8		
9		
10		
11		
12		
13		
14		
15		
16		
17		
18		
19		

(d)   (Continued)

Ruggiero Company
Balance Sheet
December 31, 2012

Assets

Liabilities and Owner's Equity

(e)

FIFO Method	Units	Unit Cost	Cost of Goods Available for Sale
1			
2			
3			
4			
5			

	Date	Units	Unit Cost	Total Cost
Ending Inventory				

Cost of Goods Sold

(f) LIFO Method

	Date	Units	Unit Cost	Total Cost
Ending Inventory				

Cost of Goods Sold

		December 26, 2009	December 27, 2008
1	(a)　Inventory (in millions)		
2			
3			
4			
5			
6	(b)　Dollar change in inventories between 2008 and 2009:		
7			
8			
9	Percent change in inventories between 2008 and 2009:		
10			
11			
12	2009 inventory as a percent of current assets:		
13			
14			
15			
16	(c)		
17			
18			
19			
20			
21			

	(d)　PepsiCo (in millions)	2009	2008	2007
22				
23				
24	Cost of goods sold			
25				
26				
27	2009 cost of goods sold as a percent of sales:			
28				
29				
30				
31				
32				
33				
34				
35				

			2011	2010	
1	(a) (1) Sales January 1 - March 31, 2012:		$ 1 8 0 0 0 0		1
2					2
3					3
4					4
5					5
6					6
7	(2) Purchases January 1 - March 31, 2012:		$ 9 4 0 0 0		7
8					8
9					9
10					10
11					11
12					12
13	*(b)		2011	2010	13
14	Net sales				14
15					15
16					16
17					17
18					18
19					19
20					20
21					21
22					22
23	Gross profit rate				23
24	Average gross profit rate				24
25					25
26	*(c) Sales				26
27					27
28					28
29					29
30					30
31					31
32					32
33					33
34					34
35					35
36					36
37					37
38					38
39					39
40					40

	Item No.	Cost	Net Realizable Value	LCNRV
1				
2				
3				
4				
5				
6				
7				
8				
9				
10				
11				
12				
13				
14				
15				
16				
17				
18				
19				
20				
21				
22				
23				
24				
25				
26				
27				
28				
29				
30				
31				
32				
33				
34				
35				
36				
37				
38				
39				
40				

BE7-4

Accounts Receivable Subsidiary Ledger

Ahuna Co.

Date	Explanation	Ref.	Debit	Credit	Balance

Aldo Co.

Date	Explanation	Ref.	Debit	Credit	Balance

Tito Co.

Date	Explanation	Ref.	Debit	Credit	Balance

General Ledger

Accounts Receivable

Date	Explanation	Ref.	Debit	Credit	Balance

1	Subsidiary balances:								1
2	Shada Company								2
3									3
4									4
5									5
6	Liam Company								6
7									7
8									8
9									9
10	Esmond Company								10
11									11
12									12
13									13
14	General ledger:								14
15	Accounts Payable								15
16									16
17									17
18									18
19									19
20									20
21									21
22									22
23									23
24									24
25									25

(a) & (b)   *General Ledger*

Accounts Receivable

Date	Explanation	Ref.	Debit	Credit	Balance
9/1	Balance	√			$ 1 0 9 6 0

Accounts Receivable Subsidiary Ledger

Minear

Date	Explanation	Ref.	Debit	Credit	Balance
9/1	Balance	√			2 0 6 0

Edlund

Date	Explanation	Ref.	Debit	Credit	Balance
9/1	Balance	√			4 8 2 0

Molina

Date	Explanation	Ref.	Debit	Credit	Balance

Gillum

Date	Explanation	Ref.	Debit	Credit	Balance
9/1	Balance	√			2 6 4 0

Gareth

Date	Explanation	Ref.	Debit	Credit	Balance
9/1	Balance	√			1 4 4 0

E7-3 (c)

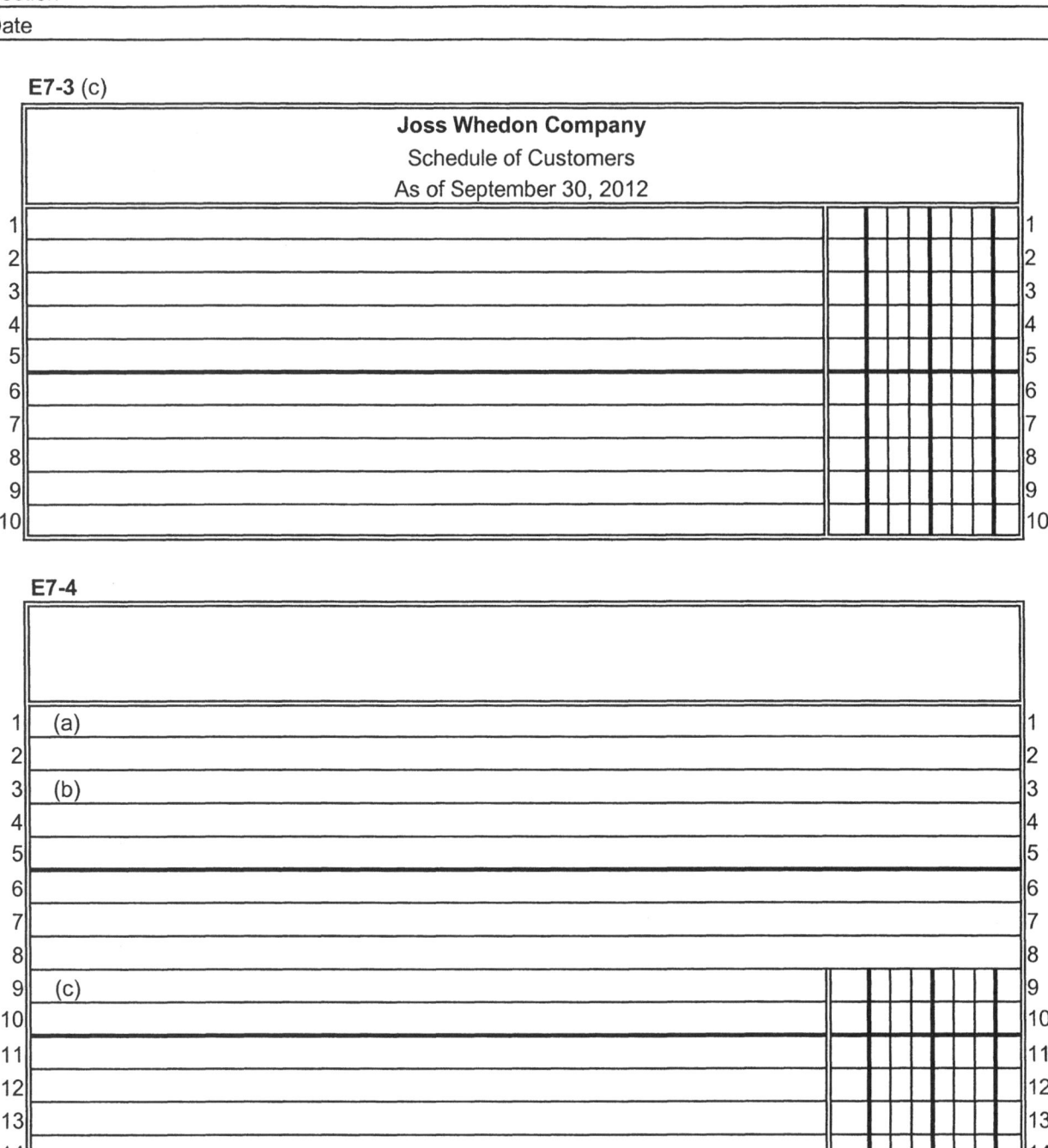

Joss Whedon Company

Schedule of Customers

As of September 30, 2012

E7-4

(a)

(b)

(c)

(d)

1	(a)
2	
3	(b)
4	
5	
6	
7	(c)
8	
9	
10	
11	
12	
13	
14	(d)
15	
16	
17	
18	
19	
20	
21	
22	
23	
24	
25	

(a) & (b)

Hoban Company

Sales Journal

S1

	Date	Account Debited	Invoice No.	Ref.	Accounts Receivable Dr. Sales Rev. Cr.	COGS Dr. Inventory Cr.	
1							1
2							2
3							3
4							4
5							5

Hoban Company

Purchases Journal

P1

	Date	Account Credited	Terms	Ref	Inventory (Dr.) Acc. Pay (Cr.)	
1						1
2						2
3						3
4						4
5						5

(a) & (b)

Inara Serra Co.

Cash Receipts Journal

CR1

Date	Account Credited	Ref.	Cash Dr.	Sales Discounts Dr.	Accounts Receivable Cr.	Sales Revenue Cr.	Other Accounts Cr.	COGS Dr. Inventory Cr.	
									1
									2
									3
									4
									5

Inara Serra Co.

Cash Payments Journal

CP1

Date	Check Number	Account Debited	Ref	Other Accounts Dr.	Accounts Payable Dr.	Cash Cr.	
							1
							2
							3
							4

(a)

	Date	Account Titles	Debit	Credit	
1	Mar 2				1
2					2
3					3
4	5				4
5					5
6					6
7	7				7
8					8
9					9
10					10
11					11
12					12

(b)

1		1
2		2
3		3
4		4
5		5
6		6
7		7
8		8
9		9
10		10
11		11
12		12
13		13
14		14
15		15
16		16
17		17
18		18
19		19
20		20
21		21
22		22
23		23

E7-12 (a)

	Date	Account Credited	Ref.	Inventory (Dr.) Acc. Pay. (Cr.)	
		Purchases Journal		P1	
1	July 3				1
2	12				2
3	14				3
4	17				4
5	20				5
6	21				6
7	29				7
8					8
9					9

(b) General Journal

	Date	Account Titles	Ref	Debit	Credit	
1	July 1					1
2						2
3						3
4						4
5	15					5
6						6
7						7
8						8
9	18					9
10						10
11						11
12	25					12
13						13

E7-13

1			1
2			2
3			3
4			4
5			5
6			6

1	(a) Accounts Payable		1
2			2
3			3
4			4
5			5
6			6
7	(b) Accounts Receivable		7
8			8
9			9
10			10
11			11
12			12
13	(c) Cash		13
14			14
15			15
16			16
17			17
18			18
19	(d) Inventory		19
20			20
21			21
22			22
23			23
24			24
25			25
26	(e) Sales Revenue		26
27			27
28			28
29			29
30			30

(a)

Cash Receipts Journal

CR1

Date	Account Credited	Ref.	Cash Dr.	Sales Discounts Dr.	Accounts Receivable Cr.	Sales Revenue Cr.	Other Accounts Cr.	COGS Dr. Inventory Cr.	
									1
									2
									3
									4
									5
									6
									7
									8
									9
									10
									11
									12
									13
									14
									15
									16
									17

(b)

General Ledger

Accounts Receivable   No. 112

Date	Explanation	Ref	Debit	Credit	Balance
Apr. 1	Balance	√			7 4 5 0

Accounts Receivable Subsidiary Ledger

Summer

Date	Explanation	Ref	Debit	Credit	Balance
Apr.1	Balance	√			1 5 5 0

Glav

Date	Explanation	Ref	Debit	Credit	Balance
Apr. 1	Balance	√			1 2 0 0

Sheppard Co.

Date	Explanation	Ref	Debit	Credit	Balance
Apr. 1	Balance	√			2 9 0 0

Book

Date	Explanation	Ref	Debit	Credit	Balance
Apr. 1	Balance	√			1 8 0 0

(c)

1		1
2		2
3		3
4		4
5		5
6		6

(a)

Cash Payments Journal

CP1

	Date	Ck. No.	Account Debited	Ref.	Other Accounts Dr.	Accounts Payable Dr.	Inventory Cr.	Cash Cr.	
1									1
2									2
3									3
4									4
5									5
6									6
7									7
8									8
9									9
10									10
11									11
12									12
13									13
14									14
15									15
16									16
17									17
18									18
19									19
20									20

(b)

General Ledger

Accounts Payable   No. 201

Date	Explanation	Ref	Debit	Credit	Balance
Oct. 1	Balance	√			1 0 7 0 0

Accounts Payable Subsidiary Ledger

Glass Company

Date	Explanation	Ref	Debit	Credit	Balance
Oct. 1	Balance	√			2 7 0 0

Ron Co.

Date	Explanation	Ref	Debit	Credit	Balance
Oct. 1	Balance	√			2 5 0 0

Hendricks Co.

Date	Explanation	Ref	Debit	Credit	Balance
Oct. 1	Balance	√			1 8 0 0

Christina Company

Date	Explanation	Ref	Debit	Credit	Balance
Oct. 1	Balance	√			3 7 0 0

(c)

1		1
2		2
3		3
4		4
5		5
6		6

(a)

					Purchases Journal			
								P1
	Date	Account Credited (Debited)	Ref.	Other Accounts Cr.		Inventory Dr.		Accounts Payable Dr.
1								
2								
3								
4								
5								
6								
7								
8								
9								
10								
11								
12								
13								
14								
15								
16								
17								
18								

				Sales Journal		
						S1
	Date	Account Debited	Ref.	Accounts Receivable Dr. Sales Rev. Cr.	COGS Dr. Inventory Cr.	
1						
2						
3						
4						
5						
6						
7						
8						
9						
10						

(a) (Continued)

General Journal   G1

	Date	Account Titles	Ref.	Debit	Credit	
1	July 8					1
2						2
3						3
4						4
5						5
6	22					6
7						7
8						8
9						9
10						10
11						11
12						12

(b)

General Ledger

Accounts Receivable   No. 112

Date	Explanation	Ref.	Debit	Credit	Balance

Inventory   No. 120

Date	Explanation	Ref.	Debit	Credit	Balance

Supplies   No. 126

Date	Explanation	Ref.	Debit	Credit	Balance

Equipment   No. 157

Date	Explanation	Ref.	Debit	Credit	Balance

(b)(Continued)

Accounts Payable   No. 201

Date	Explanation	Ref.	Debit	Credit	Balance

Sales Revenue   No. 401

Date	Explanation	Ref.	Debit	Credit	Balance

Sales Returns and Allowances   No. 412

Date	Explanation	Ref.	Debit	Credit	Balance

Cost of Goods Sold   No. 505

Date	Explanation	Ref.	Debit	Credit	Balance

Advertising Expense   No. 610

Date	Explanation	Ref.	Debit	Credit	Balance

(b)(Continued)

Accounts Receivable Subsidiary Ledger

O'Dowd Bros.

Date	Explanation	Ref.	Debit	Credit	Balance

Jen Company

Date	Explanation	Ref.	Debit	Credit	Balance

Sager Company

Date	Explanation	Ref.	Debit	Credit	Balance

Haddad Company

Date	Explanation	Ref.	Debit	Credit	Balance

(b)(Continued)   *Accounts Payable Subsidiary Ledger*

Cress Supply

Date	Explanation	Ref.	Debit	Credit	Balance

Moss Shipping

Date	Explanation	Ref.	Debit	Credit	Balance

Roy Company

Date	Explanation	Ref.	Debit	Credit	Balance

Moon Company

Date	Explanation	Ref.	Debit	Credit	Balance

Lynda Advertisements

Date	Explanation	Ref.	Debit	Credit	Balance

Anton Company

Date	Explanation	Ref.	Debit	Credit	Balance

(c)

1	Accounts receivable balance:	1
2		2
3		3
4		4
5		5
6	Subsidiary account balances:	6
7		7
8		8
9		9
10		10
11		11
12		12
13		13
14		14
15		15
16		16
17	Accounts payable balance:	17
18		18
19		19
20		20
21	Subsidiary account balances:	21
22		22
23		23
24		24
25		25
26		26
27		27
28		28
29		29
30		30
31		31
32		32
33		33
34		34
35		35
36		36
37		37
38		38
39		39
40		40

(a), (b), & (c)

Sales Journal

S1

				Accounts Receivable Dr. Sales Rev. Cr.	COGS Dr. Inventory Cr.	
	Date	Account Debited	Invoice No.	Ref.		
1							1
2							2
3							3
4							4
5							5
6							6
7							7

Purchases Journal

P1

	Date	Account Credited	Ref.	Inventory (Dr.) Acc. Pay (Cr.)	
1					1
2					2
3					3
4					4
5					5
6					6
7					7
8					8

General Journal

G1

	Date	Account Titles	Ref.	Debit	Credit	
1	Jan. 5					1
2						2
3						3
4	19					4
5						5
6						6

(a), (b), (c) (Continued)

Cash Receipts Journal

CR1

Date	Account Credited	Ref.	Cash Dr.	Sales Discounts Dr.	Accounts Receivable Cr.	Sales Revenue Cr.	Other Accounts Cr.	COGS Dr. Inventory Cr.
1								
2								
3								
4								
5								
6								
7								
8								
9								
10								
11								
12								
13								
14								
15								

(a), (b), (c) (Continued)

Cash Payments Journal

CP1

Date	Account Debited	Ref.	Other Accounts Dr.	Accounts Payable Dr.	Inventory Cr.	Cash Cr.
1						
2						
3						
4						
5						
6						
7						
8						
9						
10						
11						
12						
13						
14						
15						

(a), (d) & (g)

Cash   No. 101

Date	Explanation	Ref.	Debit	Credit	Balance

Accounts Receivable   No. 112

Date	Explanation	Ref.	Debit	Credit	Balance

Inventory   No. 120

Date	Explanation	Ref.	Debit	Credit	Balance

Supplies   No. 127

Date	Explanation	Ref.	Debit	Credit	Balance

Prepaid Rent   No. 131

Date	Explanation	Ref.	Debit	Credit	Balance

Accounts Payable   No. 201

Date	Explanation	Ref.	Debit	Credit	Balance

Owner's Capital   No. 301

Date	Explanation	Ref.	Debit	Credit	Balance

(a), (d) & (g) (Continued)

Owner's Drawings   No. 306

Date	Explanation	Ref.	Debit	Credit	Balance

Sales Revenue   No. 401

Date	Explanation	Ref.	Debit	Credit	Balance

Sales Discounts   No. 414

Date	Explanation	Ref.	Debit	Credit	Balance

Cost of Goods Sold   No. 505

Date	Explanation	Ref.	Debit	Credit	Balance

Supplies Expense   No. 631

Date	Explanation	Ref.	Debit	Credit	Balance

Rent Expense   No. 729

Date	Explanation	Ref.	Debit	Credit	Balance

(b), (c) & (d)

	Sales Journal			S1
Date	Account Debited	Ref.	Accounts Receivable Dr. Sales Rev. Cr.	COGS Dr. Inventory Cr.
1				
2				
3				
4				
5				
6				

Name

Section

Date

Richmond Co.

(b), (c) & (d) (Continued)

Cash Receipts Journal

CR1

Date	Account Credited	Ref.	Cash Dr.	Sales Discounts Dr.	Accounts Receivable Cr.	Sales Revenue Cr.	Other Accounts Cr.	COGS Dr. Inventory Cr.
1								
2								
3								
4								
5								
6								
7								
8								
9								
10								
11								
12								
13								
14								
15								

(c)

Accounts Receivable Subsidiary Ledger

Abi Co.

Date	Explanation	Ref.	Debit	Credit	Balance

H. Prince

Date	Explanation	Ref.	Debit	Credit	Balance

W. Pitts

Date	Explanation	Ref.	Debit	Credit	Balance

S. Beauty

Date	Explanation	Ref.	Debit	Credit	Balance

Accounts Payable Subsidiary Ledger

C. Tabor

Date	Explanation	Ref.	Debit	Credit	Balance

F. Noel

Date	Explanation	Ref.	Debit	Credit	Balance

M. Sneezy

Date	Explanation	Ref.	Debit	Credit	Balance

N. Fielding

Date	Explanation	Ref.	Debit	Credit	Balance

(c) (Continued)

J. Shaggy

Date	Explanation	Ref.	Debit	Credit	Balance

(e)

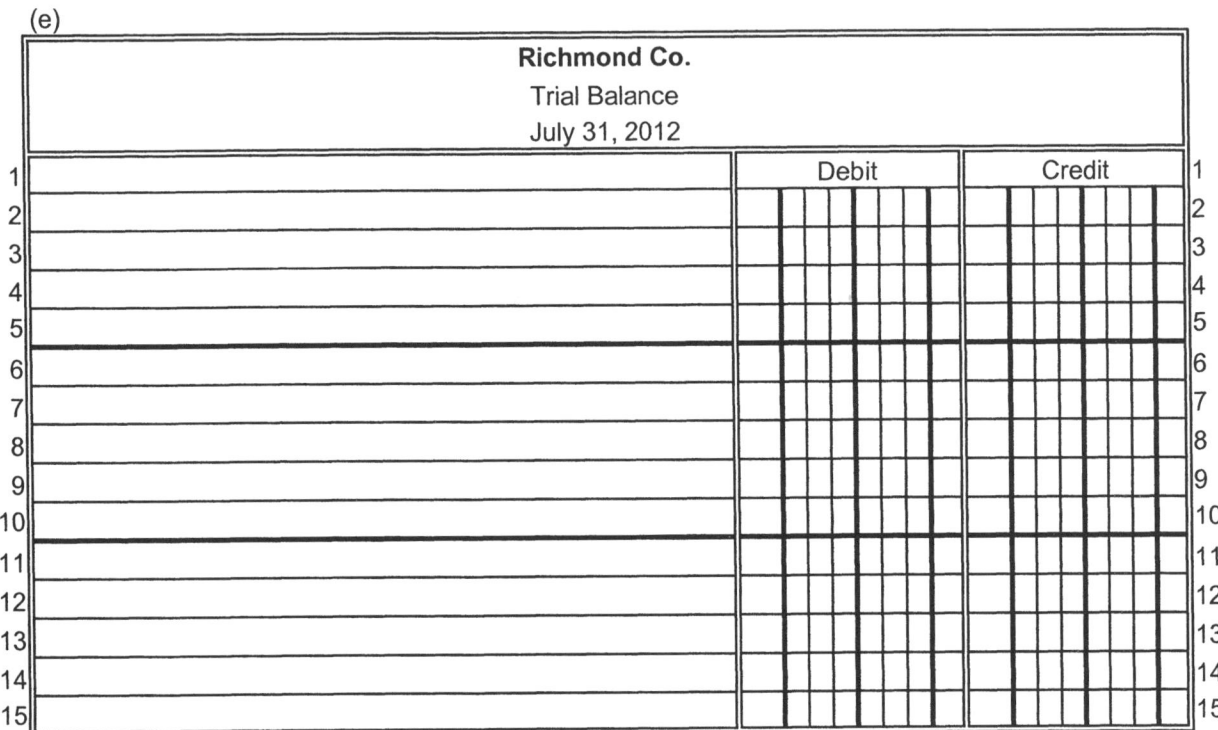

	Richmond Co. Trial Balance July 31, 2012		Debit	Credit	
1					1
2					2
3					3
4					4
5					5
6					6
7					7
8					8
9					9
10					10
11					11
12					12
13					13
14					14
15					15

(f)

1	Accounts receivable balance:	1
2		2
3	Subsidiary accounts balance:	3
4		4
5		5
6	Accounts payable balance:	6
7		7
8	Subsidiary accounts balance:	8
9		9
10		10
11		11
12		12

(g)

General Journal   G1

	Date	Account Titles	Ref.	Debit	Credit	
1	July 31					1
2						2
3						3
4	31					4
5						5
6						6

(h)

Richmond Co. Adjusted Trial Balance July 31, 2012	Debit	Credit	
1 Cash			1
2 Accounts Receivable			2
3 Inventory			3
4 Supplies			4
5 Prepaid Rent			5
6 Accounts Payable			6
7 Owner's Capital			7
8 Owner's Drawings			8
9 Sales Revenue			9
10 Sales Discounts			10
11 Cost of Goods Sold			11
12 Supplies Expense			12
13 Rent Expense			13
14			14
15			15
16			16

(b) & (c)

Cash Receipts Journal

CR1

Date	Account Credited	Ref.	Cash Dr.	Sales Discounts Dr.	Accounts Receivable Cr.	Sales Revenue Cr.	Other Accounts Cr.	COGS Dr. Inventory Cr.
1								
2								
3								
4								
5								
6								

Cash Payments Journal

CP1

Date	Account Debited	Ref.	Other Accounts Dr.	Accounts Payable Dr.	Inventory Cr.	Cash Cr.
1						
2						
3						
4						
5						
6						
7						
8						

(b) & (c) (Continued)

Sales Journal

S1

Date	Account Debited	Ref.	Accounts Receivable Dr. Sales Rev. Cr.	COGS Dr. Inventory Cr.
1				
2				
3				
4				
5				

Purchases Journal

P1

Date	Account Credited	Ref.	Inventory Dr. Acc. Pay. Cr.
1			
2			
3			
4			
5			

General Journal

G1

	Date	Account Titles	Ref.	Debit	Credit	
1	Jan 14					1
2						2
3						3
4						4
5						5
6						6
7	20					7
8						8
9						9
10	30					10
11						11
12						12
13						13

(a) and (c)   *General Ledger*

Cash   No. 101

Date	Explanation	Ref.	Debit	Credit	Balance
Jan. 1	Balance	√			4 1 5 0 0

Accounts Receivable   No. 112

Date	Explanation	Ref.	Debit	Credit	Balance
Jan. 1	Balance	√			1 5 0 0 0

Notes Receivable   No. 115

Date	Explanation	Ref.	Debit	Credit	Balance
Jan. 1	Balance	√			4 5 0 0 0

Inventory   No. 120

Date	Explanation	Ref.	Debit	Credit	Balance
Jan. 1	Balance	√			2 3 0 0 0

Equipment   No. 157

Date	Explanation	Ref.	Debit	Credit	Balance
Jan. 1	Balance	√			6 4 5 0

Accumulated Depreciation - Equipment   No. 158

Date	Explanation	Ref.	Debit	Credit	Balance
Jan. 1	Balance	√			1 5 0 0

(a) and (c) (Continued)

Notes Payable   No. 200

Date	Explanation	Ref.	Debit	Credit	Balance

Accounts Payable   No. 201

Date	Explanation	Ref.	Debit	Credit	Balance
Jan. 1	Balance	√			4 3 0 0 0

Owner's Capital   No. 301

Date	Explanation	Ref.	Debit	Credit	Balance
Jan. 1	Balance	√			8 6 4 5 0

Sales Revenue   No. 401

Date	Explanation	Ref.	Debit	Credit	Balance

Sales Returns and Allowances   No. 412

Date	Explanation	Ref.	Debit	Credit	Balance

Sales Discounts   No. 414

Date	Explanation	Ref.	Debit	Credit	Balance

Cost of Goods Sold   No. 505

Date	Explanation	Ref.	Debit	Credit	Balance

(a) and (c) (Continued)

Salaries and Wages Expense   No. 726

Date	Explanation	Ref.	Debit	Credit	Balance

Rent Expense   No. 729

Date	Explanation	Ref.	Debit	Credit	Balance

Accounts Receivable Subsidiary Ledger

B. Cordelia

Date	Explanation	Ref.	Debit	Credit	Balance
Jan. 1	Balance	√			2 5 0 0

I. Togo

Date	Explanation	Ref.	Debit	Credit	Balance
Jan. 1	Balance	√			7 5 0 0

T. Dudley

Date	Explanation	Ref.	Debit	Credit	Balance
Jan. 1	Balance	√			5 0 0 0

M. Rensing

Date	Explanation	Ref.	Debit	Credit	Balance

(a) and (c) (Continued)

Accounts Payable Subsidiary Ledger

G. Marley

Date	Explanation	Ref.	Debit	Credit	Balance

T. Igawa

Date	Explanation	Ref.	Debit	Credit	Balance
Jan. 1	Balance	√			1 0 0 0 0

D. Miranda

Date	Explanation	Ref.	Debit	Credit	Balance
Jan. 1	Balance	√			1 8 0 0 0

K. Inwood

Date	Explanation	Ref.	Debit	Credit	Balance
Jan. 1	Balance	√			1 5 0 0 0

E. Vietti

Date	Explanation	Ref.	Debit	Credit	Balance

(d)

Bugeja Co. Trial Balance January 31, 2013	Debit	Credit	
1	Cash			1
2	Accounts Receivable			2
3	Notes Receivable			3
4	Inventory			4
5	Equipment			5
6	Accumulated Depreciation - Equipment			6
7	Notes Payable			7
8	Accounts Payable			8
9	Owner's Capital			9
10	Sales Revenue			10
11	Sales Returns and Allowances			11
12	Sales Discounts			12
13	Cost of Goods Sold			13
14	Salaries and Wages Expense			14
15	Rent Expense			15
16				16
17				17
18				18

(e)

1	Accounts receivable subsidiary ledger:		1
2			2
3			3
4			4
5			5
6			6
7	Account receivable control:		7
8			8
9	Accounts payable subsidiary ledger:		9
10			10
11			11
12			12
13			13
14			14
15	Accounts payable control:		15
16			16

(a)

Cash Receipts Journal

CR1

Date	Account Credited	Ref.	Cash Dr.	Sales Discounts Dr.	Accounts Receivable Cr.	Sales Revenue Cr.	Other Accounts Cr.	COGS Dr. Inventory Cr.
1								
2								
3								
4								
5								
6								
7								
8								
9								
10								
11								
12								
13								
14								
15								
16								
17								

(b)

General Ledger

Accounts Receivable   No. 112

Date	Explanation	Ref	Debit	Credit	Balance
June 1	Balance	√			1 0 7 0 0

Accounts Receivable Subsidiary Ledger

Kwapis & Son

Date	Explanation	Ref	Debit	Credit	Balance
June 1	Balance	√			3 5 0 0

Einhorn Co.

Date	Explanation	Ref	Debit	Credit	Balance
June 1	Balance	√			2 8 0 0

Randall Bros.

Date	Explanation	Ref	Debit	Credit	Balance
June 1	Balance	√			2 4 0 0

Daniels Co.

Date	Explanation	Ref	Debit	Credit	Balance
June 1	Balance	√			2 0 0 0

(c)

1		1
2		2
3		3

(a)

Cash Payments Journal

CP1

Date	Ck. No.	Account Debited	Ref.	Other Accounts Dr.	Accounts Payable Dr.	Inventory Cr.	Cash Cr.	
								1
								2
								3
								4
								5
								6
								7
								8
								9
								10
								11
								12
								13
								14
								15
								16
								17
								18
								19
								20

(b)

General Ledger

Accounts Payable   No. 201

Date	Explanation	Ref	Debit	Credit	Balance
Nov. 1	Balance	√			8 2 0 0

Accounts Payable Subsidiary Ledger

S. Carell

Date	Explanation	Ref	Debit	Credit	Balance
Nov. 1	Balance	√			4 0 0 0

D. Schrute

Date	Explanation	Ref	Debit	Credit	Balance
Nov. 1	Balance	√			2 1 0 0

R. Wilson

Date	Explanation	Ref	Debit	Credit	Balance
Nov. 1	Balance	√			8 0 0

W. Rainn

Date	Explanation	Ref	Debit	Credit	Balance
Nov. 1	Balance	√			1 3 0 0

(c)

1	Accounts payable balance:	1
2		2
3		3
4	Subsidiary account balances:	4
5		5
6		6
7		7
8		8
9		9
10		10

(a)

| | | | | Purchases Journal | | | | | P1 |

	Date	Account Credited (Debited)	Ref.	Other Accounts Cr.	Inventory Dr.	Accounts Payable Dr.	
1							1
2							2
3							3
4							4
5							5
6							6
7							7
8							8
9							9
10							10
11							11
12							12
13							13
14							14
15							15
16							16
17							17
18							18

| | | | | Sales Journal | | S1 |

	Date	Account Debited	Ref.	Accounts Receivable Dr. Sales Rev. Cr.	COGS Dr. Inventory Cr.	
1						1
2						2
3						3
4						4
5						5
6						6
7						7
8						8
9						9
10						10

(a) (Continued)

General Journal   G1

	Date	Account Titles	Ref.	Debit	Credit	
1						1
2						2
3						3
4						4
5						5
6						6
7						7
8						8
9						9
10						10
11						11
12						12

(b)

General Ledger

Accounts Receivable   No. 112

Date	Explanation	Ref.	Debit	Credit	Balance

Inventory   No. 120

Date	Explanation	Ref.	Debit	Credit	Balance

Supplies   No. 126

Date	Explanation	Ref.	Debit	Credit	Balance

Equipment   No. 157

Date	Explanation	Ref.	Debit	Credit	Balance

(b) (Continued)

Accounts Payable   No. 201

Date	Explanation	Ref.	Debit	Credit	Balance

Sales Revenue   No. 401

Date	Explanation	Ref.	Debit	Credit	Balance

Sales Returns and Allowances   No. 412

Date	Explanation	Ref.	Debit	Credit	Balance

Cost of Goods Sold   No. 505

Date	Explanation	Ref.	Debit	Credit	Balance

Advertising Expense   No. 610

Date	Explanation	Ref.	Debit	Credit	Balance

(b)(Continued)

Accounts Receivable Subsidiary Ledger

Krasinski Company

Date	Explanation	Ref.	Debit	Credit	Balance

Coen Bros.

Date	Explanation	Ref.	Debit	Credit	Balance

Lucy Company

Date	Explanation	Ref.	Debit	Credit	Balance

(b) (Continued)   *Accounts Payable Subsidiary Ledger*

Fast Freight

Date	Explanation	Ref.	Debit	Credit	Balance

Halpert Company

Date	Explanation	Ref.	Debit	Credit	Balance

Jenna's Supplies

Date	Explanation	Ref.	Debit	Credit	Balance

Beesly Company

Date	Explanation	Ref.	Debit	Credit	Balance

Fischer Company

Date	Explanation	Ref.	Debit	Credit	Balance

Ole Advertising

Date	Explanation	Ref.	Debit	Credit	Balance

(c)

1	Accounts receivable balance:	
2		
3		
4		
5		
6	Subsidiary account balances:	
7		
8		
9		
10		
11		
12		
13		
14		
15		
16		
17	Accounts payable balance:	
18		
19		
20		
21	Subsidiary account balances:	
22		
23		
24		
25		
26		
27		
28		
29		
30		
31		
32		
33		
34		
35		
36		
37		
38		
39		
40		

(a), (b), & (c)

Sales Journal
S1

	Date	Account Debited	Invoice No.	Ref.	Accounts Receivable Dr. Sales Rev. Cr.	COGS Dr. Inventory Cr.	
1							1
2							2
3							3
4							4
5							5
6							6
7							7

Purchases Journal
P1

	Date	Account Credited	Ref.	Inventory (Dr.) Acc. Pay (Cr.)	
1					1
2					2
3					3
4					4
5					5
6					6
7					7
8					8

General Journal
G1

	Date	Account Titles	Ref.	Debit	Credit	
1	Oct 13					1
2						2
3						3
4	25					4
5						5
6						6

(a), (b), (c) (Continued)

Cash Receipts Journal

CR1

Date	Account Credited	Ref.	Cash Dr.	Sales Discounts Dr.	Accounts Receivable Cr.	Sales Revenue Cr.	Other Accounts Cr.	COGS Dr. Inventory Cr.
1								
2								
3								
4								
5								
6								
7								
8								
9								
10								

(a), (b), (c) (Continued)

Cash Payments Journal
CP1

Date	Account Debited	Ref.	Other Accounts Dr.	Accounts Payable Dr.	Inventory Cr.	Cash Cr.
1						
2						
3						
4						
5						
6						
7						
8						
9						
10						
11						

(b)

Purchases Journal

P1

Date	Account Credited	Ref.	Inventory (Dr) Acc Pay (Cr)	
				1
				2
				3
				4
				5
				6
				7

Cash Payments Journal

CP1

Date	Account Debited	Ref.	Other Accounts Dr.	Accounts Payable Dr.	Inventory Cr.	Cash Cr.	
							1
							2
							3
							4
							5
							6
							7
							8
							9
							10

(a), (d), & (g)

General Ledger

Cash   No. 101

Date	Explanation	Ref.	Debit	Credit	Balance

Accounts Receivable   No. 112

Date	Explanation	Ref.	Debit	Credit	Balance

Inventory   No. 120

Date	Explanation	Ref.	Debit	Credit	Balance

Supplies   No. 126

Date	Explanation	Ref.	Debit	Credit	Balance

Equipment   No. 157

Date	Explanation	Ref.	Debit	Credit	Balance

Accumulated Depreciation - Equipment   No. 158

Date	Explanation	Ref.	Debit	Credit	Balance

(a), (d) and (g) (Continued)

Accounts Payable   No. 201

Date	Explanation	Ref.	Debit	Credit	Balance

Owner's Capital   No. 301

Date	Explanation	Ref.	Debit	Credit	Balance

Owner's Drawings   No. 306

Date	Explanation	Ref.	Debit	Credit	Balance

Sales Revenue   No. 401

Date	Explanation	Ref.	Debit	Credit	Balance

Sales Discounts   No. 414

Date	Explanation	Ref.	Debit	Credit	Balance

Cost of Goods Sold   No. 505

Date	Explanation	Ref.	Debit	Credit	Balance

Supplies Expense   No. 631

Date	Explanation	Ref.	Debit	Credit	Balance

Depreciation Expense   No. 711

Date	Explanation	Ref.	Debit	Credit	Balance

(c)

Accounts Receivable Subsidiary Ledger

C. Lesle

Date	Explanation	Ref.	Debit	Credit	Balance

T. Baker

Date	Explanation	Ref.	Debit	Credit	Balance

S. David

Date	Explanation	Ref.	Debit	Credit	Balance

W. Oz

Date	Explanation	Ref.	Debit	Credit	Balance

Accounts Payable Subsidiary Ledger

Kansas Company

Date	Explanation	Ref.	Debit	Credit	Balance

B. Baumgartner

Date	Explanation	Ref.	Debit	Credit	Balance

A. Martin

Date	Explanation	Ref.	Debit	Credit	Balance

(c) (Continued)

D. Gale

Date	Explanation	Ref.	Debit	Credit	Balance

(e)

Hudson Co.

Trial Balance

February 28, 2012

		Debit	Credit	
1	Cash			1
2	Accounts Receivable			2
3	Inventory			3
4	Supplies			4
5	Equipment			5
6	Accounts Payable			6
7	Owner's Capital			7
8	Owner's Drawings			8
9	Sales Revenue			9
10	Sales Discounts			10
11	Cost of Goods Sold			11
12				12
13				13

(f)

1	Accounts receivable control account:		1
2			2
3	Accounts receivable subsidiary accounts:		3
4			4
5			5
6			6
7			7
8	Accounts payable control account:		8
9			9
10	Accounts payable subsidiary accounts:		10
11			11
12			12
13			13

(g)

General Journal   G1

	Date	Account Titles	Ref.	Debit	Credit	
1	Feb 28					1
2						2
3						3
4						4
5						5
6	28					6
7						7
8						8
9						9
10						10

(h)

Hudson Co.
Adjusted Trial Balance
February 28, 2012

		Debit	Credit	
1	Cash			1
2	Accounts Receivable			2
3	Inventory			3
4	Supplies			4
5	Equipment			5
6	Accumulated Depreciation - Equipment			6
7	Accounts Payable			7
8	Owner's Capital			8
9	Owner's Drawings			9
10	Sales Revenue			10
11	Sales Discounts			11
12	Cost of Goods Sold			12
13	Supplies Expense			13
14	Depreciation Expense			14
15				15
16				16
17				17
18				18
19				19
20				20
21				21

(a)

		Sales Journal			S1

	Date	Account Debited	Invoice No.	Ref.	Accounts Receiv. Dr. Sales Rev. Cr.	
1						1
2						2
3						3
4						4
5						5
6						6
7						7
8						8
9						9
10						10
11						11
12						12

		Purchases Journal			P1

	Date	Account Credited	Terms	Ref.	Purchases Dr. Acc. Pay Cr.	
1						1
2						2
3						3
4						4
5						5
6						6
7						7
8						8
9						9
10						10
11						11
12						12

Comprehensive Problem: Chapters 3 to 7 Continued

Packard Company

(a) (Continued)

Cash Receipts Journal   CR1

Date	Account Credited	Ref.	Cash Dr.	Accounts Receivable Cr.	Sales Revenue Cr.	Other Accounts Cr.
1						
2						
3						
4						
5						
6						
7						
8						
9						
10						
11						
12						
13						
14						
15						

Name

Section

Date

Packard Company

(a) (Continued)

Cash Payments Journal

CP1

Date	Account Debited	Ref.	Other Accounts Dr.	Accounts Payable Dr.	Supplies Dr.	Cash Cr.	
							1
							2
							3
							4
							5
							6
							7
							8
							9
							10
							11
							12
							13
							14
							15

(e)

	Date	Account Titles	Ref	Debit	Credit	
1	Jan. 9					1
2						2
3						3
4						4
5	18					5
6						6
7						7
8						8
9	21					9
10						10
11						11
12						12
13		Adjusting Entries				13
14	31					14
15						15
16						16
17	31					17
18						18
19						19
20	31					20
21						21
22						22
23	31					23
24						24
25						25
26						26
27						27
28						28
29						29
30						30
31						31
32						32
33						33
34						34
35						35
36						36
37						37
38						38
39						39
40						40

General Journal

G1

(a) and (e)

General Journal   G1

	Date	Account Titles	Ref	Debit	Credit	
1		Closing Entries				1
2	Jan. 31					2
3						3
4						4
5						5
6						6
7	31					7
8						8
9						9
10						10
11						11
12						12
13						13
14						14
15						15
16						16
17						17
18						18
19						19
20	31					20
21						21
22						22
23	31					23
24						24
25						25
26						26
27						27
28						28
29						29
30						30
31						31
32						32
33						33
34						34
35						35
36						36
37						37
38						38
39						39
40						40

(b) and (e)

General Ledger

Cash   No. 101

Date	Explanation	Ref.	Debit	Credit	Balance
Jan. 1	Balance	√			3 3 7 5 0

Accounts Receivable   No. 112

Date	Explanation	Ref.	Debit	Credit	Balance
Jan. 1	Balance	√			1 3 0 0 0

Notes Receivable   No. 115

Date	Explanation	Ref.	Debit	Credit	Balance
Jan. 1	Balance	√			3 9 0 0 0

Inventory   No. 120

Date	Explanation	Ref.	Debit	Credit	Balance
Jan. 1	Balance	√			2 0 0 0 0

Supplies   No. 125

Date	Explanation	Ref.	Debit	Credit	Balance
Jan. 1	Balance	√			1 0 0 0

Prepaid Insurance   No. 130

Date	Explanation	Ref.	Debit	Credit	Balance
Jan. 1	Balance	√			2 0 0 0

(b) and (e) (Continued)

Equipment   No. 157

Date	Explanation	Ref.	Debit	Credit	Balance
Jan. 1	Balance	√			6450

Accumulated Depreciation - Equipment   No. 158

Date	Explanation	Ref.	Debit	Credit	Balance
Jan. 1	Balance	√			1500

Notes Payable   No. 200

Date	Explanation	Ref.	Debit	Credit	Balance
	Balance				

Accounts Payable   No. 201

Date	Explanation	Ref.	Debit	Credit	Balance
Jan. 1	Balance	√			35000

Interest Payable   No. 230

Date	Explanation	Ref.	Debit	Credit	Balance

Owner's Capital   No. 301

Date	Explanation	Ref.	Debit	Credit	Balance
Jan. 1	Balance	√			78700

Owner's Drawings   No. 306

Date	Explanation	Ref.	Debit	Credit	Balance

(b) and (e) (Continued)

Income Summary   No. 350

Date	Explanation	Ref.	Debit	Credit	Balance

Sales Revenue   No. 401

Date	Explanation	Ref.	Debit	Credit	Balance

Sales Returns and Allowances   No. 412

Date	Explanation	Ref.	Debit	Credit	Balance

Purchases   No. 510

Date	Explanation	Ref.	Debit	Credit	Balance

Purchase Returns and Allowances   No. 512

Date	Explanation	Ref.	Debit	Credit	Balance

Freight-in   No. 516

Date	Explanation	Ref.	Debit	Credit	Balance

Salaries and Wages Expense   No. 627

Date	Explanation	Ref.	Debit	Credit	Balance

(b) and (e) (Continued)

Depreciation Expense   No. 711

Date	Explanation	Ref.	Debit	Credit	Balance

Interest Expense   No. 718

Date	Explanation	Ref.	Debit	Credit	Balance

Insurance Expense   No. 722

Date	Explanation	Ref.	Debit	Credit	Balance

Salaries and Wages Expense   No. 727

Date	Explanation	Ref.	Debit	Credit	Balance

Supplies Expense   No. 728

Date	Explanation	Ref.	Debit	Credit	Balance

Rent Expense   No. 729

Date	Explanation	Ref.	Debit	Credit	Balance

(b) (Continued)

Accounts Receivable Subsidiary Ledger

R. Draves

Date	Explanation	Ref.	Debit	Credit	Balance
Jan. 1	Balance	√			1500

J. Fine

Date	Explanation	Ref.	Debit	Credit	Balance

B. Hachinski

Date	Explanation	Ref.	Debit	Credit	Balance
Jan. 1	Balance	√			7500

S. Ingles

Date	Explanation	Ref.	Debit	Credit	Balance
Jan. 1	Balance	√			4000

B. Remy

Date	Explanation	Ref.	Debit	Credit	Balance

(b) (Continued)

Accounts Payable Subsidiary Ledger

D. Laux

Date	Explanation	Ref.	Debit	Credit	Balance

S. Kosko

Date	Explanation	Ref.	Debit	Credit	Balance
Jan. 1	Balance	√			9 0 0 0

R. Mikush

Date	Explanation	Ref.	Debit	Credit	Balance
Jan. 1	Balance	√			1 5 0 0 0

D. Moreno

Date	Explanation	Ref.	Debit	Credit	Balance
Jan. 1	Balance	√			1 1 0 0 0

S. Yost

Date	Explanation	Ref.	Debit	Credit	Balance

Comprehensive Problem: Chapters 3 to 7

Packard Company

See Appendix

(d)

	Packard Company				
	Income Statement				
	For the Month Ended January 31, 2012				

(d) (Continued)

Packard Company

Statement of Owner's Equity

For the Month Ended January 31, 2012

1	1
2	2
3	3
4	4
5	5
6	6

Packard Company

Balance Sheet

January 31, 2012

Assets	
1	1
2	2
3	3
4	4
5	5
6	6
7	7
8	8
9	9
10	10
11	11
12	12
13	13
14	14
15	15

Liabilities and Owner's Equity	
16	16
17	17
18	18
19	19
20	20
21	21
22	22
23	23
24	24
25	25
26	26
27	27
28	28
29	29
30	30

(f)

Packard Company Post-Closing Trial Balance January 31, 2012	Debit	Credit	
1 Cash			1
2 Notes Receivable			2
3 Accounts Receivable			3
4 Inventory			4
5 Supplies			5
6 Prepaid Insurance			6
7 Equipment			7
8 Accumulated Depreciation - Equipment			8
9 Notes Payable			9
10 Accounts Payable			10
11 Interest Payable			11
12 Owner's Capital			12
13			13
14			14

1 Accounts Receivable balance:		1
2		2
3 Subsidiary account balances:		3
4		4
5		5
6		6
7		7
8		8
9		9
10 Accounts Payable balance:		10
11		11
12 Subsidiary account balances:		12
13		13
14		14
15		15
16		16
17		17

	Sales Journal					S1
Date	Account Debited	Invoice No.	Ref.	Accounts Receivable Dr. Sales Rev. Cr.	COGS Dr. Inventory Cr.	
1						1
2						2
3						3
4						4
5						5
6						6
7						7
8						8
9						9
10						10
11						11
12						12

	Purchases Journal				P1
Date	Account Credited	Terms	Ref.	Inventory (Dr.) Acc. Pay (Cr.)	
1					1
2					2
3					3
4					4
5					5
6					6
7					7
8					8
9					9
10					10
11					11
12					12

(a) (Continued)

Cash Receipts Journal

CR1

Date	Account Credited	Ref.	Cash Dr.	Sales Discounts Dr.	Accounts Receivable Cr.	Sales Revenue Cr.	Other Accounts Cr.	COGS Dr. Inventory Cr.
1								
2								
3								
4								
5								
6								
7								
8								
9								
10								
11								
12								
13								
14								
15								

(a) (Continued)

Cash Payments Journal

CP1

Date	Account Debited	Ref.	Other Accounts Dr.	Accounts Payable Dr.	Supplies Dr.	Inventory Cr.	Cash Cr.
1							
2							
3							
4							
5							
6							
7							
8							
9							
10							
11							
12							
13							
14							
15							

(a) (Continued) and (e)

General Journal

G1

	Date	Account Titles	Ref	Debit	Credit	
1	Jan. 9					1
2						2
3						3
4						4
5						5
6						6
7						7
8						8
9						9
10						10
11	18					11
12						12
13						13
14						14
15	21					15
16						16
17						17
18						18
19						19
20		Adjusting Entries				20
21	31					21
22						22
23						23
24						24
25	31					25
26						26
27						27
28						28
29	31					29
30						30
31						31
32						32
33						33
34						34
35						35
36						36
37						37
38						38
39						39
40						40

(e) (Continued)

General Journal G1

	Date	Account Titles	Ref	Debit	Credit	
1		Closing Entries				1
2	Jan. 31					2
3						3
4						4
5	31					5
6						6
7						7
8						8
9						9
10						10
11						11
12						12
13						13
14						14
15						15
16						16
17						17
18						18
19						19
20						20
21						21
22						22
23						23
24						24
25						25
26						26
27						27
28						28
29						29
30						30
31						31
32						32
33						33
34						34
35						35
36						36
37						37
38						38
39						39
40						40

(b) and (e)

General Ledger

Cash   No. 101

Date	Explanation	Ref.	Debit	Credit	Balance
Jan. 1	Balance	√			3 5 7 5 0

Accounts Receivable   No. 112

Date	Explanation	Ref.	Debit	Credit	Balance
Jan. 1	Balance	√			1 3 0 0 0

Notes Receivable   No. 115

Date	Explanation	Ref.	Debit	Credit	Balance
Jan. 1	Balance	√			3 9 0 0 0

Inventory   No. 120

Date	Explanation	Ref.	Debit	Credit	Balance
Jan. 1	Balance	√			1 8 0 0 0

Supplies   No. 125

Date	Explanation	Ref.	Debit	Credit	Balance
Jan. 1	Balance	√			1 0 0 0

Prepaid Insurance   No. 130

Date	Explanation	Ref.	Debit	Credit	Balance
Jan. 1	Balance	√			2 0 0 0

(b) and (e) (Continued)

Equipment   No. 157

Date	Explanation	Ref.	Debit	Credit	Balance
Jan. 1	Balance	√			6 4 5 0

Accumulated Depreciation - Equipment   No. 158

Date	Explanation	Ref.	Debit	Credit	Balance
Jan. 1	Balance	√			1 5 0 0

Notes Payable   No. 200

Date	Explanation	Ref.	Debit	Credit	Balance

Accounts Payable   No. 201

Date	Explanation	Ref.	Debit	Credit	Balance
Jan. 1	Balance	√			3 5 0 0 0

Interest Payable   No. 230

Date	Explanation	Ref.	Debit	Credit	Balance

Owner's Capital   No. 301

Date	Explanation	Ref.	Debit	Credit	Balance
Jan. 1	Balance	√			7 8 7 0 0

Owner's Drawings   No. 306

Date	Explanation	Ref.	Debit	Credit	Balance

(b) and (e) (Continued)

Income Summary   No. 350

Date	Explanation	Ref.	Debit	Credit	Balance

Sales Revenue   No. 401

Date	Explanation	Ref.	Debit	Credit	Balance

Sales Returns and Allowances   No. 412

Date	Explanation	Ref.	Debit	Credit	Balance

Sales Discounts   No. 414

Date	Explanation	Ref.	Debit	Credit	Balance

Cost of Goods Sold   No. 505

Date	Explanation	Ref.	Debit	Credit	Balance

Salaries and Wages Expense   No. 627

Date	Explanation	Ref.	Debit	Credit	Balance

Depreciation Expense   No. 711

Date	Explanation	Ref.	Debit	Credit	Balance

(b) and (e) (Continued)

Interest Expense   No. 718

Date	Explanation	Ref.	Debit	Credit	Balance

Insurance Expense   No. 722

Date	Explanation	Ref.	Debit	Credit	Balance

Supplies Expense   No. 728

Date	Explanation	Ref.	Debit	Credit	Balance

Rent Expense   No. 729

Date	Explanation	Ref.	Debit	Credit	Balance

(b) (Continued)

Accounts Receivable Subsidiary Ledger

R. Dvorak

Date	Explanation	Ref.	Debit	Credit	Balance
Jan. 1	Balance	√			1 5 0 0

J. Forbes

Date	Explanation	Ref.	Debit	Credit	Balance

B. Garcia

Date	Explanation	Ref.	Debit	Credit	Balance
Jan. 1	Balance	√			7 5 0 0

S. LaDew

Date	Explanation	Ref.	Debit	Credit	Balance
Jan. 1	Balance	√			4 0 0 0

B. Richey

Date	Explanation	Ref.	Debit	Credit	Balance

(b) (Continued)

Accounts Payable Subsidiary Ledger

D. Lynch

Date	Explanation	Ref.	Debit	Credit	Balance

S. Hoyt

Date	Explanation	Ref.	Debit	Credit	Balance
Jan. 1	Balance	√			9000

R. Moses

Date	Explanation	Ref.	Debit	Credit	Balance
Jan. 1	Balance	√			15000

D. Omara

Date	Explanation	Ref.	Debit	Credit	Balance
Jan. 1	Balance	√			11000

S. Vogel

Date	Explanation	Ref.	Debit	Credit	Balance

Chapter 7 Financial Reporting Problem

Bluma Co.

See Appendix

(d)

Bluma Co.

Income Statement

For the Month Ended January 31, 2012

1				
2				
3				
4				
5				
6				
7				
8				
9				
10				
11				
12				
13				
14				
15				
16				
17				
18				
19				
20				
21				
22				
23				
24				
25				
26				
27				
28				
29				
30				
31				
32				
33				
34				
35				
36				
37				
38				
39				
40				

(d) (Continued)

Bluma Co.													
Owner's Equity Statement													
For the Month Ended January 31, 2012													

1							1
2							2
3							3
4							4
5							5
6							6

Bluma Co.
Balance Sheet
January 31, 2012

	Assets		
1	Assets		1
2			2
3			3
4			4
5			5
6			6
7			7
8			8
9			9
10			10
11			11
12			12
13			13
14			14
15			15
16	Liabilities and Owner's Equity		16
17			17
18			18
19			19
20			20
21			21
22			22
23			23
24			24
25			25
26			26
27			27
28			28
29			29
30			30

(f)

Bluma Co. Post-Closing Trial Balance January 31, 2012	Debit	Credit	
1 Cash			1
2 Notes Receivable			2
3 Accounts Receivable			3
4 Inventory			4
5 Supplies			5
6 Prepaid Insurance			6
7 Equipment			7
8 Accumulated Depreciation - Equipment			8
9 Notes Payable			9
10 Accounts Payable			10
11 Interest Payable			11
12 Owner's Capital			12
13			13
14			14
15			15

1 Accounts Receivable balance:		1
2		2
3 Subsidiary account balances:		3
4		4
5		5
6		6
7		7
8		8
9		9
10 Accounts Payable balance:		10
11		11
12 Subsidiary account balances:		12
13		13
14		14
15		15
16		16
17		17
18		18
19		19

BE8-6

		Account Titles	Debit	Credit	
1	1.				1
2					2
3					3
4					4
5	2.				5
6					6
7					7
8					8
9					9
10					10

	BE 8-7	Account Titles	Debit	Credit	
11					11
12					12
13					13
14					14
15					15
16					16

	BE 8-9				
17					17
18	Date	Account Titles	Debit	Credit	18
19	Mar. 20				19
20					20
21					21
22					22
23					23
24					24
25					25

	BE 8-13				
26					26
27					27
28					28
29					29
30					30
31					31
32					32

	BE 8-14				
33					33
34					34
35					35
36					36
37					37
38					38
39					39
40					40

	Date	Account Titles	Debit	Credit	
1	Aug. 1				1
2					2
3					3
4					4
5	30				5
6					6
7					7
8					8
9					9
10					10
11					11
12					12
13					13
14					14
15					15
16					16
17					17
18					18
19					19
20					20
21					21

	Date	Account Titles	Debit	Credit	
1	May 1				1
2					2
3					3
4	June 1				4
5					5
6					6
7					7
8					8
9					9
10	July 1				10
11					11
12					12
13					13
14					14
15	July 10				15
16					16
17					17
18					18
19					19
20					20

E8-8

	Date	Account Titles	Debit	Credit	
1	Mar. 1				1
2					2
3					3
4	15				4
5					5
6					6
7					7
8					8
9					9
10					10
11	20				11
12					12

E8-9 (a)

	Bob Vance Bank Reconciliation January 31			
1				1
2				2
3				3
4				4
5				5
6				6
7				7
8				8
9				9
10				10
11				11
12				12

(b)

	Date	Account Titles	Debit	Credit	
1					1
2					2
3					3
4					4
5					5
6					6

E8-10

	No.	Amount
1		
2		
3		
4		
5		

E8-11 (a)

Miner Video Company	
Bank Reconciliation	
July 31	
1	
2	
3	
4	
5	
6	
7	
8	
9	
10	
11	
12	
13	
14	
15	
16	

(b)

	Date	Account Titles	Debit	Credit
1	July 31			
2				
3				
4				
5				
6	31			
7				
8				
9				
10				

(a)

Porter Company
Bank Reconciliation
September 30

1		
2		
3		
4		
5		
6		
7		
8		
9		
10		
11		
12		
13		
14		
15		
16		
17		
18		
19		
20		

(b)

	Date	Account Titles	Debit	Credit
1	Sept. 30			
2				
3				
4				
5				
6	30			
7				
8				
9	30			
10				
11				
12	30			
13				
14				
15				

1	(a) Deposits in transit:		1
2			2
3			3
4			4
5			5
6			6
7			7
8			8
9			9
10			10
11	(b) Outstanding checks:		11
12			12
13			13
14			14
15			15
16			16
17			17
18			18
19			19
20			20
21	(c) Deposits in transit:		21
22			22
23			23
24			24
25			25
26			26
27			27
28			28
29			29
30			30
31	(d) Outstanding checks:		31
32			32
33			33
34			34
35			35
36			36
37			37
38			38
39			39
40			40

(a)

(b)

(c)

(a)

	Date	Account Titles	Debit	Credit	
1	July 1				1
2					2
3					3
4	15				4
5					5
6					6
7					7
8					8
9					9
10					10
11	31				11
12					12
13					13
14					14
15					15
16					16
17	Aug. 15				17
18					18
19					19
20					20
21					21
22					22
23					23
24	16				24
25					25
26					26
27	31				27
28					28
29					29
30					30
31					31
32					32
33					33
34					34
35					35
36					36
37					37
38					38
39					39
40					40

(b)

Petty Cash

Date	Explanation	Ref.	Debit	Credit	Balance

(c)

(a)

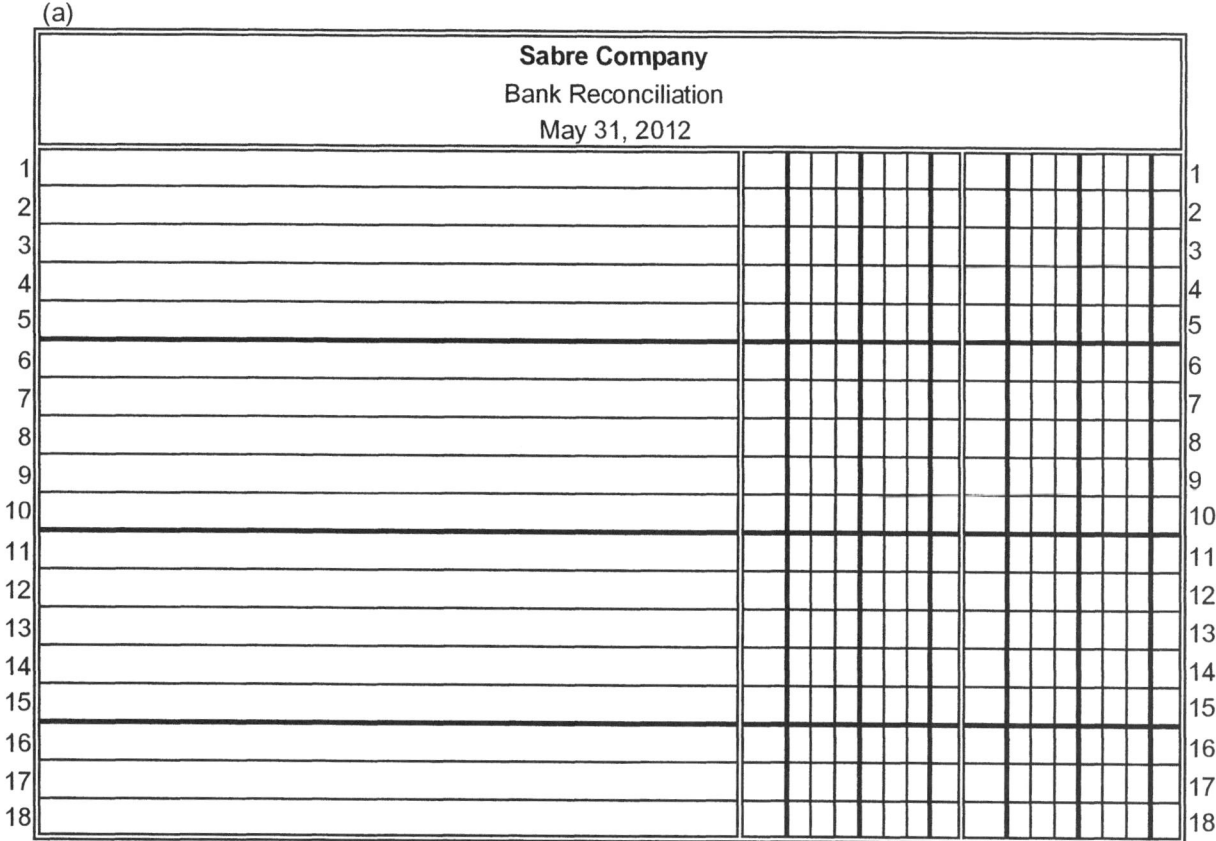

Sabre Company Bank Reconciliation May 31, 2012			
1				1
2				2
3				3
4				4
5				5
6				6
7				7
8				8
9				9
10				10
11				11
12				12
13				13
14				14
15				15
16				16
17				17
18				18

(b)

	Date	Account Titles	Debit	Credit	
1	May 31				1
2					2
3					3
4					4
5					5
6	31				6
7					7
8					8
9	31				9
10					10
11					11
12	31				12
13					13
14					14
15	31				15
16					16
17					17

(a)

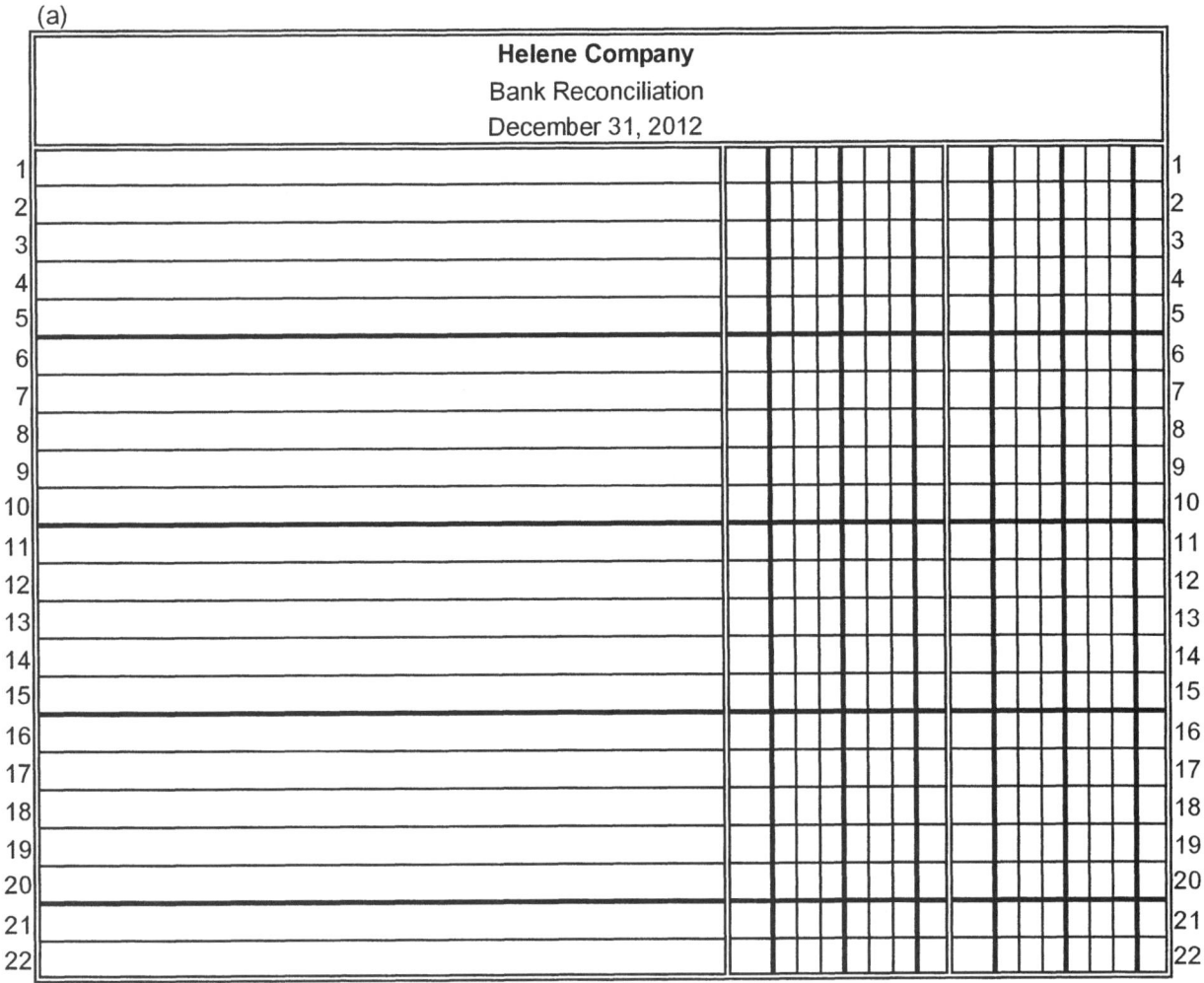

| **Helene Company** |
| Bank Reconciliation |
| December 31, 2012 |

(b)

	Date	Account Titles	Debit	Credit	
1	Dec. 31				1
2					2
3					3
4					4
5					5
6	31				6
7					7
8					8
9	31				9
10					10
11					11
12	31				12
13					13
14					14

(a)

Hidetoshi Company
Bank Reconciliation
July 31, 2012

1					1
2					2
3					3
4					4
5					5
6					6
7					7
8					8
9					9
10					10
11					11
12					12
13					13
14					14
15					15
16					16
17					17
18					18
19					19
20	Computations				20
21					21
22					22
23					23
24					24
25					25
26					26
27					27
28					28
29					29
30					30
31					31
32					32
33					33
34					34
35					35
36					36
37					37
38					38
39					39
40					40

Section

Date   Hidetoshi Company

(b)

	Date	Account Titles	Debit	Credit	
1	July 31				1
2					2
3					3
4					4
5	31				5
6					6
7					7
8	31				8
9					9
10					10
11					11
12					12
13					13
14					14
15					15
16					16
17					17
18					18
19					19
20					20

(a)

	Date	Account Titles	Debit	Credit	
1	July 1				1
2					2
3					3
4	15				4
5					5
6					6
7					7
8					8
9					9
10					10
11	31				11
12					12
13					13
14					14
15					15
16					16
17	Aug. 15				17
18					18
19					19
20					20
21					21
22					22
23					23
24	16				24
25					25
26					26
27	31				27
28					28
29					29
30					30
31					31
32					32
33					33
34					34
35					35
36					36
37					37
38					38
39					39
40					40

(b)

Petty Cash

Date	Explanation	Ref.	Debit	Credit	Balance

(c)

(a)

Rohatyn Genetics Company
Bank Reconciliation
May 31, 2012

1			
2			
3			
4			
5			
6			
7			
8			
9			
10			
11			
12			
13			
14			
15			
16			
17			

(b)

	Date	Account Titles	Debit	Credit
1	May 31			
2				
3				
4				
5				
6	31			
7				
8				
9	31			
10				
11				
12	31			
13				
14				
15	31			
16				
17				

(a)

Williams Company		
Bank Reconciliation		
November 30, 2012		
1		
2		
3		
4		
5		
6		
7		
8		
9		
10		
11		
12		
13		
14		
15		
16		
17		
18		
19		
20		
21		
22		

(b)

Date	Account Titles	Debit	Credit
Nov. 30			
30			
30			
30			

	Trong Company			
	Bank Reconciliation			
	August 31, 2012			

1				
2				
3				
4				
5				
6				
7				
8				
9				
10				
11				
12				
13				
14				
15				
16				
17				
18				
19				
20				
21	Computations			
22				
23				
24				
25				
26				
27				
28				
29				
30				
31				
32				
33				
34				
35				
36				
37				
38				
39				
40				

(b)

	Date	Account Titles	Debit	Credit	
1	Aug. 31				1
2					2
3					3
4					4
5	31				5
6					6
7					7
8	31				8
9					9
10					10
11	31				11
12					12
13					13
14					14
15					15
16					16
17					17
18					18
19					19
20					20

(a)

Braun Company
Bank Reconciliation
October 31, 2012

(b)

(c)

(a)

	Date	Account Titles	Debit	Credit	
1	Dec.7				1
2					2
3					3
4	12				4
5					5
6					6
7	17				7
8					8
9					9
10					10
11					11
12					12
13	19				13
14					14
15					15
16	22				16
17					17
18					18
19					19
20	26				20
21					21
22					22
23					23
24					24
25					25
26					26
27					27
28					28
29					29
30					30
31					31
32					32
33					33
34					34
35					35
36					36
37					37
38					38
39					39

(b) & (e)   General Ledger

Cash		Accounts Payable	
12/1 Bal	18,200		12/1 Bal 6,100

		Owner's Capital	
			12/1 Bal 64,400

Notes Receivable		Sales Revenue	
12/1Bal	2,200		

Accounts Receivable		Sales Discounts	
12/1 Bal	7,500		

Inventory		Cost of Goods Sold	
12/1 Bal	16,000		

		Depreciation Expense	

Prepaid Insurance		Salaries and Wages Expense	
12/1 Bal	1,600		

Equipment			
12/1 Bal	28,000		

Accumulated Depreciation - Equipment		Insurance Expense	
	12/1/ Bal 3,000		

(c)

	Bluemound Company			
	Bank Reconciliation			
	December 31, 2012			
1				
2				
3				
4				
5				
6				
7				
8				
9				
10				
11				
12				
13				
14				
15				
16				
17				

(d)

	Date	Account Titles	Debit	Credit
1	Dec. 31			
2				
3				
4	31			
5				
6				
7	31			
8				
9				
10				
11	31			
12				
13				
14				
15				
16				
17				

(f)

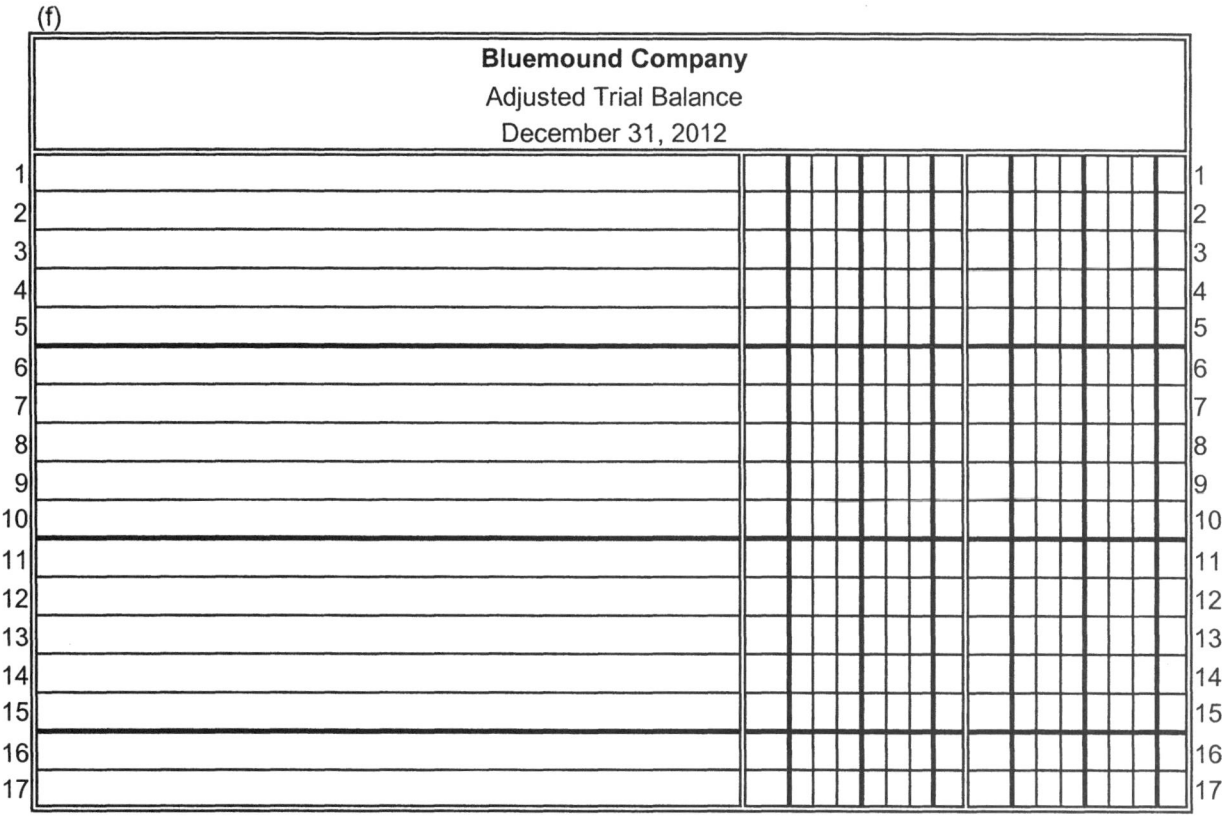

Bluemound Company

Adjusted Trial Balance

December 31, 2012

(g)

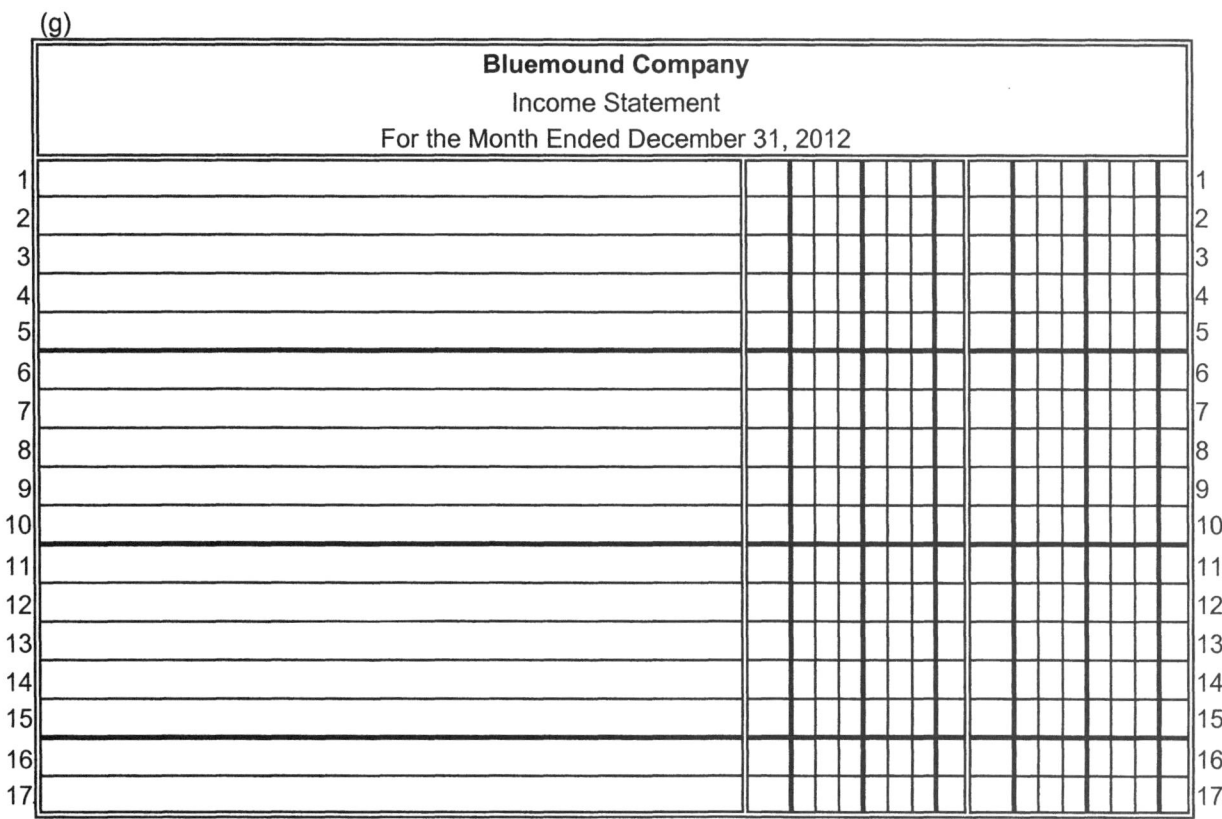

Bluemound Company

Income Statement

For the Month Ended December 31, 2012

(g)

Bluemound Company		
Balance Sheet		
December 31,2012		

	Assets		
1			1
2			2
3			3
4			4
5			5
6			6
7			7
8			8
9			9
10			10
11			11
12			12
13			13
14			14
15	Liabilities and Owners' Equity		15
16			16
17			17
18			18
19			19
20			20
21			21
22			22
23			23
24			24
25			25
26			26
27			27
28			28
29			29
30			30
31			31
32			32
33			33
34			34
35			35
36			36
37			37
38			38
39			39

	PepsiCo	Coca-Cola
(a) (In millions)		
(1) Cash and cash equivalents at year-end 2009		
(2) Increase/decrease in cash and cash equivalents from 2008 to 2009		
(3) Cash provided by operating activities during year ended Dec. 31, 2009		

(b)

BE9-1			
1	(a)		
2	(b)		
3	(c)		
4			

BE9-2	Account Titles	Debit	Credit
(a)			
(b)			
(c)			

BE9-3	Account Titles	Debit	Credit
(a)			
(b)	Current assets:		

BE9-4	Account Titles	Debit	Credit
(a)			

(b)		(1) Before Write-Off	(2) After Write-Off

BE9-5	Account Titles	Debit	Credit
1			
2			
3			
4			
5			
6			
BE9-6			
7			
8			
9			
10			
BE9-7			
(a)			
13			
14			
15			
(b)			
17			

BE9-8	Account Titles	Debit	Credit
(a)			
20			
21			
22			
(b)			
24			
25			
26			

BE9-9		Interest	Maturity Date
(a)			
(b)			
(c)			

BE9-10	Date of Note	Maturity Date	Annual Interest Rate	Total Interest
(a)	April 1		9%	
(b)	July 2			$ 600
(c)	March 7		10%	

BE9-11

	Date	Account Titles	Debit	Credit	
1	Jan. 10				1
2					2
3					3
4					4
5	Feb. 9				5
6					6
7					7
8					8
9					9
10					10

DO IT! 9-1

		Account Titles	Debit	Credit	
1					1
2					2
3					3
4					4
5					5
6					6

DO IT! 9-2

7			7
8			8
9			9
10			10

		Account Titles	Debit	Credit	
11					11
12					12
13					13
14					14
15					15
16					16

DO IT! 9-3

17		17
18	(a)	18
19		19
20		20
21	(b) The interest receivable at maturity is:	21
22		22

		Account Titles	Debit	Credit	
23					23
24					24
25					25
26					26
27					27
28					28
29					29
30					30
31					31
32					32
33					33
34					34
35					35
36					36
37					37
38					38
39					39
40					40

E9-1

	Date	Account Titles	Debit	Credit	
1	March 1				1
2					2
3					3
4	3				4
5					5
6					6
7	9				7
8					8
9					9
10					10
11	15				11
12					12
13					13
14	31				14
15					15
16					16
17	**E9-2**				17
18	(a)				18
19	Jan. 6				19
20					20
21					21
22	16				22
23					23
24					24
25					25
26	(b)				26
27	Jan. 10				27
28					28
29					29
30	Feb. 12				30
31					31
32					32
33	Mar. 10				33
34					34
35					35
36					36
37					37
38					38
39					39
40					40

E9-3

	Date	Account Titles	Debit	Credit	
1	(a)				1
2	Dec. 31				2
3					3
4					4
5	(b) (1)				5
6	Dec. 31				6
7					7
8					8
9	(2)				9
10	Dec. 31				10
11					11
12					12
13	(c) (1)				13
14	Dec. 31				14
15					15
16					16
17	(2)				17
18	Dec. 31				18
19					19
20					20

E9-4

	(a)					
22					Estimated	22
23	Accounts Receivable	Amount	%	Uncollectible	23
24	1 - 30 days				24
25					25
26	30 - 60 days				26
27					27
28	60 - 90 days				28
29					29
30	Over 90 days				30
31					31
32					32
33					33
34					34
35	(b)					35

	Date	Account Titles	Debit	Credit	
36	Date	Account Titles	Debit	Credit	36
37	Mar. 31				37
38					38
39					39
40					40

E9-5

	Date	Account Titles	Debit	Credit	
1					1
2					2
3					3
4					4
5					5
6					6
7					7
8					8
9					9
10					10
11					11
12					12
13					13
14	**E9-6**				14
15	2012				15
16	Dec. 31				16
17					17
18					18
19					19
20	2013				20
21	May 11				21
22					22
23					23
24					24
25	2013				25
26	Jun. 12				26
27					27
28					28
29					29
30					30
31					31
32					32
33					33

E9-7

	Date	Account Titles	Debit	Credit	
1	(a)				1
2	Mar. 3				2
3					3
4					4
5					5
6					6
7					7
8	(b)				8
9	May 10				9
10					10
11					11
12					12
13					13
14					14
15					15
16	**E9-8**				16
17	(a)				17
18	Apr. 2				18
19					19
20					20
21	May 3				21
22					22
23					23
24	Jun. 1				24
25					25
26					26
27	(b)				27
28	July 4				28
29					29
30					30
31					31
32					32
33					33
34					34
35					35
36					36
37					37
38					38
39					39
40					40

E9-9

	Date	Account Titles	Debit	Credit	
1	(a)				1
2	Jan. 15				2
3					3
4					4
5	20				5
6					6
7					7
8					8
9	Feb 10				9
10					10
11					11
12	15				12
13					13
14					14
15	(b)				15
16					16

E9-10

	Date	Account Titles	Debit	Credit	
17					17
18	Date	Account Titles			18
19	(a)	2012			19
20	Nov. 1		Debit	Credit	20
21					21
22					22
23	Dec. 11				23
24					24
25					25
26	16				26
27					27
28					28
29	31				29
30					30
31					31
32		Calculation of interest:			32
33					33
34					34
35					35
36					36
37	(b)	2013			37
38	Nov. 1				38
39					39
40					40
41					41

E9-11

	Date	Account Titles	Debit	Credit	
1		2012			1
2	May 1				2
3					3
4					4
5	Dec. 31				5
6					6
7					7
8	31				8
9					9
10					10
11		2013			11
12	May 1				12
13					13
14					14
15					15
16					16
17	**E9-12**				17
18	4/1/12				18
19					19
20					20
21	7/1/12				21
22					22
23					23
24	12/31/12				24
25					25
26					26
27					27
28					28
29					29
30	4/1/13				30
31					31
32					32
33					33
34					34
35					35
36	4/1/13				36
37					37
38					38
39					39
40					40

E9-13

	Date	Account Titles	Debit	Credit	
1	(a)				1
2	May 2				2
3					3
4					4
5	(b)				5
6	Nov. 2				6
7					7
8					8
9					9
10	(c)				10
11	Nov. 2				11
12					12
13					13

E9-14

(a)		
1		1
2		2
3		3
4		4
5		5
6		6
7		7
8		8
9	(b) Accounts receivable	9
10	turnover ratio =	10
11		11
12		12
13		13
14		14
15	(c) Average collection	15
16	period in days =	16
17		17
18		18
19		19
20		20
21		21
22		22

		Account Titles	Debit	Credit	
1	1.				1
2					2
3					3
4	2.				4
5					5
6					6
7	3.				7
8					8
9					9
10	4.				10
11					11
12					12
13	5.				13
14					14
15					15
16					16
17					17
18					18
19					19
20					20

(b)

Accounts Receivable	
Bal. 960,000	

Allowance for Doubtful Accounts	
	Bal. 80,000

(c)

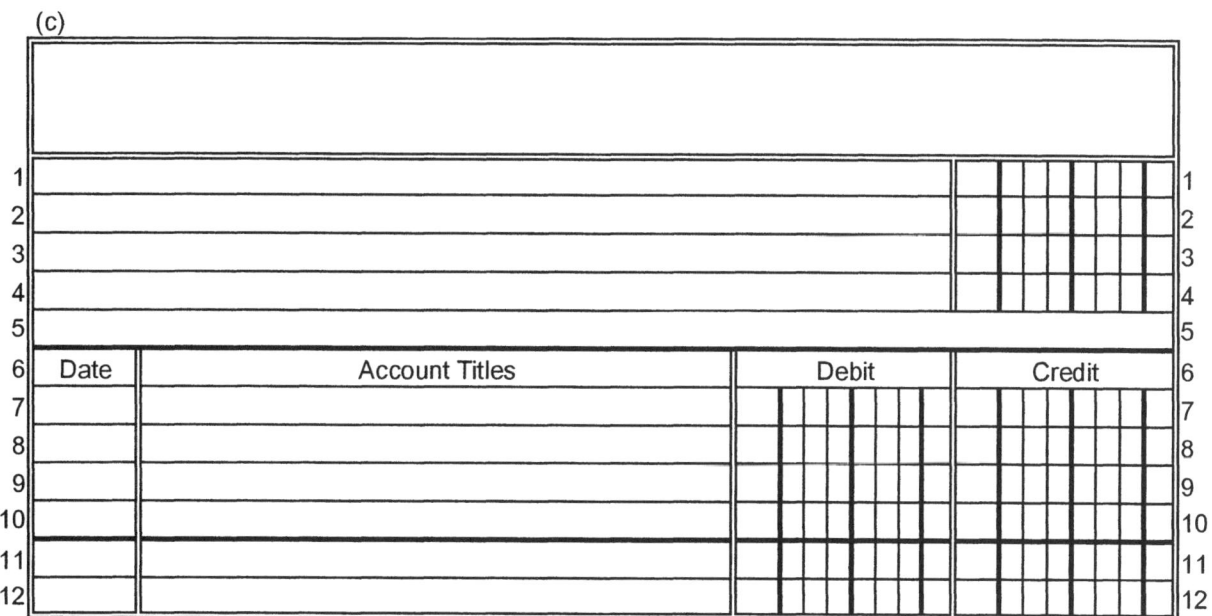

	Date	Account Titles	Debit	Credit	
1					1
2					2
3					3
4					4
5					5
6					6
7					7
8					8
9					9
10					10
11					11
12					12

(d)

1	Accounts receivable turnover ratio =	1
2		2
3		3
4		4
5		5
6		6
7		7
8		8
9		9
10		10

(a), (b), and (c)

	Date	Account Titles	Debit	Credit	
1	(a)				1
2	Dec. 31				2
3					3
4					4
5					5
6	(b)	(1) 2013			6
7	Mar. 31				7
8					8
9					9
10					10
11		(2)			11
12	May 31				12
13					13
14					14
15	31				15
16					16
17					17
18					18
19	(c)	2013			19
20	Dec. 31				20
21					21
22					22

(a) & (b)

Bad Debts Expense

	Date	Explanation	Ref.	Debit	Credit	Balance	
1							1
2							2
3							3

Allowance for Doubtful Accounts

	Date	Explanation	Ref.	Debit	Credit	Balance	
1	2012						1
2	Dec. 31	Balance	√			1 2 0 0 0	2
3							3
4							4
5							5
6							6
7							7

(a)

	Total	Number of Days Outstanding				
		0 - 30	31 - 60	61 - 90	91 - 120	Over 120
1 Accounts receivable	$ 2 0 0 0 0 0	$ 7 7 0 0 0	$ 4 6 0 0 0	$ 3 9 0 0 0	$ 2 3 0 0 0	$ 1 5 0 0 0	1
2							2
3 % uncollectible		1%	4%	5%	8%	10%	3
4							4
5 Estimated Bad Debts							5

	Date	Account Titles	Debit	Credit	
1	(b)				1
2					2
3					3
4	(c)				4
5					5
6					6
7	(d)				7
8					8
9					9
10					10
11					11
12					12
13					13
14					14
15					15

(e)

1		1
2		2
3		3
4		4
5		5

	Date	Account Titles	Debit	Credit	
1	(a)				1
2					2
3					3
4					4
5	Date	Account Titles	Debit	Credit	5
6	(b) (1)				6
7	Dec. 31				7
8					8
9					9
10	(2)				10
11	Dec. 31				11
12					12
13					13
14					14
15	(c) (1)				15
16	Dec. 31				16
17					17
18					18
19					19
20	(2)				20
21	Dec. 31				21
22					22
23					23
24					24
25					25
26	(d)				26
27					27
28					28
29					29
30					30
31	(e)				31
32					32
33					33
34					34
35					35
36	(f)				36
37					37
38					38
39					39
40					40

(a)

	Date	Account Titles	Debit	Credit	
1	Oct. 7				1
2					2
3					3
4	12				4
5					5
6					6
7					7
8	15				8
9					9
10					10
11	15				11
12					12
13					13
14					14
15					15
16	24				16
17					17
18					18
19					19
20					20
21	31				21
22					22
23					23
24					24
25					25
26					26
27					27
28					28
29					29
30					30
31					31
32					32
33					33
34					34
35					35
36					36
37					37
38					38
39					39
40					40

(b)

Notes Receivable

	Date	Explanation	Ref.	Debit	Credit	Balance	
1	Oct 1	Balance	√			3 3 0 0 0	1
2							2
3							3
4							4

Accounts Receivable

	Date	Explanation	Ref.	Debit	Credit	Balance	
1							1
2							2
3							3
4							4

Interest Receivable

	Date	Explanation	Ref.	Debit	Credit	Balance	
1	Oct 1	Balance	√			1 7 0	1
2							2
3							3
4							4
5							5

(c)

	Assets		
1			1
2	Current Assets		2
3			3
4			4
5			5
6			6
7			7
8			8

	Date	Account Titles	Debit	Credit	
1	Jan. 5				1
2					2
3					3
4	20				4
5					5
6					6
7					7
8	Feb. 18				8
9					9
10					10
11	Apr. 20				11
12					12
13					13
14					14
15	30				15
16					16
17					17
18					18
19	May 25				19
20					20
21					21
22	Aug. 18				22
23					23
24					24
25					25
26	25				26
27					27
28					28
29					29
30	Sept. 1				30
31					31
32					32
33					33
34					34
35					35
36					36
37					37
38					38
39					39
40					40

		Account Titles	Debit	Credit	
1	1.				1
2					2
3					3
4	2.				4
5					5
6					6
7	3.				7
8					8
9					9
10	4.				10
11					11
12					12
13	5.				13
14					14
15					15
16					16
17					17
18					18
19					19
20					20

(b)

Accounts Receivable	
Bal. 250,000	

Allowance for Doubtful Accounts	
	Bal. 15,000

(c)

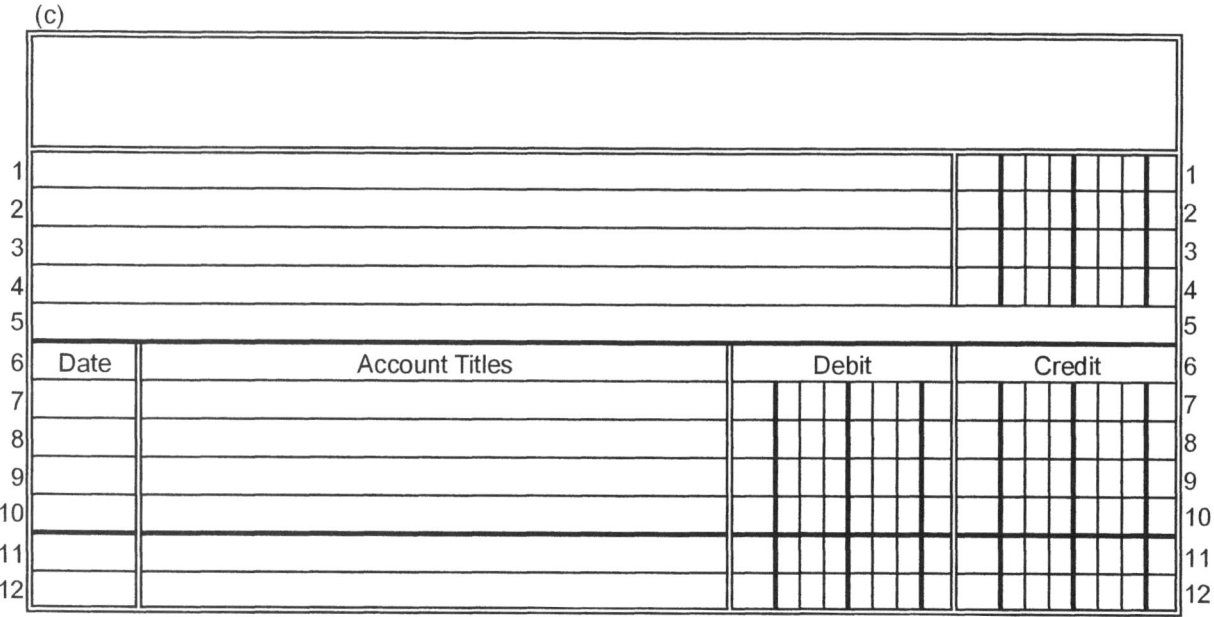

	Date	Account Titles	Debit	Credit	
1					1
2					2
3					3
4					4
5					5
6					6
7					7
8					8
9					9
10					10
11					11
12					12

(d)

1	Accounts Receivable turnover ratio =	1
2		2
3		3
4		4
5		5
6		6
7		7
8		8
9		9
10		10

(a), (b), and (c)

	Date	Account Titles	Debit	Credit	
1	(a)				1
2	Dec. 31				2
3					3
4					4
5					5
6	(b)	(1) 2013			6
7	Mar. 1				7
8					8
9					9
10					10
11		(2)			11
12	May 1				12
13					13
14					14
15	1				15
16					16
17					17
18					18
19	(c)	2013			19
20	Dec. 31				20
21					21
22					22

(a) & (b)

Bad Debts Expense

	Date	Explanation	Ref.	Debit	Credit	Balance	
1							1
2							2
3							3

Allowance for Doubtful Accounts

	Date	Explanation	Ref.	Debit	Credit	Balance	
1	2012						1
2	Dec. 31	Balance	√			1 6 0 0 0	2
3							3
4							4
5							5
6							6
7							7

(a)

	Total	Number of Days Outstanding				
		0 - 30	31 - 60	61 - 90	91 - 120	Over 120
1 Accounts receivable	$ 375000	$ 220000	$ 90000	$ 40000	$ 100000	$ 15000
2						
3 % uncollectible		1%	4%	5%	8%	10%
4						
5 Estimated Bad Debts						

	Date	Account Titles	Debit	Credit	
1	(b)				1
2					2
3					3
4	(c)				4
5					5
6					6
7	(d)				7
8					8
9					9
10					10
11					11
12					12
13					13
14					14
15					15

(e)

	Date	Account Titles	Debit	Credit	
1	(a) (1)				1
2	Dec. 31				2
3					3
4					4
5					5
6	(2)				6
7	Dec. 31				7
8					8
9					9
10					10
11	(b) (1)				11
12	Dec. 31				12
13					13
14					14
15					15
16	(2)				16
17	Dec. 31				17
18					18
19					19
20	(c)				20
21					21
22					22
23					23
24					24
25	(d)				25
26					26
27					27
28					28
29					29
30					30
31	(e)				31
32	(1)				32
33					33
34					34
35	(2)				35
36					36
37					37

(a)

	Date	Account Titles	Debit	Credit	
1	July 5				1
2					2
3					3
4	14				4
5					5
6					6
7					7
8	14				8
9					9
10					10
11	15				11
12					12
13					13
14					14
15					15
16	25				16
17					17
18					18
19					19
20					20
21	31				21
22					22
23					23
24					24
25					25
26					26
27					27
28					28
29					29
30					30
31					31
32					32
33					33
34					34
35					35
36					36
37					37
38					38
39					39
40					40

(b)

Notes Receivable

	Date	Explanation	Ref.	Debit	Credit	Balance	
1	July 1	Balance	√			5 7 0 0 0	1
2							2
3							3
4							4

Accounts Receivable

	Date	Explanation	Ref.	Debit	Credit	Balance	
1							1
2							2
3							3
4							4

Interest Receivable

	Date	Explanation	Ref.	Debit	Credit	Balance	
1	July 1	Balance	√			4 2 0	1
2							2
3							3
4							4
5							5

(c)

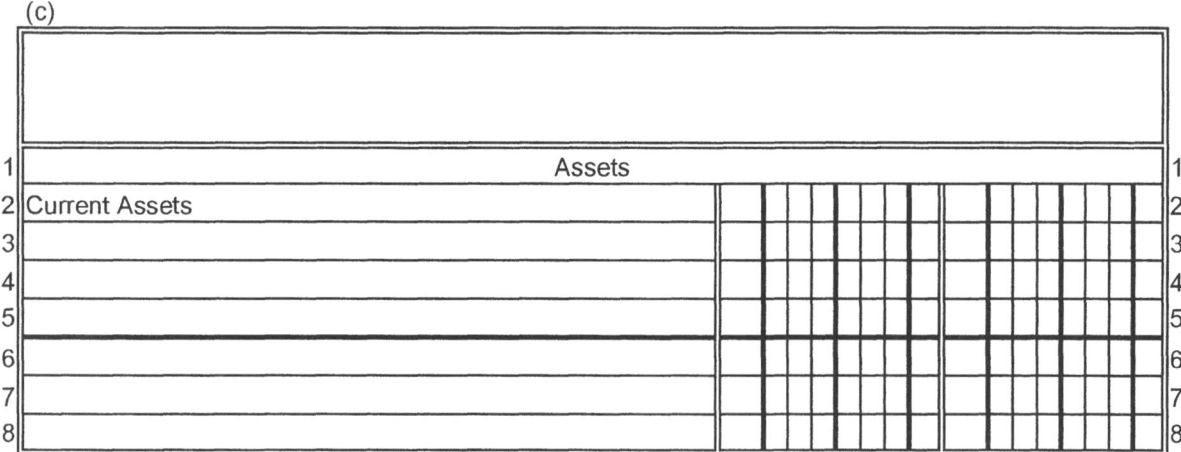

	Assets		
1			1
2	Current Assets		2
3			3
4			4
5			5
6			6
7			7
8			8

	Date	Account Titles	Debit	Credit	
1	Jan. 5				1
2					2
3					3
4	Feb. 2				4
5					5
6					6
7	12				7
8					8
9					9
10	26				10
11					11
12					12
13	Apr. 5				13
14					14
15					15
16	12				16
17					17
18					18
19					19
20	June 2				20
21					21
22					22
23					23
24	July 5				24
25					25
26					26
27					27
28	15				28
29					29
30					30
31	Oct. 15				31
32					32
33					33
34					34
35					35
36					36
37					37
38					38
39					39
40					40

(a)

	Date	Account Titles	Debit	Credit	
1	Jan. 1				1
2					2
3					3
4					4
5	3				5
6					6
7					7
8	8				8
9					9
10					10
11	11				11
12					12
13					13
14					14
15					15
16					16
17	15				17
18					18
19					19
20					20
21					21
22					22
23					23
24	17				24
25					25
26					26
27	21				27
28					28
29					29
30	24				30
31					31
32					32
33					33
34					34
35					35
36	27				36
37					37
38					38
39	31				39
40					40

(a) (Continued)

	Date	Account Titles	Debit	Credit	
1		Adjusting Entries			1
2	Jan. 31				2
3					3
4					4
5	31				5
6					6
7					7
8	31				8
9					9
10					10

(b)

Porter Company
Adjusted Trial Balance
January 31, 2012

		Debit	Credit	
1				1
2	Cash			2
3	Notes Receivable			3
4	Accounts Receivable			4
5	Allowance for Doubtful Accounts			5
6	Interest Receivable			6
7	Inventory			7
8	Supplies			8
9	Accounts Payable			9
10	Owner's Capital			10
11	Sales Revenue			11
12	Cost of Goods Sold			12
13	Supplies Expense			13
14	Bad Debts Expense			14
15	Service Charge Expense			15
16	Other Operating Expenses			16
17	Interest Revenue			17
18				18
19				19
20				20
21				21
22				22
23				23
24				24
25				25

(b)   Optional T accounts for accounts with multiple transactions

Cash		Supplies	
1/1 Bal	13,100		

		Accounts Payable	
		1/1 Bal.	8,750

Accounts Receivable			
1/1Bal	19,780		

		Sales Revenue	

Allowance for Doubtful Accounts		Cost of Goods Sold	
	1/1 Bal. 800		

Inventory			
1/1 Bal.	9,400		

(c)

Porter Company
Income Statement
For the Month Ending January 31, 2012

1			
2			
3			
4			
5			
6			
7			
8			
9			
10			
11			
12			
13			
14			
15			

Porter Company
Owner's Equity Statement
For the Month Ending January 31, 2012

1	
2	
3	
4	
5	
6	
7	
8	
9	
10	
11	
12	
13	
14	
15	
16	
17	
18	
19	
20	

(c) (Continued)

Porter Company
Balance Sheet
January 31, 2012

	Assets					
1						
2						
3						
4						
5						
6						
7						
8						
9						
10						
11						
12						
13	Liabilities and Owner's Equity					
14						
15						
16						
17						
18						
19						
20						
21						
22						
23						
24						
25						
26						
27						
28						
29						
30						
31						
32						
33						
34						
35						
36						
37						
38						
39						
40						

(a)

		SEK Company						
		Accounts Receivable Aging Schedule						
		May 31, 2012						
		Proportion of Total %	Amount in Category		Probability of Non-Collection %	Estimated Uncollectible Amount		
1	Not yet due							1
2								2
3	Less than 30 days past due							3
4								4
5	30 to 60 days past due							5
6								6
7	61 to 120 days past due							7
8								8
9	121 to 180 days past due							9
10								10
11	Over 180 days past due							11
12								12
13	Totals							13
14								14

(b)

	SEK Company				
	Analysis of Allowance for Doubtful Accounts				
	May 31, 2012				
1					1
2					2
3					3
4					4
5					5
6					6
7					7
8					8
9					9
10	Account Titles	Debit		Credit	10
11					11
12					12
13					13
14					14
15					15

(c)

	1. Steps to Improve the Accounts Receivable Situation	2. Risks and Costs Involved	
1			1
2			2
3			3
4			4
5			5
6			6
7			7
8			8
9			9
10			10
11			11
12			12
13			13
14			14
15			15
16			16
17			17
18			18
19			19
20			20
21			21
22			22
23			23
24			24
25			25
26			26
27			27
28			28
29			29
30			30
31			31
32			32
33			33
34			34
35			35
36			36
37			37
38			38
39			39
40			40

(a)	2012	2011	2010
1 Net credit sales			
2			
3 Credit and collection expenses			
4 Collection agency fees			
5 Salary of accounts receivable clerk			
6 Uncollectible accounts			
7 Billing and mailing costs			
8 Credit investigation fees			
9			
10 Total			
11			
12			
13 Total expenses as a percentage			
14 of net credit sales			
15			
16 (b) Average accounts receivable			
17			
18 Investment earnings			
19			
20 Total credit and collection			
21 expenses per above			
22 Add: Investment earnings			
23 Net credit and collection			
24 expenses			
25			
26 Net expenses as a percentage			
27 of net credit sales			
28			
29 (c)			
30			
31			
32			
33			
34			
35			
36			
37			
38			
39			
40			

BE10-5

	Year	Book Value	X	Rate	=	Depreciation
	1					
	2					

BE10-6

Depreciation cost per unit:

	Year	Calculation	Amount
	1		
	2		

BE10-7

1			
2			
3			
4			
5			
6			

BE10-8	Account Titles	Debit	Credit
1.			
2.			

BE10-9	Account Titles	Debit	Credit
(a)			
(b)			

Calculations:

BE10-10

	Account Titles	Debit	Credit	
1				1
2	(a)			2
3				3
4				4
5	(b)			5
6				6
7				7
8				8
9				9
10	Calculations:			10
11				11
12				12
13				13
14				14
15				15
16				16

BE10-11

17

18 (a)   Depletion cost per unit =

19

20

21   Depletion expense =

22

23

24

	Account Titles	Debit	Credit	
25				25
26				26
27				27
28				28
29	(b)			29
30				30
31				31

	BE10-12 Account Titles	Debit	Credit	
32				32
33	(a)			33
34				34
35				35
36	(b)			36
37				37
38				38
39				39
40				40

BE10-13

Lucy Company			
Balance Sheet (Partial)			
December 31, 2012			

		Debit	Credit
1			
2			
3			
4			
5			
6			
7			
8			
9			
10			
11			
12			
13			
14			
15			
16			
17			

*BE10-15

Account Titles	Debit	Credit

Calculations:

*BE10-16	Account Titles	Debit	Credit
1			
2			
3			
4			
5			
6			
7	Calculations:		
8			
9			
10			
11			
12			
13			
14			
15			
16			
17			
18			
19			
20			
21			
22			
23			
24			
25			
26			
27			
28			
29			
30			
31			
32			
33			
34			
35			
36			
37			
38			
39			
40			

DO IT! 10-1

1. Cost of truck:
2.
3.
4.
5.
6.
7.
8. Other costs:
9.
10.
11.
12.

DO IT! 10-2

14. Depreciation expense =
15.
16.

	Account Titles	Debit	Credit

DO IT! 10-3

24. Original depreciation expense =
25.
26. Accumulated depreciation after 3 years =
27.
28. Revised annual depreciation:
29.
30.
31.
32.
33.
34.
35.
36.
37.
38.
39.
40.

		Account Titles	Debit	Credit	
1	(a)	Sale of truck for cash at a gain:			1
2					2
3					3
4					4
5					5
6					6
7	(b)	Sale of truck for cash at a loss:			7
8					8
9					9
10					10
11					11
12					12
13					13
14					14
15					15
16					16
17					17
18					18
19					19
20					20
21					21
22					22
23					23
24					24
25					25
26					26
27					27
28					28
29					29
30					30

E10-3

1	(a)　Cost of land:	
2		
3		
4		
5		
6		
7		
8		
9	(b)	
10		
11		
12		
13		
14		
15		

E10-5

(a)　Depreciation cost per unit =

(b) Year	Computation Units of Activity	X	Depreciation Cost/Unit	=	Annual Depreciation Expense	End of Year Accumulated Depreciation	Book Value
2012							
2013							
2014							
2015							

(a)

(1)	2012:	
	2013:	
(2)	Calculation of depreciation cost per unit:	
	2012:	
	2013:	
(3)	2012:	
	2013:	

(b)	Account Tiles	Debit	Credit
(1)			
(2)	Balance sheet presentation:		

E10-8

	Building	Warehouse	
1 (a)			1
2			2
3			3
4			4
5			5
6			6
7			7
8			8
9			9

10 (b)				10
11	Date	Account Titles	Debit	Credit	11
12	Dec. 31				12
13					13
14					14
15					15

E10-9

16					16
17	Date	Account Titles	Debit	Credit	17
18	Jan. 1				18
19					19
20					20
21	June 30				21
22					22
23					23
24	30				24
25					25
26					26
27					27
28					28
29	Dec. 31				29
30					30
31					31
32	31				32
33					33
34					34
35					35
36					36
37					37
38					38
39					39
40					40

		Account Titles	Debit	Credit	
1	(a)				1
2					2
3					3
4					4
5					5
6					6
7	(b)				7
8					8
9					9
10					10
11					11
12					12
13					13
14					14
15					15
16	(c)				16
17					17
18					18
19					19
20					20
21					21
22	(d)				22
23					23
24					24
25					25
26					26
27					27
28					28
29					29
30					30
31					31
32					32
33					33
34					34
35					35
36					36
37					37
38					38
39					39
40					40

E10-11

	Date	Account Titles	Debit	Credit	
1	(a)				1
2	Dec. 31				2
3					3
4					4
5	Calculations				5
6					6
7					7
8					8
9					9
10	(b)				10
11					11
12					12

E10-12

	Date	Account Titles	Debit	Credit	
14	Date	Account Titles	Debit	Credit	14
15	Dec. 31				15
16					16
17					17

E10-13

	Date	Account Titles	Debit	Credit	
19	Date	Account Titles	Debit	Credit	19
20	1/2/12				20
21					21
22					22
23	4/1/12				23
24					24
25					25
26	7/1/12				26
27					27
28					28
29	9/1/12				29
30					30
31					31
32	12/31/12				32
33					33
34					34
35					35
36					36
37	Ending balances:				37
38	Patent				38
39	Goodwill				39
40	Franchise				40
41	R&D expense				41

*E10-15

	Account Titles	Debit	Credit	
1	(a)			1
2				2
3				3
4				4
5				5
6				6

	Calculations:			
7				7
8				8
9				9
10				10
11				11
12				12
13				13
14				14
15				15
16				16
17				17

	Account Titles	Debit	Credit	
18	(b)			18
19				19
20				20
21				21
22				22
23				23

	Calculations:			
24				24
25				25
26				26
27				27
28				28
29				29
30				30
31				31
32				32
33				33
34				34
35				35
36				36
37				37
38				38
39				39
40				40

	Date	Account Titles	Debit	Credit	
1	(a)				1
2					2
3					3
4					4
5					5
6					6
7	Calculations:				7
8					8
9					9
10					10
11					11
12					12
13					13
14	(b)	Account Titles	Debit	Credit	14
15					15
16					16
17					17
18					18
19					19
20	Calculations:				20
21					21
22					22
23					23
24					24
25					25
26					26
27					27
28					28
29					29
30					30
31					31
32					32
33					33
34					34
35					35
36					36
37					37
38					38
39					39
40					40

Item	Land	Building	Other Accounts	
			Amount	Account Titles
1.				
2.				
3.				
4.				
5.				
6.				
7.				
8.				
9.				
10.				

		Year	Computation	Cumulative, 12/31	
1	(a)		BUS 1		1
2					2
3		2010			3
4					4
5		2011			5
6					6
7		2012			7
8					8
9					9
10					10
11					11
12			BUS 2		12
13					13
14		2010			14
15					15
16		2011			16
17					17
18		2012			18
19					19
20					20
21			BUS 3		21
22					22
23		2011			23
24					24
25		2012			25
26					26
27					27
28					28
29					29
30	(b)	Year	Depreciation Computation	Expense	30
31			BUS 2		31
32		(1) 2010			32
33					33
34		(2) 2011			34
35					35
36					36
37					37
38					38
39					39
40					40

Total cost of machinery:

(a) (1)

Account Titles	Debit	Credit

(2) Annual depreciation:

Account Titles	Debit	Credit

(b) (1)

(2)	Year	Book Value at Beginning of Year	DDB Rate	Annual Depreciation Expense	Accumulated Depreciation
	2012				
	2013				
	2014				
	2015				

(b) (Continued) and (c)

1 (b) (3) Depreciation cost per unit:

2

3

4

5

6

7

8

	Year	Computation	Depreciation Expense
9			
10			
11			
12	2012		
13			
14	2013		
15			
16	2014		
17			
18	2015		
19			

20 (c)

21

22

23

24

25

26

27

28

29

30

31

32

33

34

35

36

37

38

39

40

	Year		Depreciation Expense	Accumulated Depreciation	
1	2010				1
2	2011				2
3	2012				3
4	2013				4
5	2014				5
6	2015				6
7	2016				7
8					8
9					9
10					10
11					11
12	Supporting calculations:				12
13					13
14					14
15					15
16					16
17					17
18					18
19					19
20					20
21					21
22					22
23					23
24					24
25					25
26					26
27					27
28					28
29					29
30					30
31					31
32					32
33					33
34					34
35					35
36					36
37					37
38					38
39					39
40					40

(a)

	Date	Account Titles	Debit	Credit	
1	Apr. 1				1
2					2
3					3
4	May 1				4
5					5
6					6
7	1				7
8					8
9					9
10					10
11					11
12	Calculations:				12
13					13
14					14
15					15
16					16
17					17
18					18
19	June 1				19
20					20
21					21
22					22
23	July 1				23
24					24
25					25
26	Dec. 31				26
27					27
28					28
29	31				29
30					30
31					31
32	Calculations:				32
33					33
34					34
35					35
36					36
37					37
38					38
39					39
40					40

(b)

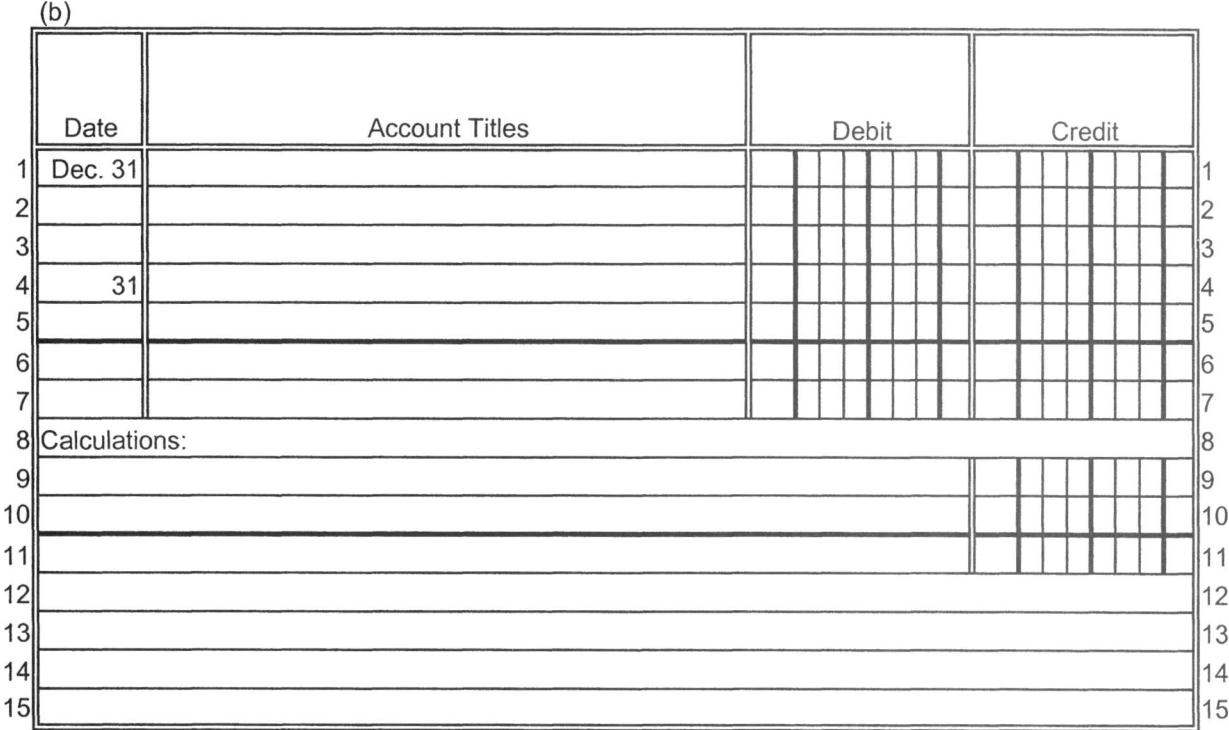

	Date	Account Titles	Debit	Credit	
1	Dec. 31				1
2					2
3					3
4	31				4
5					5
6					6
7					7
8	Calculations:				8
9					9
10					10
11					11
12					12
13					13
14					14
15					15

(c)

Alina Company

Partial Balance Sheet

December 31, 2013

1			1
2			2
3			3
4			4
5			5
6			6
7			7
8			8
9			9
10			10
11			11
12			12
13			13
14			14
15			15
16			16
17			17
18			18
19			19
20			20

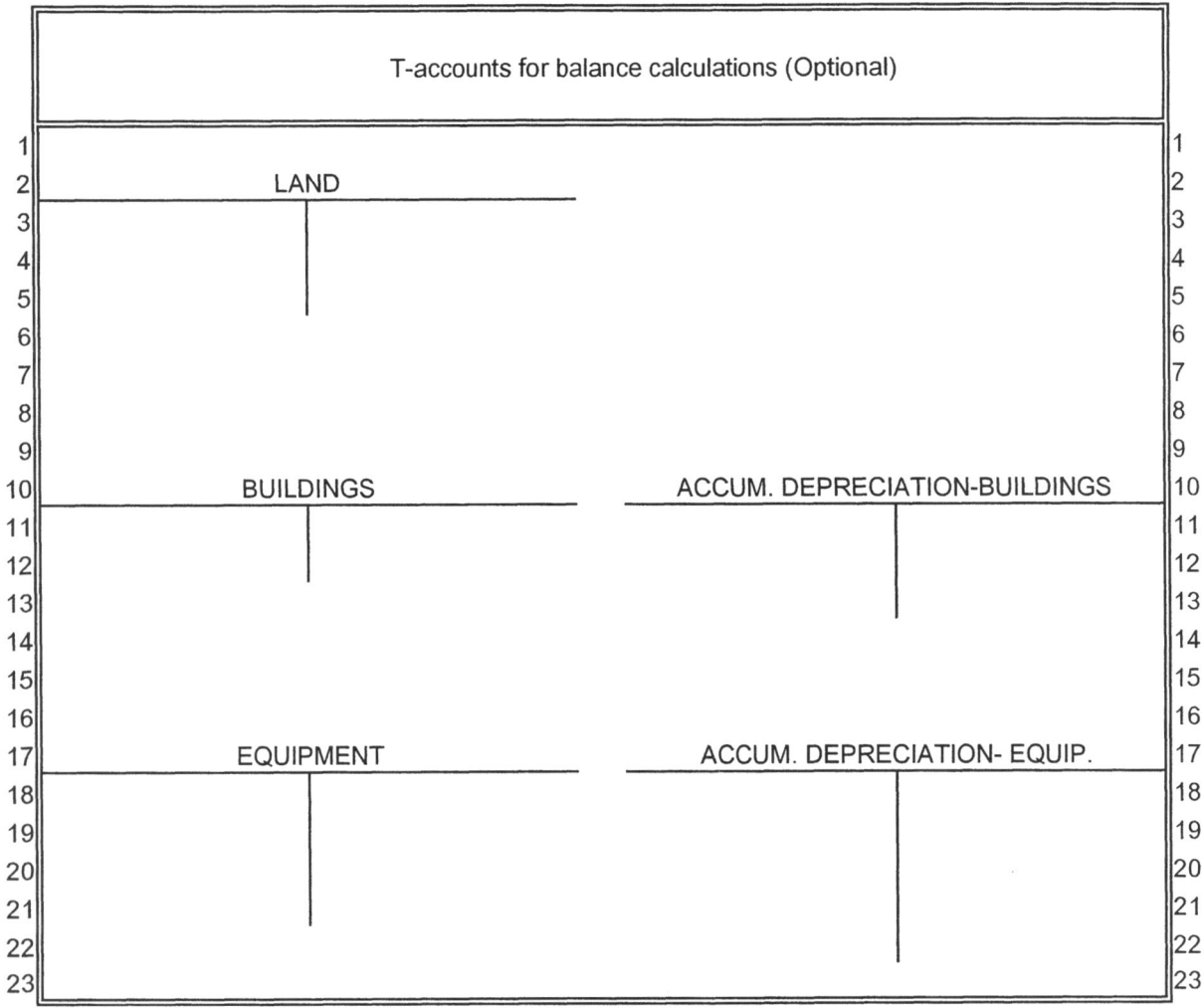

T-accounts for balance calculations (Optional)

LAND

BUILDINGS   ACCUM. DEPRECIATION-BUILDINGS

EQUIPMENT   ACCUM. DEPRECIATION- EQUIP.

	Account Titles	Debit	Credit	
1	(a)			1
2				2
3				3
4				4
5				5
6				6
7				7
8	(b)			8
9				9
10				10
11				11
12				12
13				13
14				14
15				15
16	(c)			16
17				17
18				18
19				19
20				20
21				21
22				22
23				23
24				24
25				25
26				26
27				27
28				28
29				29
30				30
31				31
32				32
33				33
34				34
35				35
36				36
37				37
38				38
39				39
40				40

	Date	Account Titles	Debit	Credit	
1	(a)				1
2	Jan. 2				2
3					3
4					4
5	Jan. -				5
6	June				6
7					7
8					8
9	Sept. 1				9
10					10
11					11
12	Oct. 1				12
13					13
14					14
15					15
16	(b)				16
17	Dec. 31				17
18					18
19	31				19
20					20
21					21
22					22
23	(c)	Intangible Assets:			23
24					24
25					25
26					26
27					27
28					28
29					29
30					30
31					31
32					32
33					33
34					34
35					35
36					36
37					37
38					38
39					39
40					40

		Account Titles	Debit	Credit	
1	1.				1
2					2
3					3
4					4
5					5
6					6
7					7
8					8
9					9
10	2.				10
11					11
12					12
13					13
14					14
15					15
16					16
17					17
18					18
19					19
20					20
21					21
22					22
23					23
24					24
25					25
26					26
27					27
28					28
29					29
30					30

Item	Land	Building	Other Accounts	
			Amount	Account Titles
1				
2	1.			
3				
4	2.			
5				
6	3.			
7				
8	4.			
9				
10	5.			
11				
12	6.			
13				
14	7.			
15				
16	8.			
17				
18	9.			
19				
20	10.			
21				
22				
23				
24				
25				

	Year	Computation	Cumulative, 12/31	
(a)		MACHINE 1		1
				2
	2009			3
				4
	2010			5
				6
	2011			7
				8
	2012			9
				10
				11
		MACHINE 2		12
				13
	2010			14
				15
	2011			16
				17
	2012			18
				19
				20
		MACHINE 3		21
				22
	2012			23
				24
				25
				26
				27
				28
				29
(b)	Year	Depreciation Computation	Expense	30
		MACHINE 2		31
	(1) 2010			32
				33
	(2) 2011			34
				35
				36
				37
				38
				39
				40

Total cost of machinery:

(a) (1)

Account Titles	Debit	Credit

(2) Annual depreciation:

Account Titles	Debit	Credit

(b) (1)

(2) Year	Book Value at Beginning of Year	DDB Rate	Annual Depreciation Expense	Accumulated Depreciation
2012				
2013				
2014				
2015				

(b) (Continued) and (c)

(b) (3) Depreciation cost per unit:

	Year	Computation	Depreciation Expense
	2012		
	2013		
	2014		
	2015		

(c)

	Year		Depreciation Expense	Accumulated Depreciation	
1	2010				1
2	2011				2
3	2012				3
4	2013				4
5	2014				5
6	2015				6
7	2016				7
8					8
9					9
10					10
11					11
12	Supporting calculations:				12
13					13
14					14
15					15
16					16
17					17
18					18
19					19
20					20
21					21
22					22
23					23
24					24
25					25
26					26
27					27
28					28
29					29
30					30
31					31
32					32
33					33
34					34
35					35
36					36
37					37
38					38
39					39
40					40

(a)

	Date	Account Titles	Debit	Credit	
1	Apr. 1				1
2					2
3					3
4	May 1				4
5					5
6					6
7	1				7
8					8
9					9
10					10
11					11
12	Calculations:				12
13					13
14					14
15					15
16					16
17					17
18					18
19	June 1				19
20					20
21					21
22					22
23	July 1				23
24					24
25					25
26	Dec. 31				26
27					27
28					28
29	31				29
30					30
31					31
32	Calculations:				32
33					33
34					34
35					35
36					36
37					37
38					38
39					39
40					40

(b)

	Date	Account Titles	Debit	Credit	
1	Dec. 31				1
2					2
3					3
4	31				4
5					5
6					6
7					7
8	Calculations:				8
9					9
10					10
11					11
12					12
13					13
14					14
15					15

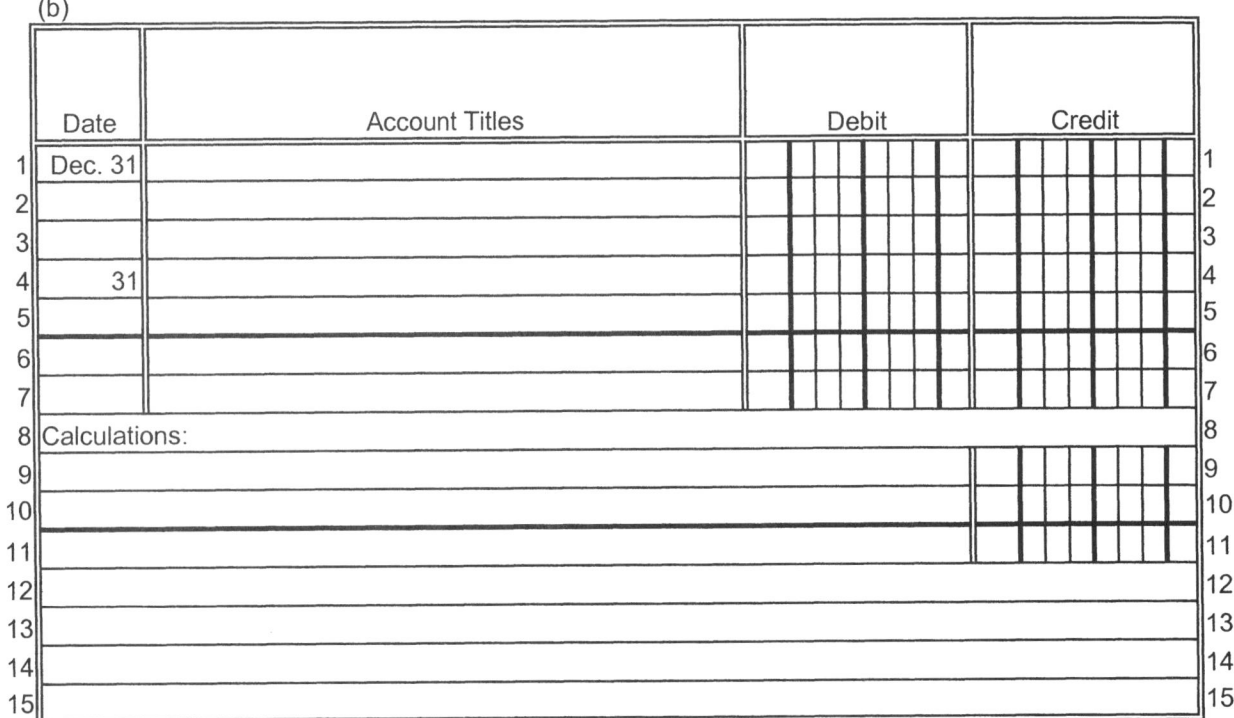

(c)

Ramaswami Company

Partial Balance Sheet

December 31, 2013

1			1
2			2
3			3
4			4
5			5
6			6
7			7
8			8
9			9
10			10
11			11
12			12
13			13
14			14
15			15
16			16
17			17
18			18
19			19
20			20

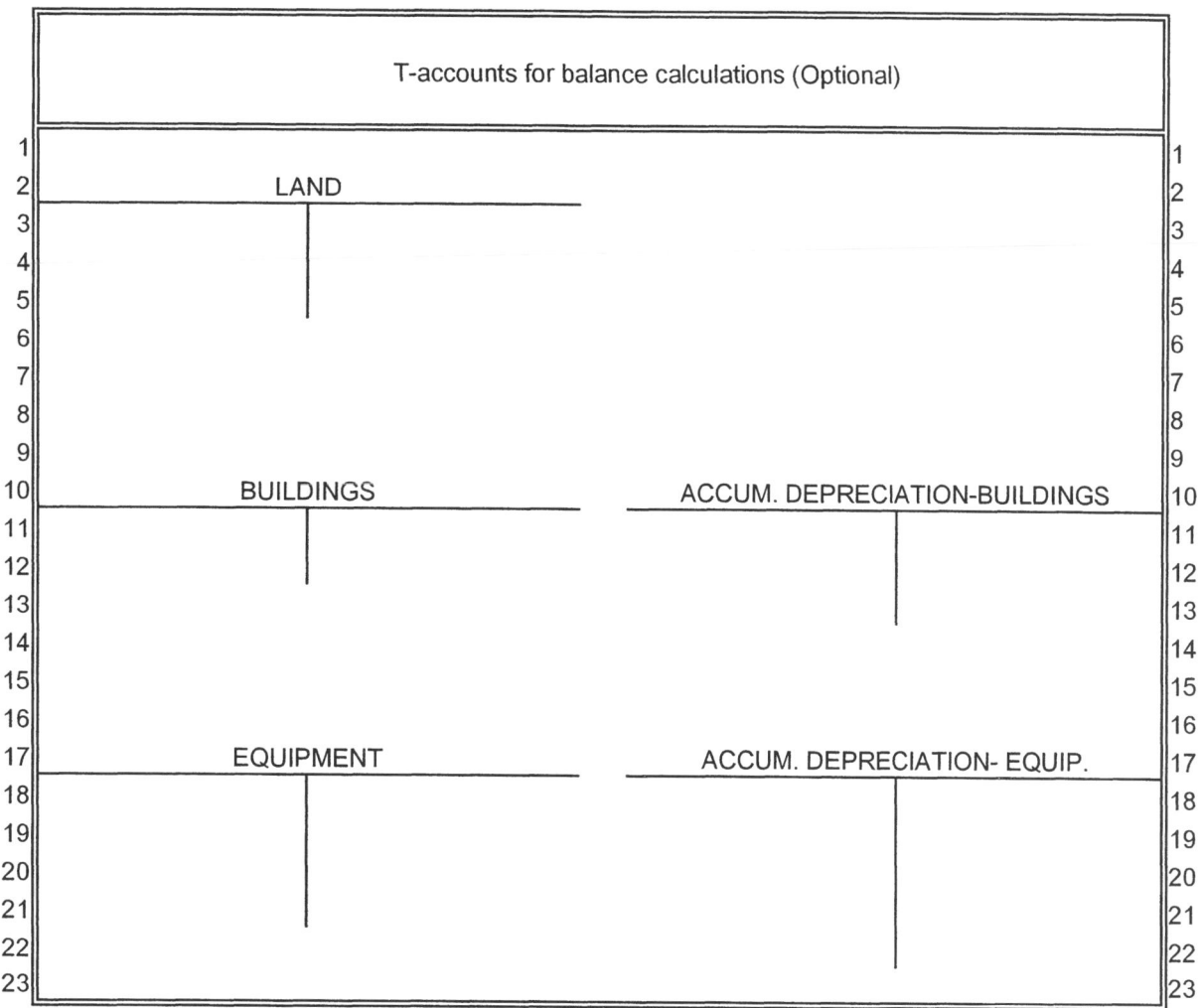

Account Titles	Debit	Credit
1 (a)		
2		
3		
4		
5		
6		
7		
8 (b)		
9		
10		
11		
12		
13		
14		
15		
16 (c)		
17		
18		
19		
20		

	Date	Account Titles	Debit	Credit	
1	(a)				1
2	Jan. 2				2
3					3
4					4
5	Jan -				5
6	June				6
7					7
8					8
9	Sept. 1				9
10					10
11					11
12					12
13	Oct. 1				13
14					14
15					15
16	(b)				16
17	Dec. 31				17
18					18
19					19
20	31				20
21					21
22					22
23	(c)	Intangible Assets:			23
24					24
25					25
26					26
27					27
28					28
29					29
30					30
31	(d)				31
32					32
33					33
34					34
35					35
36					36
37					37
38					38
39					39
40					40

		Account Titles	Debit	Credit	
1	1.				1
2					2
3					3
4					4
5					5
6					6
7					7
8					8
9					9
10	2.				10
11					11
12					12
13					13
14					14
15					15
16					16
17					17
18					18
19					19
20					20
21					21
22					22
23					23
24					24
25					25
26					26
27					27
28					28
29					29
30					30

(a)

		Account Titles	Debit	Credit	
1	1.				1
2					2
3					3
4	2.				4
5					5
6					6
7					7
8					8
9					9
10					10
11					11
12	3.				12
13					13
14					14
15					15
16					16
17					17
18	4.				18
19					19
20					20
21	5.				21
22					22
23					23
24	6.				24
25					25
26					26
27	7.				27
28					28
29					29
30	8.				30
31					31
32					32
33	9.				33
34					34
35					35
36	10.				36
37					37
38					38
39					39
40					40

(a) (Continued)

		Account Titles	Debit	Credit	
1	11.				1
2					2
3					3
4	12.				4
5					5
6					6
7	13.				7
8					8
9					9
10					10
11					11
12					12
13					13
14					14
15					15
16					16
17					17
18					18
19					19
20					20
21					21
22					22
23					23
24					24
25					25
26					26
27					27
28					28
29					29
30					30
31					31
32					32
33					33
34					34
35					35
36					36
37					37
38					38
39					39
40					40

(b)

Winterschid Company Trial Balance December 31, 2012	Debits	Credits	
1	Cash			1
2	Accounts Receivable			2
3	Notes Receivable			3
4	Interest Receivable			4
5	Inventory			5
6	Prepaid Insurance			6
7	Land			7
8	Buildings			8
9	Equipment			9
10	Patents			10
11	Allowance for Doubtful Accounts			11
12	Accumulated Depreciation - Buildings			12
13	Accumulated Depreciation - Equipment			13
14	Accounts Payable			14
15	Salaries and Wages Payable			15
16	Unearned Rent Revenue			16
17	Notes Payable (due in 2013)			17
18	Interest Payable			18
19	Notes Payable (due after 2013)			19
20	Owner's Capital			20
21	Owner's Drawing			21
22	Sales Revenue			22
23	Interest Revenue			23
24	Rent Revenue			24
25	Gain on Disposal of Plant Assets			25
26	Bad Debts Expense			26
27	Cost of Goods Sold			27
28	Depreciation Expense			28
29	Insurance Expense			29
30	Interest Expense			30
31	Other Operating Expense			31
32	Amortization Expense			32
33	Salaries and Wages Expense			33
34	Totals			34
35				35
36				36
37				37
38				38
39				39

(c)

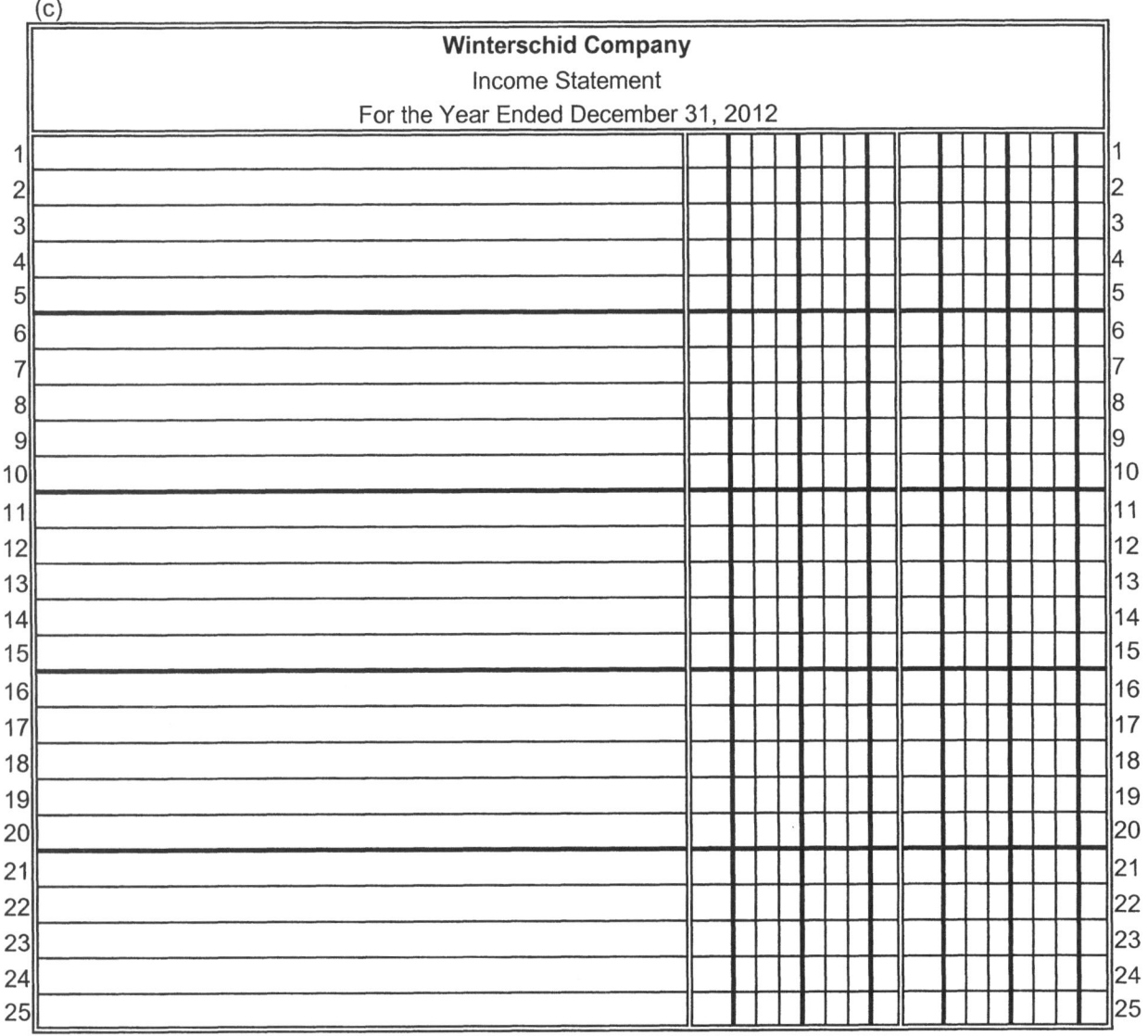

Winterschid Company

Income Statement

For the Year Ended December 31, 2012

Winterschid Company

Owner's Equity Statement

For the Year Ended December 31, 2012

(d)

Winterschid Company
Balance Sheet
December 31, 2012

Assets

Liabilities and Owner's Equity

1	(a)	Reimer Company- Straight-line method				
2						
3						
4						
5						
6						
7						
8						

Lingo Company- Double-declining-balance method

Year	Asset	Computation	Annual Depreciation	Accumulated Depreciation
2010	Building			
	Equipment			
2011	Building			
	Equipment			
2012	Building			
	Equipment			

(b) Year	Reimer Company Net Income	Lingo Co. Net Inc. as Adjusted	Computations for Lingo Company
2010			
2011			
2012			
Total			

(c)

(c) (Continued)

1	1
2	2
3	3
4	4
5	5
6	6
7	7
8	8
9	9
10	10
11	11
12	12
13	13
14	14
15	15
16	16
17	17
18	18
19	19
20	20
21	21
22	22
23	23
24	24
25	25
26	26
27	27
28	28
29	29
30	30
31	31
32	32
33	33
34	34
35	35
36	36
37	37
38	38
39	39
40	40

1	(a)
2	
3	
4	
5	
6	
7	
8	(b)
9	
10	
11	
12	
13	
14	
15	
16	
17	
18	
19	
20	
21	(c)
22	Old
23	Estimates
24	
25	
26	
27	
28	
29	
30	Revised
31	Estimates
32	
33	
34	
35	
36	
37	
38	
39	
40	

IFRS10-4

1	Warehouse component:		1
2			2
3	HVAC component:		3
4			4
5	Total component depreciation in first year:		5
6			6

IFRS10-5

Date	Account Titles	Debit	Credit	
(a)				9
				10
				11
				12
				13
(b)				14
				15
				16
				17
				18

IFRS10-6

Date	Account Titles	Debit	Credit	
				25
				26
				27
				28
				29

1	(a)		1
2			2
3			3
4	(b)		4
5			5
6			6
7			7
8	(c)		8

9	Date	Account Titles	Debit	Credit	9
10					10
11					11
12					12
13					13
14					14
15					15

16		16
17		17
18		18
19		19
20		20
21		21
22		22
23		23
24		24
25		25
26		26
27		27
28		28
29		29
30		30
31		31
32		32
33		33
34		34
35		35
36		36
37		37
38		38
39		39
40		40

BE11-2

	Date	Account Titles	Debit	Credit	
1	July 1				1
2					2
3					3
4	Dec 31				4
5					5
6					6
7					7
8					8
9	**BE11-3**				9
10					10
11					11
12					12
13					13
14					14
15	Date	Account Titles	Debit	Credit	15
16	Mar. 16				16
17					17
18					18
19					19
20					20
21					21
22					22
23					23
24					24
25					25
26					26
27					27
28					28
29					29
30					30

BE11-4

	Date	Account Titles	Debit	Credit	
1					1
2					2
3					3
4					4
5					5
6					6
7					7
8					8
9					9
10					10
11					11
12					12
13					13
14					14
15					15

BE11-6

	Date	Account Titles	Debit	Credit	
17	Date	Account Titles	Debit	Credit	17
18	Dec. 31				18
19					19
20					20
21					21

BE11-7

			Debit	Credit	
23	Gross earnings:				23
24					24
25					25
26					26
27					27
28					28
29					29
30					30
31					31
32					32
33					33
34					34

BE11-8

	Date	Account Titles	Debit	Credit	
1	Jan. 15				1
2					2
3					3
4					4
5					5
6	15				6
7					7
8					8
9					9

BE11-9

	Date	Account Titles	Debit	Credit	
11	Jan. 31				11
12					12
13					13
14					14
15					15
16					16
17					17
18					18
19					19
20					20
21					21
22					22
23					23
24					24
25					25

*BE11-11

	Date	Account Titles	Debit	Credit	
28	Jan. 31				28
29					29
30					30
31					31
32					32
33					33
34					34
35					35
36					36
37					37
38					38
39					39
40					40

DO IT! 11-2

1	(a)	Current liabilities:	1
2			2
3			3
4			4
5			5
6			6
7			7
8			8
9			9
10			10
11	(b)	Working capital:	11
12			12
13			13
14			14
15			15
16		Current ratio:	16
17			17
18			18

DO IT! 11-3

20	(a)	Net pay:	20
21			21
22			22
23			23
24			24
25			25

		Account Titles	Debit	Credit	
27					27
28	(b)				28
29					29
30					30
31					31
32					32
33					33
34					34
35					35
36					36
37					37
38					38
39					39
40					40

		Account Titles	Debit	Credit	
1					1
2					2
3					3
4					4
5					5
6					6
7					7
8					8
9					9
10					10
11					11
12					12
13					13
14					14
15					15
16					16
17					17
18					18
19					19
20					20
21					21
22					22
23					23
24					24
25					25
26					26
27					27
28					28
29					29
30					30
31					31
32					32
33					33
34					34
35					35
36					36
37					37
38					38
39					39
40					40

	Date	Account Titles	Debit	Credit	
1		July 1, 2012			1
2					2
3					3
4					4
5		November 1, 2012			5
6					6
7					7
8					8
9		December 31, 2012			9
10					10
11					11
12					12
13					13
14					14
15					15
16		February 1, 2013			16
17					17
18					18
19					19
20					20
21					21
22		April 1, 2013			22
23					23
24					24
25					25
26					26
27					27
28					28
29					29
30					30
31					31
32					32
33					33
34					34
35					35
36					36
37					37
38					38
39					39
40					40

E11-2

	Date	Account Titles	Debit	Credit	
1	(a)				1
2	June 1				2
3					3
4					4
5	(b)				5
6	June 30				6
7					7
8					8
9	(c)				9
10	Dec. 1				10
11					11
12					12
13					13
14	(d)				14
15					15
16					16

E11-3

	Date	Account Titles	Debit	Credit	
18	Date	Account Titles	Debit	Credit	18
19		**Miraz Company**			19
20	Apr. 10				20
21					21
22					22
23					23
24		**Trumpkin Company**			24
25	15				25
26					26
27					27
28					28
29					29
30					30
31					31
32					32
33					33
34					34
35					35
36					36
37					37
38					38
39					39
40					40

E11-4

	Date	Account Titles	Debit	Credit	
1	(a)				1
2	Nov. 30				2
3					3
4					4
5	(b)				5
6	Dec. 31				6
7					7
8					8
9	(c)				9
10	Mar. 31				10
11					11
12					12

E11-5

(a)   Estimated warrranties outstanding:

		Month	Estimate	Units Defective	Outstanding	
15						15
16						16
17		November				17
18		December				18
19		Total				19
20						20

Estimated warranty liability:

	Date	Account Titles	Debit	Credit	
24	(b)				24
25					25
26					26
27					27
28					28
29					29
30					30
31	(c)				31
32					32
33					33
34					34
35					35
36					36
37					37
38					38
39					39
40					40

(a)

Warwick Online Company		
Partial Balance Sheet		

1			
2			
3			
4			
5			
6			
7			
8			
9			
10			

(b)

11	
12	
13	
14	
15	
16	
17	
18	
19	
20	

(a)

1	(1)	Regular	
2		Overtime	
3		Gross earnings	
4	(2)	FICA taxes	
5	(3)	Federal income taxes	
6	(4)	State income taxes	
7	(5)	Net pay	

(b)

Date	Account Titles	Debit	Credit

(a)

Alvarez Company Payroll Register For the Week Ending January 31				
		Earnings		
Employee	Total Hours	Regular	Overtime	Gross Pay
1 L. Donnon					1
2					2
3 L. Gregoire					3
4					4
5 D. Alcazar					5
6 Totals					6

(a) Continued

Alvarez Company Payroll Register (continued) For the Week Ending January 31					
	Deductions				
	FICA Taxes	Federal Income Taxes	Health Insurance	Total	Net Pay
1 Donnon						1
2						2
3 Gregoire						3
4						4
5 Alcazar						5
6 Totals						6

(b)

	Date	Account Titles	Debit	Credit	
1	Jan 31				1
2					2
3					3
4					4
5					5
6					6
7	31				7
8					8
9					9
10					10
11					11
12					12

E11-13

(a)

1	Gross earnings:	$	8 9 0 0	State income taxes		1
2	Regular			Union dues	1 0 0	2
3	Overtime			Total deductions		3
4	Total			Net pay	$ 7 6 6 0	4
5	Deductions:			Accounts debited:		5
6	FICA taxes		8 0 0	Salaries and wages expense		6
7	Federal income taxes		1 1 4 0			7
8						8

(b)

	Date	Account Titles	Debit	Credit	
11	Feb 28				11
12					12
13					13
14					14
15					15
16					16
17					17
18					18
19	28				19
20					20
21					21

E11-14

(a)

23			23
24			24
25			25
26			26
27			27
28			28

(b)

	Date	Account Titles	Debit	Credit	
31					31
32					32
33					33
34					34
35					35
36					36
37					37
38					38
39					39
40					40

*E11-15

	Date	Account Titles	Debit	Credit	
1	Mar. 31				1
2					2
3					3
4	31				4
5					5
6					6
7					7

*E11-16

	Date	Account Titles	Debit	Credit	
1	1.				1
2					2
3					3
4					4
5	2.				5
6					6
7					7
8					8
9					9
10	3.				10
11					11
12					12
13					13
14					14
15					15
16					16
17					17
18					18
19					19
20					20
21					21
22					22
23					23
24					24
25					25
26					26
27					27
28					28

	Date	Account Titles	Debit	Credit	
1	(a)				1
2	Jan 5				2
3					3
4					4
5					5
6	12				6
7					7
8					8
9	14				9
10					10
11					11
12	20				12
13					13
14					14
15					15
16	21				16
17					17
18					18
19	25				19
20					20
21					21
22					22
23	(b) (1)				23
24	Jan 31				24
25					25
26					26
27					27
28	(2)				28
29	31				29
30					30
31					31
32					32
33					33
34					34
35					35
36					36
37					37

(c)

Montoya Company			
Balance Sheet (Partial)			
January 31, 2012			
1	Current liabilities:		
2			
3			
4			
5			
6			
7			
8			
9			
10			
11			
12			
13			
14			
15			

(a)

	Date	Account Titles	Debit	Credit	
1	Jan 2				1
2					2
3					3
4	Feb 1				4
5					5
6					6
7	Mar 31				7
8					8
9					9
10	Apr 1				10
11					11
12					12
13					13
14	July 1				14
15					15
16					16
17					17
18	Sept 30				18
19					19
20					20
21	Oct 1				21
22					22
23					23
24					24
25	Dec 1				25
26					26
27					27
28	Dec 31				28
29					29
30					30

(c)

	Andreu Company Balance Sheet (Partial) December 31			
1	Current liabilities:			1
2				2
3				3
4				4
5				5

(b)

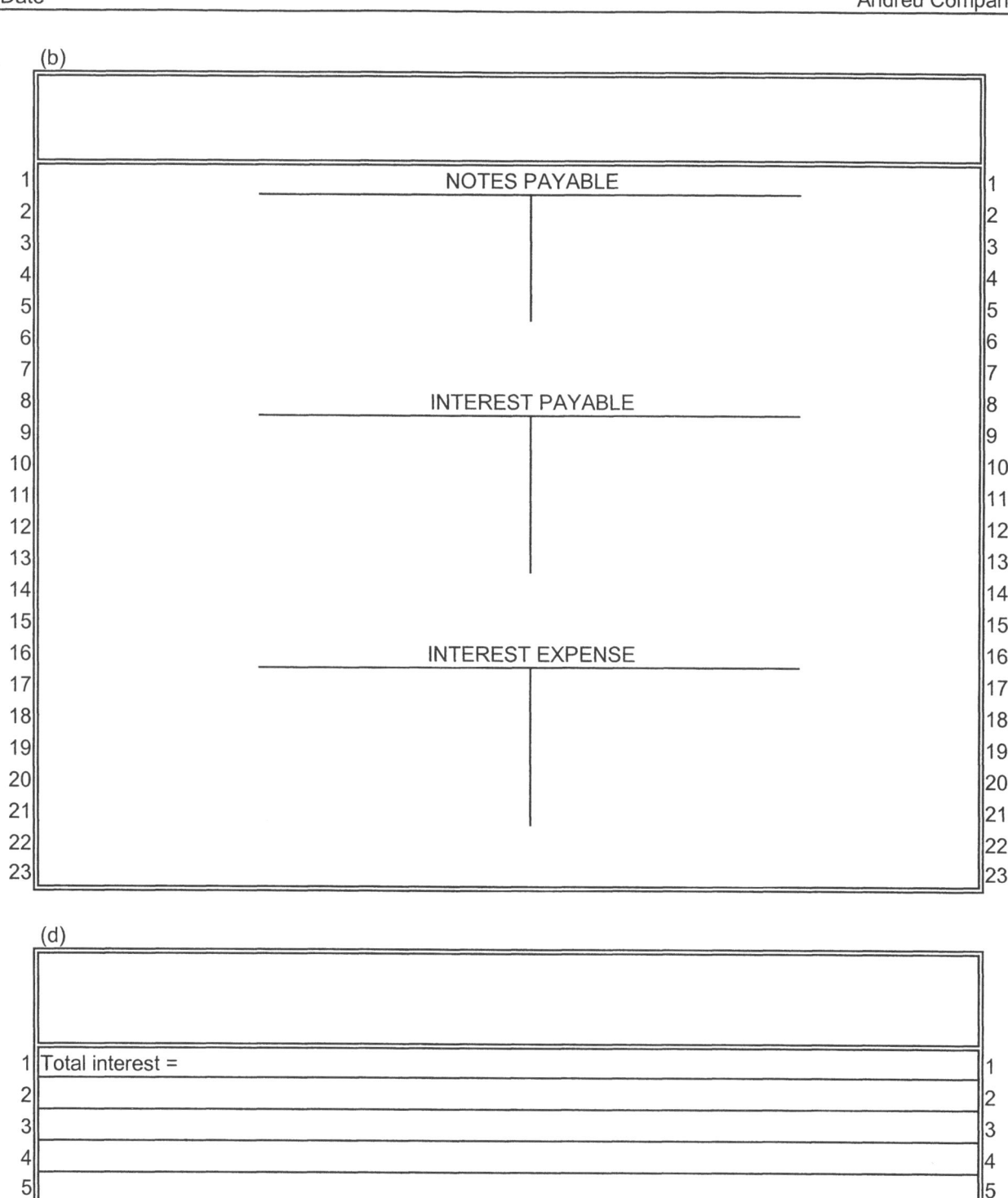

NOTES PAYABLE

INTEREST PAYABLE

INTEREST EXPENSE

(d)

1	Total interest =
2	
3	
4	
5	

(a)

Hira Hardware
Payroll Register
For the Week Ended March 15, 2010

	Employee	Hours	Earnings				
			Regular	Over-time	Gross Pay	
1	Joe Hana	4 0				1
2						2
3	Mary Alina	4 2				3
4						4
5	Andy Silva	4 4				5
6						6
7	Kim Gomez	4 6				7
8						8
9	Totals					9

Deductions					
	FICA Taxes	Fed. Inc. Tax	State Inc. Tax	United Fund	Total
1				$ 5	1
2					2
3				5	3
4					4
5		6 0		8	5
6					6
7		6 1		5	7
8					8
9					9

	Net Pay	Salaries and Wages Expense	
1			1
2			2
3			3
4			4
5			5
6			6
7			7
8			8
9			9

	Date	Account Titles	Debit	Credit	
1	(b)				1
2	Mar 15				2
3					3
4					4
5					5
6					6
7					7
8					8
9					9
10					10
11	15				11
12					12
13					13
14					14
15					15
16					16
17					17
18					18
19					19
20					20
21	(c)				21
22	Mar 16				22
23					23
24					24
25					25
26					26
27					27
28					28
29					29
30					30
31	(d)				31
32	Mar 31				32
33					33
34					34
35					35
36					36
37					37
38					38
39					39
40					40

	Date	Account Titles	Debit	Credit	
1	(a)				1
2	Jan 10				2
3					3
4					4
5	12				5
6					6
7					7
8					8
9	15				9
10					10
11					11
12	17				12
13					13
14					14
15	20				15
16					16
17					17
18					18
19	31				19
20					20
21					21
22					22
23					23
24					24
25					25
26					26
27					27
28	31				28
29					29
30					30
31	(b) 1.				31
32	Jan 31				32
33					33
34					34
35					35
36					36
37	*2.				37
38	31				38
39					39
40					40

Date	Account Titles	Debit	Credit
(a)			
(b)			

(c)

Employee	Wages, Tips, Other Compensation	Federal Income Tax Withheld	State Income Tax Withheld	FICA Wages	FICA Tax Withheld
Lucie Solarova	$ 5 9 0 0 0	$ 2 8 5 0 0			
Kristina Madericova	2 6 0 0 0	1 0 2 0 0			

	Date	Account Titles	Debit	Credit	
1	(a)				1
2	Jan 1				2
3					3
4					4
5	5				5
6					6
7					7
8					8
9	12				9
10					10
11					11
12	14				12
13					13
14					14
15	20				15
16					16
17					17
18					18
19	25				19
20					20
21					21
22					22
23	(b) (1)				23
24	Jan 31				24
25					25
26					26
27					27
28	(2)				28
29	31				29
30					30
31					31
32					32
33					33
34					34
35					35
36					36
37					37

(c)

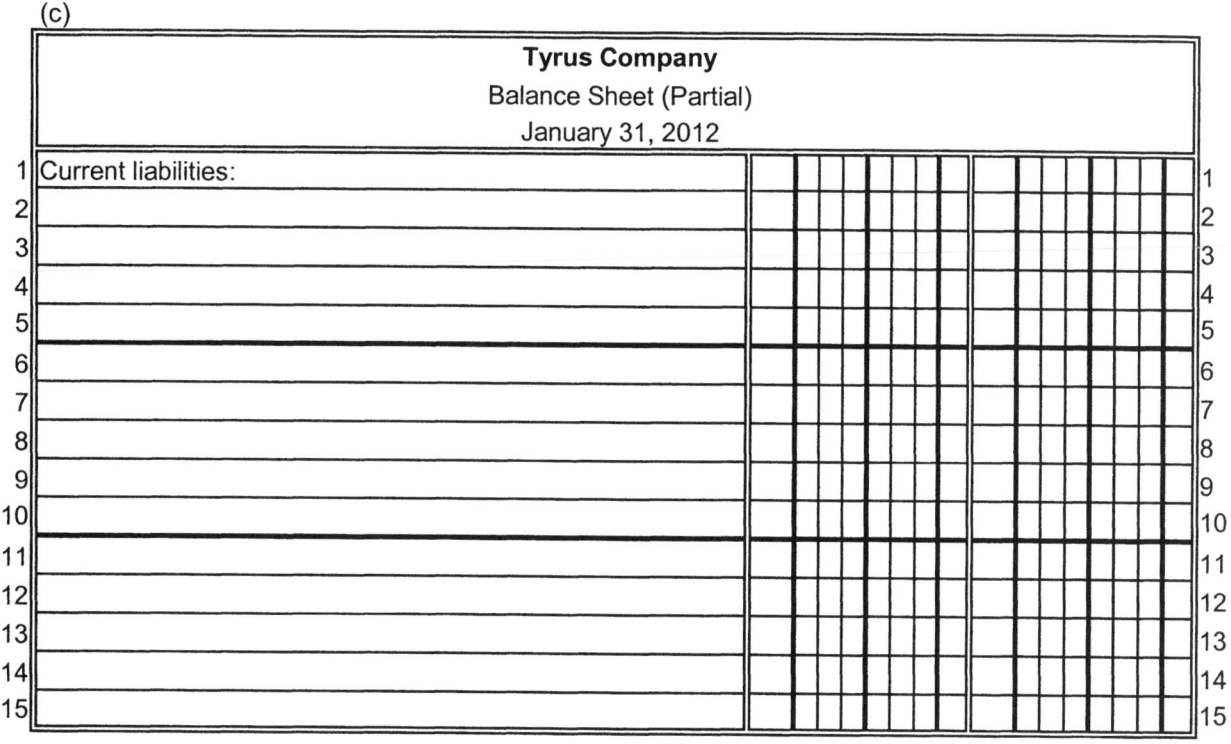

Tyrus Company
Balance Sheet (Partial)
January 31, 2012

Current liabilities:		

(a)

	Date	Account Titles	Debit	Credit	
1	Jan 2				1
2					2
3					3
4	Feb 1				4
5					5
6					6
7	Mar 31				7
8					8
9					9
10	Apr 1				10
11					11
12					12
13					13
14	July 1				14
15					15
16					16
17					17
18	Sept 30				18
19					19
20					20
21	Oct 1				21
22					22
23					23
24					24
25	Dec 1				25
26					26
27					27
28	Dec 31				28
29					29
30					30

(c)

Karolina Company

Balance Sheet (Partial)

December 31

1	Current liabilities:		1
2			2
3			3
4			4
5			5

(b)

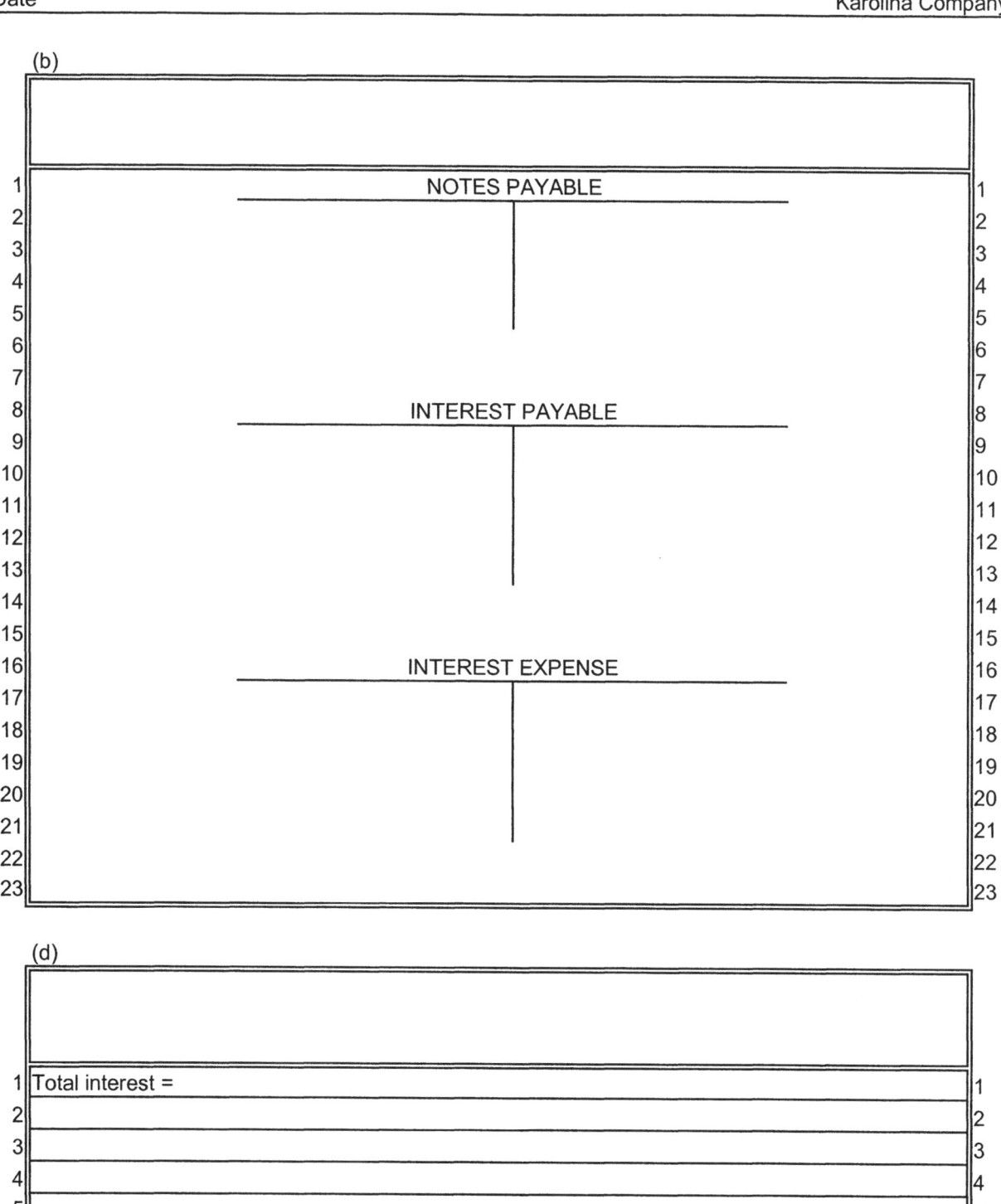

	NOTES PAYABLE	
	INTEREST PAYABLE	
	INTEREST EXPENSE	

(d)

1	Total interest =	1
2		2
3		3
4		4
5		5

(a)

Yemi's Drug Store
Payroll Register
For the Week Ended February 15, 2012

		Earnings		
Employee	Hours	Regular	Over-time	Gross Pay
1 M. Dvorska	3 9			
2				
3 D. Motti	4 2			
4				
5 L. Abbasova	4 4			
6				
7 A. Lee	4 6			
8				
9 Totals				

Deductions				
FICA Taxes	Fed. Inc. Tax	State Inc. Tax	United Fund	Total
1	3 4		$ 0	
2				
3	2 0		1 0 00	
4				
5	5 1		5 00	
6				
7	3 6		5 00	
8				
9				

Net Pay	Salaries and Wages Expense	
1		
2		
3		
4		
5		
6		
7		
8		
9		

	Date	Account Titles	Debit	Credit	
1	(b)				1
2	Feb 15				2
3					3
4					4
5					5
6					6
7					7
8					8
9					9
10					10
11	15				11
12					12
13					13
14					14
15					15
16					16
17					17
18					18
19					19
20					20
21	(c)				21
22	Feb 16				22
23					23
24					24
25					25
26					26
27					27
28					28
29					29
30					30
31	(d)				31
32	Feb 28				32
33					33
34					34
35					35
36					36
37					37
38					38
39					39
40					40

	Date	Account Titles	Debit	Credit	
1	(a)				1
2	Jan 10				2
3					3
4					4
5	12				5
6					6
7					7
8					8
9	15				9
10					10
11					11
12	17				12
13					13
14					14
15	20				15
16					16
17					17
18					18
19	31				19
20					20
21					21
22					22
23					23
24					24
25					25
26					26
27					27
28	31				28
29					29
30					30
31	(b) 1.				31
32	Jan 31				32
33					33
34					34
35					35
36					36
37	*2.				37
38	31				38
39					39
40					40

	Date	Account Titles	Debit	Credit	
1	(a)				1
2	Dec. 31				2
3					3
4					4
5					5
6					6
7					7
8					8
9					9
10					10
11					11
12					12
13	(b)				13
14	Dec. 31				14
15					15
16					16
17					17
18					18
19					19
20					20
21					21
22					22
23					23
24					24
25					25

(c)

	Employee	Wages, Tips, Other Compensation	Federal Income Tax Withheld	State Income Tax Withheld	FICA Wages	FICA Tax Withheld	
1							1
2	A. Valdez	$ 50000	$ 18300				2
3							3
4	E. Izzard	24000	4800				4
5							5
6							6
7							7
8							8
9							9
10							10

(a)

	Date	Account Titles	Debit	Credit	
1	1.				1
2					2
3					3
4	2.				4
5					5
6					6
7	3.				7
8					8
9					9
10					10
11					11
12					12
13					13
14	4.				14
15					15
16					16
17	5.				17
18					18
19					19
20	6.				20
21					21
22					22
23	7.				23
24					24
25					25
26					26
27					27
28					28
29					29
30					30
31					31
32					32
33					33
34					34
35					35
36					36
37					37
38					38
39					39
40					40

(a) (Continued)

	Date	Account Titles	Debit	Credit	
1		Adjusting Entries			1
2	8.				2
3					3
4					4
5	9.				5
6					6
7					7
8	10.				8
9					9
10					10
11					11
12	11.				12
13					13
14					14
15					15
16					16
17					17
18					18
19					19
20					20
21					21
22					22
23					23
24					24
25					25
26					26
27					27
28					28
29					29
30					30
31					31
32					32
33					33
34					34
35					35
36					36
37					37
38					38
39					39
40					40

(a) and (b)

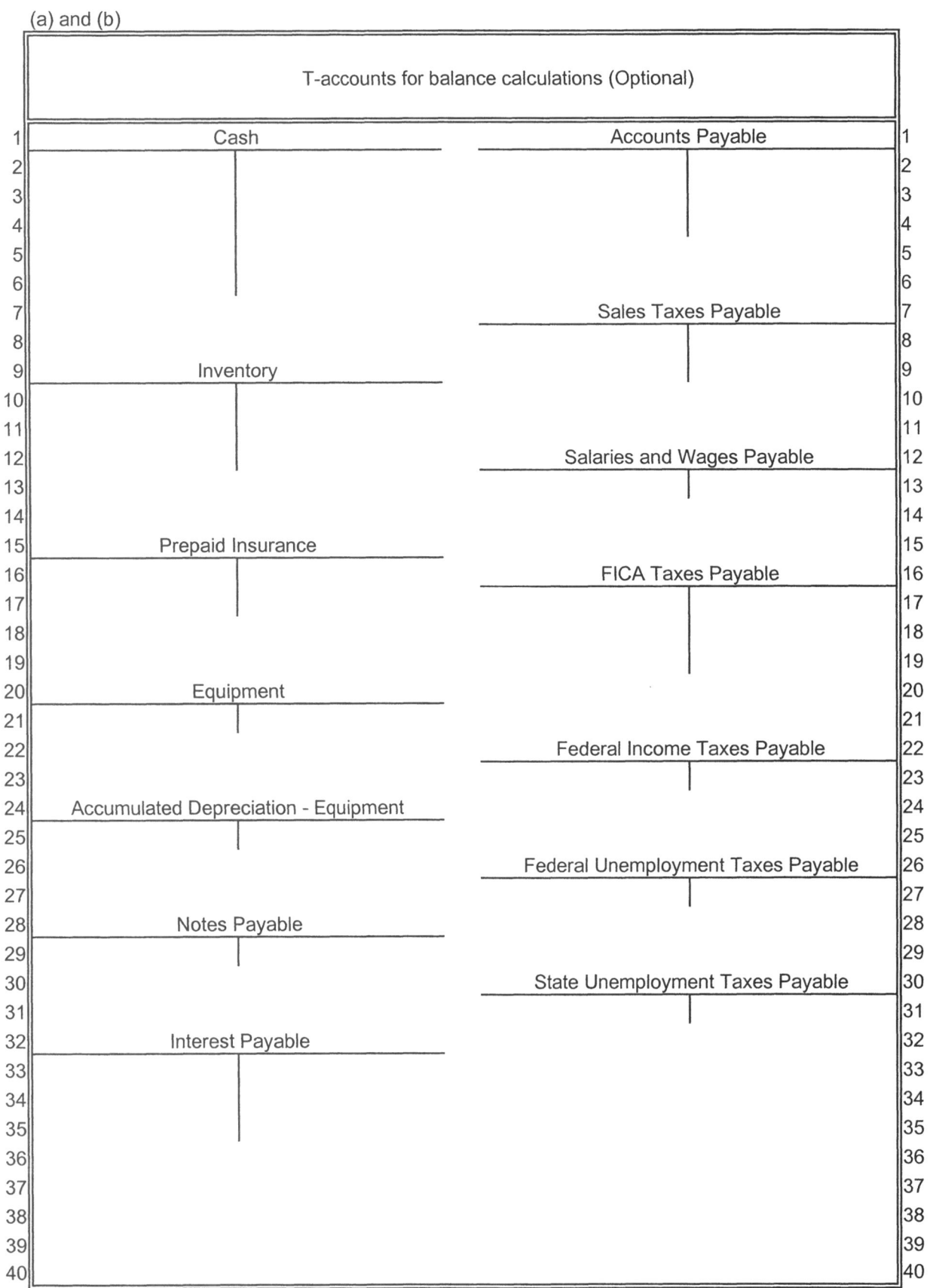

T-accounts for balance calculations (Optional)	
Cash	Accounts Payable
Inventory	Sales Taxes Payable
Prepaid Insurance	Salaries and Wages Payable
Equipment	FICA Taxes Payable
Accumulated Depreciation - Equipment	Federal Income Taxes Payable
Notes Payable	Federal Unemployment Taxes Payable
Interest Payable	State Unemployment Taxes Payable

(a) and (b) (Continued)

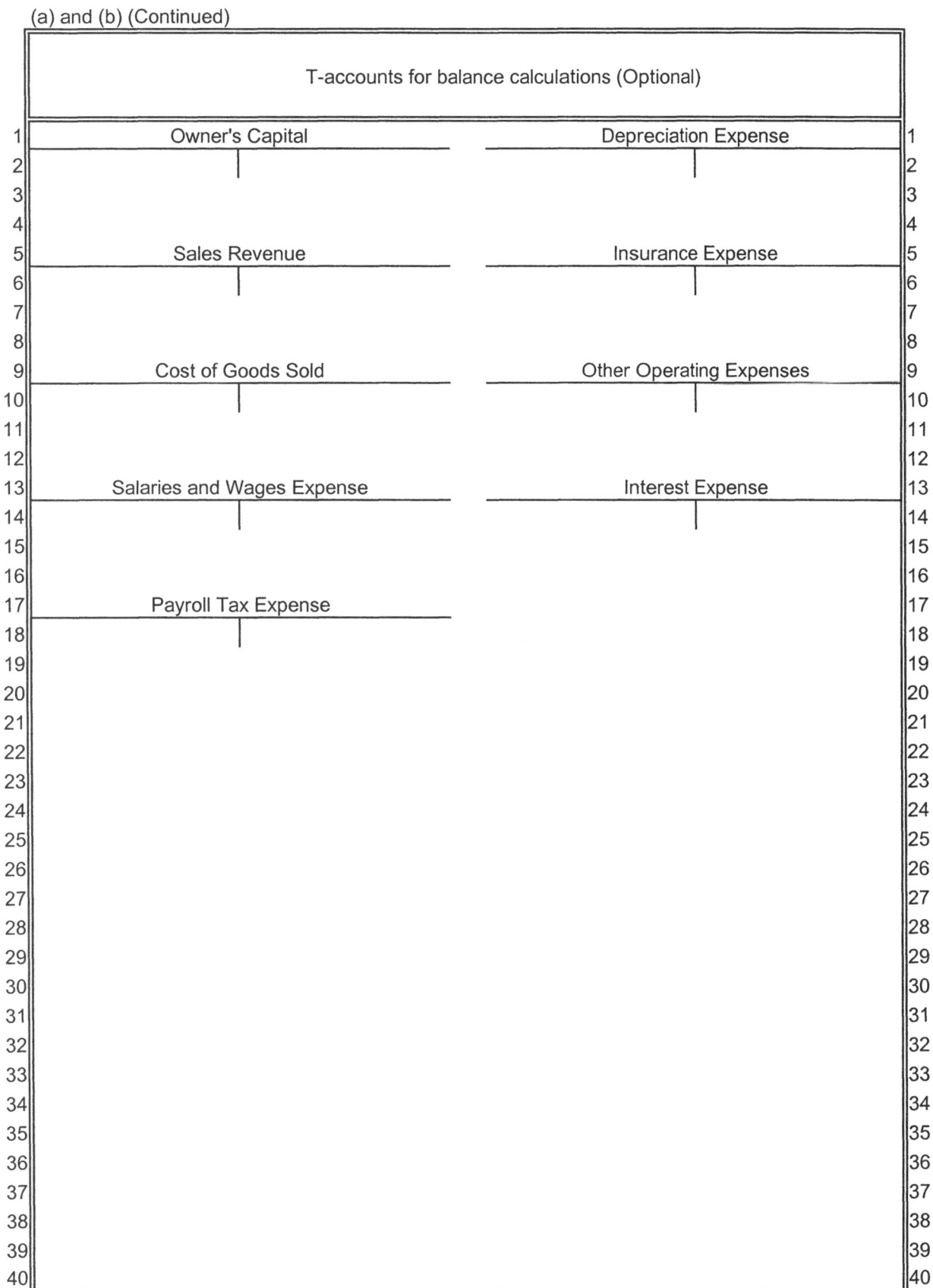

	T-accounts for balance calculations (Optional)	
Owner's Capital		Depreciation Expense
Sales Revenue		Insurance Expense
Cost of Goods Sold		Other Operating Expenses
Salaries and Wages Expense		Interest Expense
Payroll Tax Expense		

(b)

	Wright Company Adjusted Trial Balance January 31, 2012			
1	Account	Debit	Credit	1
2	Cash			2
3	Inventory			3
4	Prepaid Insurance			4
5	Equipment			5
6	Accumulated Depreciation - Equipment			6
7	Accounts Payable			7
8	Interest Payable			8
9	Sales Taxes Payable			9
10	Salaries and Wages Payable			10
11	FICA Taxes Payable			11
12	Federal Income Taxes Payable			12
13	Federal Unemployment Taxes Payable			13
14	State Unemployment Taxes Payable			14
15	Notes Payable			15
16	Owner's Capital			16
17	Sales Revenue			17
18	Cost of Goods Sold			18
19	Salaries and Wages Expense			19
20	Payroll Tax Expense			20
21	Depreciation Expense			21
22	Insurance Expense			22
23	Other Operating Expenses			23
24	Interest Expense			24
25				25
26				26
27				27
28				28
29				29
30				30
31				31
32				32
33				33
34				34
35				35
36				36
37				37
38				38
39				39
40				40

(c)

Wright Company		
Income Statement		
For the Month Ended January 31, 2012		
1		
2		
3		
4		
5		
6		
7		
8		
9		
10		
11		
12		
13		
14		
15		
16		
17		
18		
19		
20		

Wright Company	
Owner's Equity Statement	
For the Month Ended January 31, 2012	
1	
2	
3	
4	
5	
6	
7	
8	
9	
10	
11	
12	
13	
14	
15	

	Wright Company		
	Balance Sheet		
	January 31, 2012		
1	Assets		
2			
3			
4			
5			
6			
7			
8			
9			
10			
11			
12			
13			
14			
15	Liabilities and Owner's Equity		
16			
17			
18			
19			
20			
21			
22			
23			
24			
25			
26			
27			
28			
29			
30			
31			
32			
33			
34			
35			
36			
37			
38			
39			
40			

1	(a)	1
2		2
3		3
4		4
5		5
6	(b)	6
7		7
8		8
9	(c)	9
10		10
11		11
12		12
13		13
14		14
15		15
16		16
17		17
18		18
19		19
20		20

(a)

Metcalfe Services Inc.

Month	Number of Employees	Days Worked	Daily Rate	Cost
January - March				
April - May				
June - October				
November - December				
Total Cost				

Payroll Costs for Metcalf's Permanent Employees

(b)

1	(a)
2	
3	
4	
5	
6	
7	
8	
9	
10	(b)
11	
12	(c)
13	
14	
15	
16	
17	
18	(d)
19	
20	
21	(e)
22	
23	(f)
24	
25	
26	
27	
28	
29	
30	
31	
32	
33	
34	
35	
36	
37	
38	

(g)

1	Total taxes:	1
2		2
3		3
4		4
5		5
6		6
7		7
8		8
9		9
10		10
11	The percentage of total taxes to income is:	11
12		12
13		13
14		14
15		15
16		16
17		17
18		18
19		19
20		20
21		21
22		22
23		23
24		24
25		25
26		26
27		27
28		28
29		29
30		30
31		31
32		32
33		33
34		34
35		35
36		36
37		37
38		38

	Debit	Credit
BE12-1		
1		
2		
3		
4		
5		

	Debit	Credit
BE12-2		
6		
7		
8		
9		
10		
11		

BE12-3

Calculation of net income division:

	Debit	Credit
15		
16		
17		
18		
19		
20		

BE12-4

	Division of Net Income			
	Sweet	Drinian	Tauros	Total
23				
24				
25				
26				
27				
28				
29				
30				
31				
32				
33				
34				
35				
36				
37				
38				
39				
40				

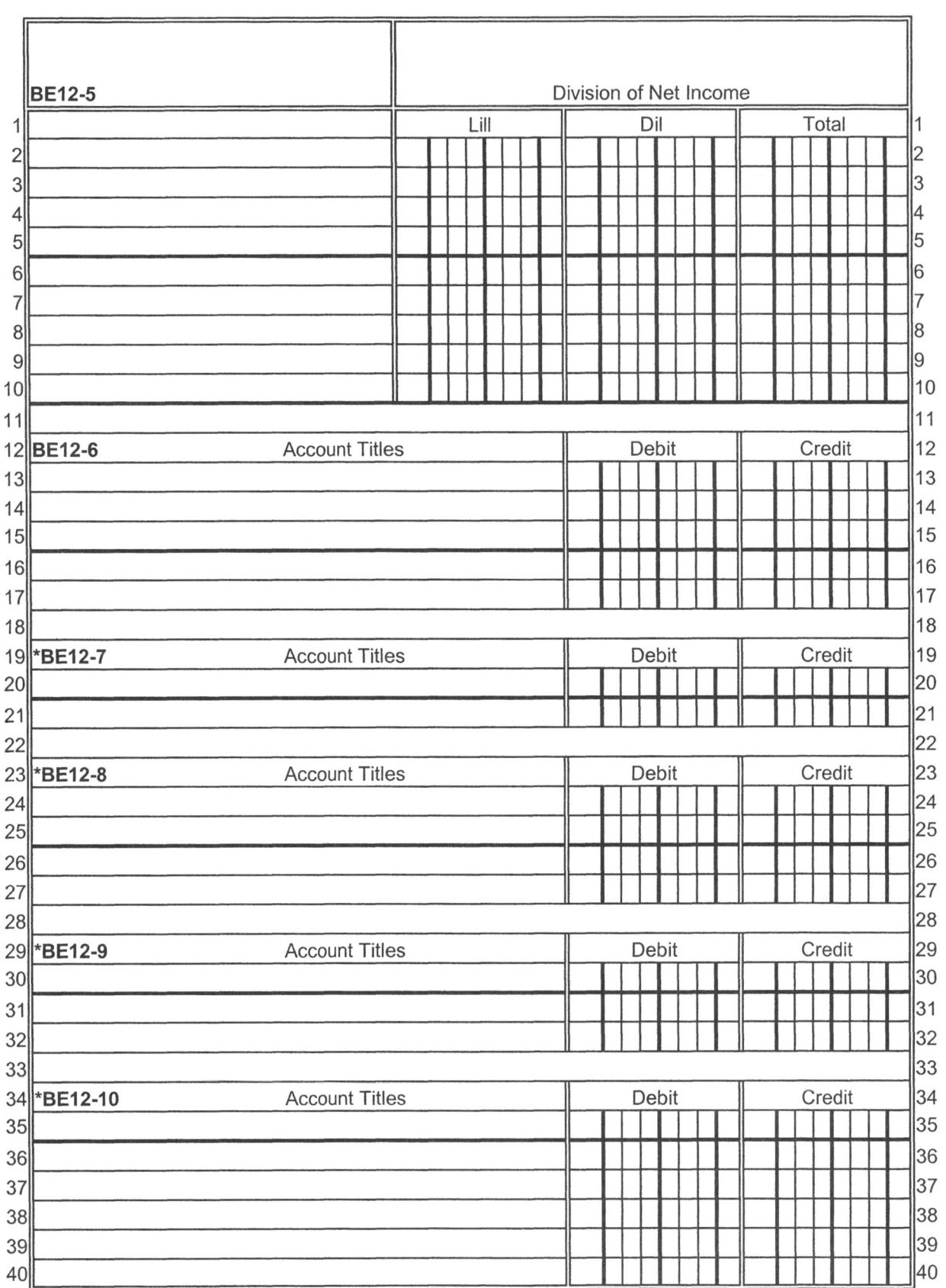

BE12-5		Division of Net Income		
		Lill	Dil	Total
1				
2				
3				
4				
5				
6				
7				
8				
9				
10				

BE12-6	Account Titles	Debit	Credit
12			
13			
14			
15			
16			
17			

*BE12-7	Account Titles	Debit	Credit
19			
20			
21			

*BE12-8	Account Titles	Debit	Credit
23			
24			
25			
26			
27			

*BE12-9	Account Titles	Debit	Credit
29			
30			
31			
32			

*BE12-10	Account Titles	Debit	Credit
34			
35			
36			
37			
38			
39			
40			

DO IT! 12-2

	Division of Net Income		
	Kibra	Devrish	Total
1			
2			
3			
4			
5			
6			
7			
8			

	Account Titles	Debit	Credit
9			
10			
11			
12			
13			
14			
15			

DO IT! 12-4

	Account Titles	Debit	Credit
16			
17			
18			
19			
20			
21			
22			
23			
24			
25			
26			
27			
28			
29			
30			
31			
32			
33			
34			
35			
36			
37			
38			

CS Company
Schedule of Cash Payments

	Item	Cash	Non-cash Assets	Liabilities	Arabella Capital	Dufflepud Capital	Davies Capital
1	Balances before liquidation	15000	90000	40000	20000	32000	13000
2	Sale of noncash assets and						
3	allocation of gain						
4	New balances						
5	Pay liabilities						
6	New balances						
7	Cash distribution to partners						
8	Final balances						
9							
10							
11							
12							
13							
14							
15							
16							
17							
18							
19							
20							

	Account Titles	Debit	Credit	
1	(a)			1
2				2
3				3
4				4
5				5
6				6
7				7
8				8
9				9
10				10
11				11
12				12
13				13
14				14
15				15
16	(b)			16
17				17
18				18
19				19
20				20
21				21
22				22
23				23
24				24
25				25

E12-3

	Date	Account Titles	Debit	Credit	
1	Jan 1				1
2					2
3					3
4					4
5					5
6					6
7					7

E12-6 (a)

		D. Noble	A. Bond	Total	
	Starrite Co. Partners' Capital Statement For the Year Ended December 31, 2012				
1					1
2					2
3					3
4					4
5					5
6					6
7					7
8					8

(b)

	Starrite Co. Partial Balance Sheet December 31, 2012			
1	Owner's Equity			1
2				2
3				3
4				4
5				5
6				6

(a)

	F. Calvert	G. Powers	Total
(1) Net income is $50,000:			
(2) Net income is $36,000:			

(b)

	Debit	Credit
(1) Net income is $50,000:		
(2) Net income is $36,000:		

Account Titles	Debit	Credit
(a)		
(b)		
(c)		
(d)		

The Doctor Paretnership

Balance Sheet

December 31, 2012

	Assets						
1							1
2							2
3							3
4							4
5							5
6							6
7							7
8							8
9							9
10							10
11							11
12							12
13							13
14							14
15							15
16							16
17							17
18							18
19							19
20							20
21	Liabilities and Owner's Equity						21
22							22
23							23
24							24
25							25
26							26
27							27
28							28
29							29
30							30
31							31
32							32
33							33
34							34
35							35
36							36
37							37
38							38
39							39
40							40

The Freema Company
Schedule of Cash Payments

Item	Cash	Non-cash Assets	Liabilities	Dalek Capital	Briggs Capital
1					
2					
3					
4					
5					
6					
7					
8					
9					
10					
11					
12					
13					
14					
15					
16					
17					
18					
19					
20					

E12-9

		Account Titles	Debit	Credit	
1	(a)				1
2					2
3					3
4					4
5	(b)				5
6					6
7					7
8					8
9	(c)				9
10					10
11					11
12	(d)				12
13					13
14					14
15					15

E12-10

		Account Titles	Debit	Credit	
1	(a) (1)				1
2					2
3					3
4					4
5	(2)				5
6					6
7					7
8					8
9	(b) (1)				9
10					10
11					11
12					12
13	(2)				13
14					14
15					15
16					16
17					17
18					18
19					19
20					20

*E12-11

		Account Titles	Debit	Credit	
1	(a)				1
2					2
3					3
4	(b)				4
5					5
6					6
7	(c)				7
8					8
9					9
10					10

*E12-13

		Account Titles	Debit	Credit	
1	1.				1
2					2
3					3
4					4
5					5
6	2.				6
7					7
8					8
9					9
10	3.				10
11					11
12					12
13					13
14					14
15					15

	Account Titles	Debit	Credit	
1 (a)				1
2				2
3				3
4				4
5				5
6	Calculation of Trinity's capital account and bonus to old partners:			6
7				7
8				8
9				9
10				10
11				11
12				12
13				13
14				14
15				15
16				16
17				17
18				18
19 (b)	Account Titles	Debit	Credit	19
20				20
21				21
22				22
23				23
24				24
25	Calculation of Trinity's capital account and bonus to new partner:			25
26				26
27				27
28				28
29				29
30				30
31				31
32				32
33				33
34				34
35				35
36				36
37				37
38				38
39				39
40				40

		Account Titles	Debit	Credit	
1	1.				1
2					2
3					3
4					4
5					5
6		Calculation of bonus to retiring partner and allocation of bonus to remaining partners:			6
7					7
8					8
9					9
10					10
11					11
12					12
13					13
14					14
15					15
16					16
17					17
18	2.		Debit	Credit	18
19					19
20					20
21					21
22					22
23					23
24		Calculation of bonus to remaining partners and allocation of bonus:			24
25					25
26					26
27					27
28					28
29					29
30					30
31					31
32					32
33					33
34					34
35					35
36					36
37					37
38					38
39					39
40					40

		Account Titles	Debit	Credit	
1	(a)				1
2					2
3					3
4					4
5					5
6					6
7					7
8	(b)				8
9					9
10					10
11					11
12					12
13					13
14					14
15					15
16					16
17					17
18					18
19					19
20					20
21					21
22					22
23					23
24					24
25					25
26					26
27					27
28					28
29					29
30					30
31					31

(a)

	Date	Account Titles	Debit	Credit	
1	Jan 1				1
2					2
3					3
4					4
5					5
6					6
7					7
8					8
9					9
10					10
11	1				11
12					12
13					13
14					14
15					15
16					16
17					17
18					18
19					19
20					20

(b)

	Date	Account Titles	Debit	Credit	
1	Jan 1				1
2					2
3					3
4					4
5					5
6	1				6
7					7
8					8
9					9
10					10

(c)

	Wijo Company
	Balance Sheet
	January 1, 2012

Assets

1								
2								
3								
4								
5								
6								
7								
8								
9								
10								
11								
12								
13								
14								
15								

Liabilities and Owners' Equity

16								
17								
18								
19								
20								
21								
22								
23								
24								
25								
26								
27								
28								
29								
30								

(a)

	Account Titles	Debit	Credit
(1)			
(2)			

Calculation to support net income distribution for (a)(2) above:

(3)			

Calculations to support net income distribution for (a)(3) above:

(b)

LAD Company				
Division of Net Income				
	Rory Lachelle	Andy Andoh	Francine Dalek	Total
1				
2				
3				
4				
5				
6				
7				
8				
9				
10				
11				
12				
13				
14				
15				
16				
17				
18				
19				
20				

(c)

LAD Company				
Partners' Capital Statement				
For the Year Ended December 31, 2012				
	Rory Lachelle	Andy Andoh	Francine Dalek	Total
1				
2				
3				
4				
5				
6				
7				
8				
9				
10				

(a)

	Account Titles	Debit	Credit	
(1)				
(2)	Account Titles	Debit	Credit	
(3)				
(4)				
(5)				

(b)

Cash		A. Mangold, Capital	
Bal	27,500	Bal.	33,000

S. Otis, Capital		P. Tyler, Capital	
Bal	21,000	Bal.	3,000

(c)

		Account Titles	Debit	Credit	
1	(1)				1
2					2
3					3
4					4
5					5
6	(2)				6
7					7
8					8
9					9
10					10
11					11
12					12
13					13
14					14
15					15
16					16
17					17
18					18
19					19

(a)

	Account Titles	Debit	Credit
(1)			
(2)			
(3)			
Calculations of bonus paid by new partner and distribution to old partners:			
(4)			
Calculation of bonus to new partner:			

1	(b)		1
2			2
3	(1)		3
4			4
5			5
6			6
7			7
8			8
9			9
10	(2)		10
11			11
12			12
13			13
14			14
15			15
16			16
17			17
18			18
19			19
20			20

(a)

		Account Titles	Debit	Credit	
1	(1)				1
2					2
3					3
4					4
5	(2)				5
6					6
7					7
8	(3)				8
9					9
10					10
11					11
12	Calculation of bonus to Ruscoe in (a)(3) above:				12
13					13
14					14
15					15
16					16
17	(4)				17
18					18
19					19
20					20
21	Calculation of bonus to old partners in (a)(4) above:				21
22					22
23					23
24					24
25					25
26	(b) (1)				26
27					27
28					28
29					29
30					30
31					31
32					32
33					33
34	(2)				34
35					35
36					36
37					37
38					38
39					39
40					40

(a)

Date	Account Titles	Debit	Credit	
1	Jan 1				1
2					2
3					3
4					4
5					5
6					6
7					7
8					8
9					9
10					10
11	1				11
12					12
13					13
14					14
15					15
16					16
17					17
18					18
19					19
20					20

(b)

Date	Account Titles	Debit	Credit	
1	Jan 1				1
2					2
3					3
4					4
5					5
6	1				6
7					7
8					8
9					9
10					10

(c)

Commander Company
Balance Sheet
January 1, 2012

	Assets				
1					
2					
3					
4					
5					
6					
7					
8					
9					
10					
11					
12					
13					
14					
15					
16	Liabilities and Owners' Equity				
17					
18					
19					
20					
21					
22					
23					
24					
25					
26					
27					
28					
29					
30					

(a)

	Account Titles	Debit	Credit	
(1)				1
				2
				3
				4
				5
				6
(2)				7
				8
				9
				10

Calculation to support net income distribution for (a)(2) above:

(3)

Calculation to support net income distribution for (a)(3) above:

(b)

	Staal	Harris	Blaine	Total
SHB Company Division of Net Income				
1				
2				
3				
4				
5				
6				
7				
8				
9				
10				
11				
12				
13				
14				
15				
16				
17				
18				
19				
20				

(c)

	Staal	Harris	Blaine	Total
SHB Company Partners' Capital Statement For the Year Ended December 31, 2010				
1				
2				
3				
4				
5				
6				
7				
8				
9				
10				

Tallis Company

Schedule of Cash Payments

Item	Cash	Non-cash Assets	Liabilities	Laszlo Capital	Alaya Capital	Octavian Capital
1						
2						
3						
4						
5						
6						
7						
8						
9						
10						
11						
12						
13						
14						
15						
16						
17						
18						
19						
20						

(b)

	Account Titles	Debit	Credit	
1	(1)			1
2				2
3				3
4				4
5				5
6				6
7				7
8				8
9	Gain/loss on sale of noncash assets:			9
10				10
11				11
12				12
13				13
14				14
15	(2)			15
16				16
17				17
18				18
19				19
20				20
21	(3)			21
22				22
23				23
24				24
25				25
26				26
27	(4)			27
28				28
29				29
30				30
31				31
32				32
33				33
34				34
35				35
36				36
37				37
38				38
39				39
40				40

(c)

Cash			Alaya, Capital	
4/30 Bal 30,000			4/30 Bal 13,650	

Laszlo, Capital			Octavian, Capital	
	4/30 Bal 28,000			4/30 Bal 5,850

(a)

	Account Titles	Debit	Credit
1	(1)		
2			
3			
4	(2)		
5			
6			
7	(3)		
8			
9			
10			
11			
12	Calculation of bonus paid to new partner:		
13			
14			
15			
16			
17			
18			
19			
20			
21			
22			
23			
24	(4)		
25			
26			
27			
28			
29	Calculation of bonus paid by new partner and distribution to old partners:		
30			
31			
32			
33			
34			
35			
36			
37			
38			
39			
40			

1	(b)									1
2										2
3	(1)									3
4										4
5										5
6										6
7										7
8										8
9										9
10	(2)									10
11										11
12										12
13										13
14										14
15										15
16										16
17										17
18										18
19										19
20										20

(a)

		Account Titles	Debit	Credit	
1	(1)				1
2					2
3					3
4					4
5	(2)				5
6					6
7					7
8	(3)				8
9					9
10					10
11					11
12	Calculation of bonus to Ogden in (a)(3) above:				12
13					13
14					14
15					15
16					16
17	(4)				17
18					18
19					19
20					20
21	Calculation of bonus to old partners in (a)(4) above:				21
22					22
23					23
24					24
25					25
26	(b) (1)				26
27					27
28					28
29					29
30					30
31					31
32					32
33					33
34	(2)				34
35					35
36					36
37					37
38					38
39					39
40					40

Name

Section

Date

Orlando Bloom and Co.

DO IT! 1-3

		Assets				Liabilities			Owner's Equity										
		Cash	+	Accounts Receivable	=	Accounts Payable	+	Owner's Capital	-	Owner's Drawings	+	Revenues	-	Expenses	
1	(1)														1
2	(2)														2
3	(3)														3
4	(4)														4
5															5
6															6
7															7
8															8
9															9
10															10

(a)

		Assets							=	Liabilities			+	Owner's Equity						
Ramona Castro, Veterinarian																				
Trans-actions	Cash	+	Accounts Receivable	+	Supplies	+	Office Equipment	=	Notes Payable	+	Accounts Payable	+	Owner's Capital	-	Owner's Drawings	+	Revenues	-	Expenses	
1 Bal.	$ 9 0 0 0		$ 1 7 0 0		$ 6 0 0		$ 6 0 0 0				$ 3 6 0 0		$ 1 3 7 0 0							1
2 1.																				2
3																				3
4 2.																				4
5																				5
6 3.																				6
7																				7
8 4.																				8
9																				9
10 5.																				10
11																				11
12																				12
13																				13
14 6.																				14
15																				15
16 7.																				16
17																				17
18 8.																				18
19																				19
20																				20

(a)

		Beckham Deliveries																	
		Assets						=	Liabilities			+	Owner's Equity						
	Date	Cash	+	Accounts Receivable	+	Supplies	+	Equipment	=	Notes Payable	+	Accounts Payable	+	Owner's Capital	-	Owner's Drawings	+	Revenues	-	Expenses
1	June 1																		
2	2																		
3	3																		
4	5																		
5	9																		
6	12																		
7	15																		
8	17																		
9	20																		
10	23																		
11	26																		
12	29																		
13	30																		
14																			
15																			
16																			
17																			
18																			
19																			
20																			

Name _____   Problem 1-1B
Section _____
Date _____   Vince's Travel Agency

(a)

	Vince's Travel Agency												
	Assets						=	Liabilities	+	Owner's Equity			
Trans-actions	Cash	+	Accounts Receivable	+	Supplies	+	Equipment	=	Accounts Payable	+	Owner's Capital	-	Owner's Drawings	+	Revenues	-	Expenses
1.													
2.													
3.													
4.													
5.													
6.													
7.													
8.													
9.													
10.													

Name _____

Section _____

Date _____ Juanita Pierre, Attorney at Law

(a)

			Juanita Pierre, Attorney at Law										
		Assets				**=**	**Liabilities**		**+**	**Owner's Equity**				
Trans-actions	Cash	+	Accounts Receivable	+	Supplies	+	Equipment	=	Notes Payable	+	Accounts Payable	+	Owner's Capital	-	Owner's Drawings	+	Revenues	-	Expenses
1 Bal.	$ 5000		$ 1500		$ 500		$ 6000				$ 4200		$ 8800						
2 1.																			
3																			
4 2.																			
5																			
6 3.																			
7																			
8 4.																			
9																			
10 5.																			
11																			
12																			
13																			
14 6.																			
15																			
16 7.																			
17																			
18 8.																			
19																			
20																			

Name

Section

Date

(a)

	Quentin Consulting																
	Assets						=	Liabilities			+	Owner's Equity					
Date	Cash	+	Accounts Receivable	+	Supplies	+	Equipment	=	Notes Payable	+	Accounts Payable	+	Owner's Capital	-	Owner's Drawings	+	Revenues	-	Expenses
May 1																	
2																	
3																	
5																	
9																	
12																	
15																	
17																	
20																	
23																	
26																	
29																	
30																	

BE4-2

	Account Titles	Trial Balance		Adjustments		Adjusted Trial Balance		Income Statement		Balance Sheet		
		Debit	Credit	Debit	Credit	Debit	Credit	Debit	Credit	Debit	Credit	
1	Prepaid Insurance	3 0 0 0										1
2	Service Revenue		5 8 0 0 0									2
3	Salaries and Wages											3
4	Expense	2 5 0 0 0										4
5	Accounts Receivable											5
6	Salaries and Wages											6
7	Payable											7
8	Insurance Expense											8
9												9
10												10

Saddler Company
Worksheet

(a)

	Account Titles	Trial Balance		Adjustments		Adjusted Trial Balance		Income Statement		Balance Sheet		
		Dr.	Cr.	Dr.	Cr.	Dr.	Cr.	Dr.	Cr.	Dr.	Cr.	
1	Cash	2320										1
2	Accounts Receivable	2440										2
3	Supplies	1880										3
4	Accounts Payable		1120									4
5	Unearned Service Rev.		240									5
6	Owner's Capital		3600									6
7	Service Revenue		2400									7
8	Salaries & WagesExp.	560										8
9	Miscellaneous Expense	160										9
10	Totals	7360	7360									10
11	Supplies Expense											11
12	Salaries & Pay.											12
13	Totals											13
14	Net Loss											14
15	Totals											15
16												16
17												17
18												18
19												19
20												20

Tinoisamoa Company
Worksheet
For The Month Ended June 30, 2012

(a)

Noah Amusement Park
Worksheet
For The Year Ended September 30, 2012

	Account Titles	Trial Balance Dr.	Trial Balance Cr.	Adjustments Dr.	Adjustments Cr.	Adjusted Trial Balance Dr.	Adjusted Trial Balance Cr.	Income Statement Dr.	Income Statement Cr.	Balance Sheet Dr.	Balance Sheet Cr.	
1	Cash	41400				41400						1
2	Supplies	18600				2200						2
3	Prepaid Insurance	31900				10900						3
4	Land	80000				80000						4
5	Equipment	120000				120000						5
6	Accum. Depr. - Equip.		36200				42200					6
7	Accounts Payable		14600				14600					7
8	Unearned Ticket Rev.		3700				1000					8
9	Mortgage Note Payable		50000				50000					9
10	Owner's Capital		109700				109700					10
12	Owner's Drawings	14000				14000						12
13	Ticket Revenue		277500				280200					13
14	Salaries & Wages Exp.	105000				105000						14
15	Maint. & Repairs Exp.	30500				30500						15
16	Advertising Expense	9400				9400						16
17	Utilities Expense	16900				16900						17
18	Property Taxes Expense	18000				21000						18
19	Interest Expense	6000				10000						19
20	Totals	491700	491700									20
21												21
22	Insurance Expense					21000						22
23	Supplies Expense					16400						23
24	Interest Payable						4000					24
25	Depreciation Expense					6000						25
26	Property Taxes Payable						3000					26
27	Totals					504700	504700					27
28	Net Income											28
29	Totals											29

(b) & (c)

	Devine's Carpet Cleaners									
	Worksheet									
	For the Month Ended March 31, 2012									
Account Titles	Trial Balance		Adjustments		Adjusted Trial Balance		Income Statement		Balance Sheet	
	Dr.	Cr.	Dr.	Cr.	Dr.	Cr.	Dr.	Cr.	Dr.	Cr.
1 Cash										
2 Accounts Receivable										
3 Supplies										
4 Prepaid Insurance										
5 Equipment										
6 Accounts Payable										
7 Owner's Capital										
8 Owner's Drawings										
9 Service Revenue										
10 Gasoline Expense										
11 Salaries & Wages Exp.										
12 Totals										
13 Depreciation Expense										
14 Accum. Depreciation - Equip.										
15 Insurance Expense										
16 Supplies Expense										
17 Salaries & Wages Pay.										
18 Totals										
19 Net Income										
20 Totals										
21										

(a)

	Acie Cable								
	(1) Incorrect Entry			**(2) Correct Entry**			**(3) Correcting Entry**		
	Account Titles	Dr.	Cr.	Account Titles	Dr.	Cr.	Account Titles	Dr.	Cr.
1	1.								
2									
3									
4	2.								
5									
6									
7	3.								
8									
9									
10									
11									
12	4.								
13									
14									
15	5.								
16									
17									
18									
19									
20									

(a)

		Gibson Roofing										
		Worksheet										
		For The Month Ended March 31, 2010										
	Account Titles	Trial Balance		Adjustments		Adjusted Trial Balance		Income Statement		Balance Sheet		
		Dr.	Cr.	Dr.	Cr.	Dr.	Cr.	Dr.	Cr.	Dr.	Cr.	
1	Cash	4500										1
2	Accounts Receivable	3200										2
3	Supplies	2000										3
4	Equipment	11000										4
5	Accum. Depr.-Equip.		1250									5
6	Accounts Payable		2500									6
7	Unearned Service Rev.		550									7
8	Owner's Capital		12900									8
9	Owner's Drawings	1100										9
10	Service Revenue		6300									10
11	Salaries & Wages Exp.	1300										11
12	Misc. Expense	400										12
13	Totals	23500	23500									13
14	Supplies Expense											14
15	Depr. Expense											15
16	Salaries & Wages Pay.											16
17	Totals											17
18	Net Income											18
19	Totals											19
20												20

(a)

Law Management Services
Worksheet
For the Year Ended December 31, 2012

	Account Titles	Trial Balance Dr.	Trial Balance Cr.	Adjustments Dr.	Adjustments Cr.	Adjusted Trial Balance Dr.	Adjusted Trial Balance Cr.	Income Statement Dr.	Income Statement Cr.	Balance Sheet Dr.	Balance Sheet Cr.	
1	Cash	13800				13800						1
2	Accounts Receivable	28300				28300						2
3	Prepaid Insurance	3600				2400						3
4	Land	67000				67000						4
5	Buildings	127000				127000						5
6	Equipment	59000				59000						6
7	Accounts Payable		12500				12500					7
8	Unearned Rent Revenue		6000				1500					8
9	Mortgage Note Payable		120000				120000					9
10	Owner's Capital		144000				144000					10
11	Owner's Drawings	22000				22000						11
12	Service Revenue		90700				90700					12
13	Rent Revenue		29000				33500					13
14	Salaries & Wages Exp.	42000				42000						14
15	Advertising Expense	20500				20500						15
16	Utilities Expense	19000				19000						16
17	Totals	402200	402200									17
18	Insurance Expense					1200						18
19	Depr. Expense					6600						19
20	Accum. Depreciation - Bldgs.						3000					20
21	Acum. Depreciation - Equip.						3600					21
22	Interest Expense					10000						22
23	Interest Payable						10000					23
24	Totals					418800	418800					24
25	Net Income											25
26	Totals											26
27												27
28												28

Name

Section

Date

(b) and (c)

Pargo's Cleaning Service
Worksheet
For The Month Ended July 31, 2012

Account Titles	Trial Balance		Adjustments		Adjusted Trial Balance		Income Statement		Balance Sheet	
	Dr.	Cr.	Dr.	Cr.	Dr.	Cr.	Dr.	Cr.	Dr.	Cr.
1 Cash										
2 Accounts Receivable										
3 Supplies										
4 Prepaid Insurance										
5 Equipment										
6 Accounts Payable										
7 Owner's Capital										
8 Owner's Drawings										
9 Service Revenue										
10 Gasoline Expense										
11 Salaries & Wages Exp.										
12 Totals										
13										
14 Depreciation Expense										
15 Accum. Depr. - Equip.										
16 Insurance Expense										
17 Supplies Exp.										
18 Salaries & Wages Pay.										
19 Totals										
20 Net Income										
21 Totals										
22										

(b) & (c)

Julie's Maids Cleaning Service
Worksheet
For the Month Ended July 31, 2012

	Trial Balance		Adjustments		Adjusted Trial Balance		Income Statement		Balance Sheet	
Account Titles	Dr.	Cr.	Dr.	Cr.	Dr.	Cr.	Dr.	Cr.	Dr.	Cr.
1 Cash										
2 Accounts Receivable										
3 Supplies										
4 Prepaid Insurance										
5 Equipment										
6 Accounts Payable										
7 Owner's Capital										
8 Owner's Drawings										
9 Service Revenue										
10 Gasoline Expense										
11 Salaries Expense										
12 Totals										
14 Depreciation Expense										
15 Accum. Depreciation - Equip.										
16 Insurance Expense										
17 Supplies Expense										
18 Salaries & Wages Pay.										
19 Totals										
20 Net Income										
21 Totals										
22										
23										
24										

Linus Company
Worksheet
For the Month Ended June 30, 2012

	Account Titles	Trial Balance Dr.	Trial Balance Cr.	Adjustments Dr.	Adjustments Cr.	Adjusted Trial Balance Dr.	Adjusted Trial Balance Cr.	Income Statement Dr.	Income Statement Cr.	Balance Sheet Dr.	Balance Sheet Cr.	
1	Cash	1920										1
2	Accounts Receivable	2440										2
3	Inventory	11640										3
4	Accounts Payable		1120									4
5	Owner's Capital		3500									5
6	Sales Revenue		42500									6
7	Cost of Goods Sold	20560										7
8	Operating Expenses	10560										8
9	Totals	47120	47120									9
10	Net Income											10
11	Totals											11
12												12
13												13
14												14
15												15

Name

Section

Date

(a)

Mr. Eko Fashion Center
Worksheet
For the Year Ended November 30, 2012

	Account Titles	Trial Balance Dr.	Trial Balance Cr.	Adjustments Dr.	Adjustments Cr.	Adjusted Trial Balance Dr.	Adjusted Trial Balance Cr.	Income Statement Dr.	Income Statement Cr.	Balance Sheet Dr.	Balance Sheet Cr.	
1	Cash	8700										1
2	Accounts Receivable	30700										2
3	Inventory	44700										3
4	Supplies	6200										4
5	Equipment	133000										5
6	Accum. Depr. - Equip.		28000									6
7	Notes Payable		51000									7
8	Accounts Payable		48500									8
9	Owner's Capital		90000									9
10	Owner's Drawings	12000										10
11	Sales Revenue		755200									11
12	Sales Returns and Allow.	8800										12
13	Cost of Goods Sold	497400										13
14	Salaries & Wages Exp.	140000										14
15	Advertising Expense	24400										15
16	Utilities Expense	14000										16
17	Maintenance & Repairs Exp.	12100										17
18	Delivery Expense	16700										18
19	Rent Expense	24000										19
20	Totals	972700	972700									20
21	Supplies Expense											21
22	Depreciation Expense											22
23	Interest Expense											23
24	Interest Payable											24
25	Totals											25
26	Net Loss											26
27	Totals											27
28												28
29												29
30												30

(c)

	Packard Company										
	Work Sheet										
	For the Month Ended January 31, 2012										
Account Titles	Trial Balance		Adjustments		Adjusted Trial Balance		Income Statement		Balance Sheet		
	Dr.	Cr.	Dr.	Cr.	Dr.	Cr	Dr.	Cr	Dr.	Cr.	
1 Cash											1
2 Accounts Receivable											2
3 Notes Receivable											3
4 Inventory											4
5 Supplies											5
6 Prepaid Insurance											6
7 Equipment											7
8 Accum. Depr. - Equip.											8
9 Notes Payable											9
10 Accounts Payable											10
11 Interest Payable											11
12 Owner's Capital											12
13 Owner's Drawings											13
14 Sales											14
15 Sales Rtns. and Allow.											15
16 Purchases											16
17 Purch. Rtns and Allow.											17
18 Freight-in											18
19 Salaries & Wages Exp.											19
20 Rent Expense											20
21 Totals											21
22 Supplies Exp.											22
23 Insurance Exp.											23
24 Depreciation Exp.											24
25 Interest Exp.											25
26 Totals											26
27 Net Income											27
28 Totals											28
29											29

(c)

	Bluma Company									
	Work Sheet									
	For the Month Ended January 31, 2012									
Account Titles	Trial Balance		Adjustments		Adjusted Trial Balance		Income Statement		Balance Sheet	
	Dr.	Cr.	Dr.	Cr.	Dr.	Cr	Dr.	Cr	Dr.	Cr.
1 Cash										
2 Accounts Receivable										
3 Notes Receivable										
4 Inventory										
5 Supplies										
6 Prepaid Insurance										
7 Equipment										
8 Accum. Depr. - Equip.										
9 Notes Payable										
10 Accounts Payable										
11 Interest Payable										
12 Owner's Capital										
13 Owner's Drawings										
14 Sales Revenue										
15 Sales Rtns. and Allow.										
16 Sales Discounts										
17 Cost of Goods Sold										
18 Salaries & Wages Exp.										
19 Rent Exp.										
20 Totals										
21 Supplies Exp.										
22 Insurance Exp.										
23 Depreciation Exp.										
24 Interest Exp.										
25 Totals										
26 Net Income										
27 Totals										
28										
29